CANADIANS AT LAST:
CANADA INTEGRATES NEWFOUNDLAND
AS A PROVINCE

History provides some interesting case studies of what happens when trade barriers come down. Among them is the story told in this book of Newfoundland's integration into Canada in the aftermath of the province's 1948 referendum. Raymond B. Blake takes a refreshing approach to this episode in Canadian history, avoiding the old shibboleths of conspiracy and local nationalism, and instead making a down-to-earth study of economic and political events.

Canadians at Last explores the efforts of the many Canadians and Newfoundlanders who tried to make Confederation work. Blake argues that Canada wanted union, to remove any uncertainty in its dealings with Newfoundland over civil aviation, defence, and trade. Newfoundland opted for union largely because Canada's burgeoning social welfare system promised a more secure existence. Investigating the complex problems encountered during negotiations, Blake details changes in trade, fishing, and manufacturing and in the political process in Newfoundland. He also looks at the introduction and impact of social programs, and the terms of the US military presence there. Finally, he demonstrates that by 1957 Newfoundland's integration into Canada was essentially complete; it was being treated the same as the other provinces, subject to the terms of union.

By beginning with the 1949 Confederation rather than the activities leading up to it, and by thoroughly documenting areas of agreement, contention, and neglect, Blake writes a solid, contemporary history of Newfoundland's integration into Canada. Virtually the only complete academic treatment of this subject, *Canadians at Last* offers much basic information that so far has not been made available.

RAYMOND B. BLAKE is Assistant Professor, Department of History, St Thomas University, Fredericton.

RAYMOND B. BLAKE

Canadians at Last: Canada Integrates Newfoundland as a Province

UNIVERSITY OF TORONTO PRESS
Toronto Buffalo London

© University of Toronto Press Incorporated 1994
Toronto Buffalo London
Printed in Canada

ISBN 0-8020-0554-3 (cloth)
ISBN 0-8020-6978-9 (paper)

Printed on acid-free paper

Canadian Cataloguing in Publication Data

Blake, Raymond Benjamin
  Canadians at Last: Canada integrates Newfoundland
  as a province

  Includes bibliographical references and index.
  ISBN 0-8020-0554-3 (bound) ISBN 0-8020-6978-9 (pbk.)

  1. Newfoundland – History – 1949– .* I. Title.

  FC 2175.B53 1994   971.8'04   C94-930016-0
  F1123.B53 1994

University of Toronto Press acknowledges the financial assistance to its
publishing program of the Canada Council and the Ontario Arts Council.

This book has been published with the help of a grant from the Social
Science Federation of Canada, using funds provided by the Social Sciences
and Humanities Research Council of Canada.

For Mom and for Wanda

Contents

PREFACE ix

Introduction 3

1
The stage is set: from dominion to province 7

2
Back to politics: political organization in post-Confederation
Newfoundland, 1948–1951 44

3
Sharing the wealth: Canadian social programs come to
Newfoundland 70

4
Going it alone: the federal government and secondary
manufacturing in Newfoundland, 1948–1953 94

5
Canada establishes sovereignty in Newfoundland, 1948–1952 122

6
The problem of Newfoundland: Ottawa and the fisheries,
1948-1957 146

viii Contents

Conclusion 177

NOTES 185

ILLUSTRATION SOURCES AND CREDITS 226

BIBLIOGRAPHY 227

INDEX 241

Preface

When Canadians are asked when their country became a nation, most will answer 1 July 1867. However, it was not until 31 March 1949 when Newfoundland, the last of the former British colonies in North America, gained provincial status that the vision of the country held by the original Fathers of Confederation was finally fulfilled and the nation complete. This book is about that more recent Confederation and the role the federal government played in nation building from 1948 to 1957. It examines how the Canadian government attempted to integrate Newfoundland into the union and how it made a province of the former dominion.

Historical research and writing are always costly and often lonely pursuits. In the course of my research and writing, I received a lot of help, without which this book might never have been completed. I want to acknowledge, first, the generous financial assistance of the Government of Newfoundland and Labrador, which awarded me the J.W. Pickersgill Fellowship, and also the Institute of Social and Economic Research at Memorial University for its generous doctoral fellowship. Also in St John's, I want to thank Sherry Anderson and her various roommates – Allison, Tina, Verna, and Murray – for providing shelter while I completed my research there. Dr Andy den Otter provided me with office space at Memorial, and Bill and Eileen Kearns were helpful as usual. Their generosity did not go unnoticed.

I am grateful to the staff at the National Archives of Canada in Ottawa, especially Jocelyn LeGough, Paul Marsden, and Geoff Ott; and, at the Centre for Newfoundland Studies Archives, to Nancy Grenville and Bert Riggs. I had my doubts about how much I would accomplish at the Provincial Archives of Newfoundland and Labrador when

I was told one rainy day shortly after my arrival that they did not retrieve documents stored in a separate building when it was wet outside. Luckily, it was a dry summer. I also thank those who were kind enough to grant me interviews in St John's and Ottawa and the interlibrary loan staff at York University, notably Mary Hudecki.

It is to Jack Granatstein that I owe the greatest gratitude. He was involved with this project from the beginning when he supervised my dissertation at York University. He directed me to archival collections that I would surely have missed, raised crucial questions about interpretation, and, more important, tried to teach me something about what he knows best – writing history books. He was demanding, but for his time and patience I will be eternally grateful. The members of my dissertation supervisory committee, Drs Christopher Armstrong, H.V. Nelles, and Reginald Whitaker, were also extremely helpful, offering reasoned insights and thoughtful suggestions that made this a better book. Peter Neary knows more about Newfoundland history than anyone, and his comments and advice helped me avoid numerous pitfalls. I would also like to thank the editorial staff at University of Toronto Press: Gerry Hallowell for his encouragement and support, Agnes Ambrus and Theresa Griffin for all their help, and Margaret Allen for her splendid copy-editing.

At York, I was fortunate to make some very good friends. Several of them were kind enough to read parts of the book and provide useful commentary. For this, I thank them. Gregory Johnson, David Lenarcic, Dan Azoulay, and Dean Oliver did more than comment on various chapters: their friendship and our shared non-academic interests provided a useful diversion from the dissertation. Perhaps our Saturday mornings could have been more effectively spent reading history books, but road hockey is important too.

I owe my greatest thanks to my family. My mother, my brothers and sister and their families, and my in-laws have, each in his or her own way, been very supportive. But to Wanda I owe the most. Her support, her encouragement, her faith in me, and her love have sustained me throughout this period, and this book is as much hers as it is mine. It is to her and to my mother that I dedicate this book.

The first page of the souvenir edition of the St John's *Daily News*, 31 March 1949

Prime Minister Louis St Laurent and Albert J. Walsh sign the Terms of Union on 11 December 1948. Standing behind them (left to right) are M.F. Gregg, J.J. McCann, Brooke Claxton, F.G. Bradley, G.A. Winter, Philip Gruchy, J.R. Smallwood, and J.B. McEvoy.

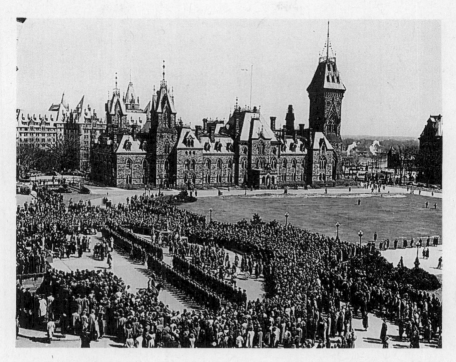

A crowd gathered on the grounds of Parliament Hill in Ottawa to witness
the ceremony welcoming Newfoundland as the tenth province of Canada,
1 April 1949

Prime Minister St Laurent welcomes Newfoundland as the tenth province of Canada during the celebrations at Ottawa on 1 April 1949. Seated in the foreground are the Hon. F.G. Bradley, secretary of state for Canada, former prime minister W.L.M. King, who had made the decision earlier to accept the results of the second Newfoundland referendum, and behind him the Hon. J.H. King, speaker of the Senate.

Joseph R. Smallwood meets with reporters after being sworn in as Newfoundland's first premier, 1 April 1949.

Colin Gibson, Canadian minister of mines and resources, presents Newfoundland's lieutenant-governor, Sir Albert Walsh, with a general certificate
of Canadian citizenship at the ceremony in St John's on 1 April 1949 to cel-
ebrate union with Canada. The province's chief justice, Sir Edward Emerson, looks on.

Prime Minister Louis St Laurent and Premier Joseph R. Smallwood on the campaign trail in the 1949 federal election

A Progressive Conservative campaign poster for the 1949 provincial election

A typical Newfoundland fishing village at the time of union with Canada. There were more than 1,000 such isolated communities demanding normal amenities such as electricity and full-time, qualified teachers.

Fishermen preparing codfish for salting on the Harbour Grace waterfront

The Newfoundland fishery involved more than the catching of cod, as the fishermen and their families were generally responsible for salting and drying the codfish. After Confederation many fishermen lost interest in the traditional fishery and wanted to sell their fish directly to the fish-processing plants.

Women were often responsible for tending the codfish while it was on the flakes drying. By 1949, many fishermen had realized that the traditional fishery based on dried cod had not given them a decent standard of living.

Workers wrapping fillets in cellophane for quick freezing at the Job Brothers and Co. Limited's fish-packing plant at St John's in 1949. Both the federal and the provincial governments believed that the fishery could survive only if it modernized.

Construction of a modern fish-processing plant at LaScie in 1957. This was a joint federal-provincial project designed to modernize the Newfoundland fishery.

Gertrude Everard, Phoebe Moore, and Doris Moore were among the first federal civil servants in Newfoundland. They were hired as filing clerks at the Department of National Health and Welfare in St John's to register children for family allowances. The office was opened in November 1948.

The Canadian National coastal boat ss *Burgeo* calling at Pushthrough in 1949. Before union, steamship service was provided by the Newfoundland Railway, but after 1949 the CN 'steamer' was a welcomed arrival, bringing mail, passengers, and freight to isolated communities.

Immediately following union there was a small boom in local construction. Much of it involved building new post offices, such as the one pictured here, which was completed at Change Island in 1953.

Joseph R. Smallwood and J.W. Pickersgill campaigning during the 1953 federal election. Pickersgill became Newfoundland's representative in the cabinet following Bradley's appointment to the Senate in 1953.

CANADIANS AT LAST:
CANADA INTEGRATES NEWFOUNDLAND
AS A PROVINCE

Introduction

Confederation had not come easily to Newfoundland. After the hysteria and fear whipped up in 1869, when the party advocating union with Canada was resoundingly trounced in a national election, politicians stayed clear of the issue for decades. Generations of Newfoundlanders were weaned on anti-Confederate songs that had been popularized during the first Confederation debate:

> Men, hurrah for our native Isle, Newfoundland –
> Not a stranger shall hold one inch of her strand;
> Her face turns to Britain, her back to the Gulf,
> Come near at your peril, Canadian Wolf!

By the late 1940s, however, much in Newfoundland had changed. The bonds that had tied it to Britain were finally coming undone as a result of the increased contact with Canada and the United States brought by the Second World War. The war had also brought unprecedented prosperity, largely a result of defence spending by Canada and the United States, which had recognized the dominion's[1] strategic value. With the war finally won, however, the economic future for the country was far from certain. It was doubtful that the peacetime economy could sustain the level of growth experienced during the war.

Newfoundland was peculiar among the British dominions. To avert economic collapse and bankruptcy, at the height of the Depression it had surrendered responsible government in favour of a British-appointed Commission of Government. With the return of economic prosperity and peace, the country had to settle its constitutional affairs. After months of debate and discussion both inside and outside a National Convention, the people were asked to vote on the future of their dominion in a national referendum called for 3 June 1948. They were faced with a difficult decision. Should they choose the uncertainties of independence and nationhood that came with a return to responsible government? Should they opt for the relative financial and social security that came from being a province of Canada? Or should they retain the Commission of Government that had governed the country since 1934? On the one hand, union with Canada would mean the end of Newfoundland as a separate dominion; on the other, provincial status promised a fair measure of security from the deprivation and want that many people remembered all too well from the 1930s. The results of the referendum were inconclusive. Nothing was decided save that few Newfoundlanders wanted to continue with the Commission of Government, but the stage was set for a run-off vote on 22 July 1948 between Confederation with Canada and a return to responsible government. This time, a slender majority opted for the more secure course with Canada.[2]

Once Newfoundland had voted for Confederation, Ottawa wanted to complete the process as quickly as possible. A delegation appointed by the Newfoundland government travelled to Ottawa and negotiated the final terms of union, after which the appropriate British, Canadian, and Newfoundland legislation to make union possible received royal assent. Once it became clear that Newfoundland would become the tenth province, the Canadian government began immediately the process of integrating the new province into the federal system. Over the years, the two countries had developed quite differently. But with union, it became Ottawa's responsibility to integrate Newfoundland into the federation by extending the benefits of Canadian citizenship to the new province and bringing it to an acceptable Canadian standard.

This book is about that process. It examines how Newfoundland was made a province and how it was integrated into the federal system. Because the union between Newfoundland and Canada affected so many areas, this book is necessarily selective in focus. While organized thematically, it attempts to maintain some semblance of chronology. After a brief discussion of the events that led to victory for the supporters of Confederation in the second referendum, chapter one turns to the negotiations, between a seven-member delegation appointed by the governor of Newfoundland and a cabinet committee of the Canadian government, to complete union. Post-Confederation political organization is the subject of chapter two. Chapter three covers the implementation of social programs necessitated by union. Even before the negotiations between Newfoundland and Ottawa were completed, Canadian civil servants were itching to begin their task in Newfoundland. They were responsible for ensuring that as many of Canada's federal social programs as possible were ready for 1 April 1949, family allowances being the most recognized and most publicized of these. Chapter four examines how Newfoundland's secondary industries underwent a period of readjustment after Confederation. Chapter five looks at some of the international implications of union. The integration of Newfoundland into the Canadian system of defence threatened the harmonious relationship between Canada and the United States, in particular when Canada attempted to win modifications to the 1941 Leased Bases Agreement that gave the Americans sovereignty over three military bases in Newfoundland. Chapter six examines Ottawa's attempts to deal with the problems of the Newfoundland fishery.

This book does not pretend to cover every aspect of Newfoundland's integration into Canada. There is no attempt here to discuss the contentious issue of freight rates, though this was one of the few issues that brought cooperation between Newfoundland and its Atlantic neighbours, with Newfoundland following the lead of the Maritime provinces in criticizing Ottawa for an unfavourable transportation policy. Likewise, the province's quarrel with Ottawa that pitted Premier Joseph R. Smallwood against Prime Minister John Diefenbaker over Term 29 and the reassessment of the province's financial needs in 1959 are not covered, since that dispute's resolution lies outside the time period of this project. Other historians interested in the subject of integration might quarrel with the focus of this book. No matter what aspects of union are examined, however, it is clear that Newfoundland was rapidly integrated into Canada and that by 1957 it was being treated the way the other provinces were, subject to the provisions of the Terms of Union.

By the time Newfoundland joined with Canada, the policy objectives of the federal government had changed radically from what they had been in the early years following the original union in 1867. The heyday of rapid industrial development fostered by successive federal governments under Sir John A. Macdonald and Sir Wilfrid Laurier had long passed. The National Policy had been largely displaced by the social policies of the federal government after the Second World War. While Macdonald promised in 1867 to build a strong, vibrant economy, Prime Minister Louis St Laurent promised in 1949 equality of opportunity and social benefits for all while maintaining full employment in a strong economy. As the economy prospered throughout most of the 1940s and 1950s, the federal government was concerned with improving the lives of Canadians. This shift in federal policy meant that the benefits accruing to Newfoundland from Confederation were radically different from those that its Maritime neighbours had hoped for nearly eighty-five years earlier. The Maritimes had opted for union in large part because it promised greater economic opportunity.[3] For a short period at least, their goals were realized. Newfoundland, on the other hand, never demanded economic development, its people were never promised it, and Newfoundland never received it. Instead, it was promised greater social benefits, and it is in the area of social welfare policy that Newfoundland gained, in the short term at least, from Confederation with Canada. By 1949, the promise of Confederation no longer had the same meaning it had had in 1867, and this affected the nature of Newfoundland's integration into Canada.

One should be under no illusion that Newfoundland joined Confederation because of any lofty ideals associated with being Canadian: Newfoundlanders joined for purely pragmatic reasons, as Canada offered the best insurance against the problems of the past. Being Canadian promised a brighter and more secure future than being an independent nation. Newfoundland's decision in 1948 to throw away the status of a self-governing dominion for that of a province demonstrates clearly the difficulties facing small nations in an uncertain world. Newfoundland realized that economic and political integration into a larger entity was necessary to achieve a secure future. Union succeeded in improving the standard of living in Newfoundland, but in the process the province shifted its dependence from London to Ottawa.

1

The stage is set: from dominion to province

Newfoundland's first full day in Canada was surprisingly quiet. A moment before midnight the previous evening, 31 March 1949, Newfoundland officially became the tenth and newest province of Canada. The celebrations usually associated with constitutional events of such magnitude simply did not occur in Newfoundland, a fact all the more amazing considering that the dominion's constitutional status had been settled by a narrow margin in two bitterly fought referenda. That there were no serious public expressions of opposition in St John's, where support for a return to independence and responsible government had been strongest, implies that many who had supported constitutional options other than union with Canada had accepted the results of the second referendum or had resigned themselves to becoming Canadian citizens. The lack of universal rejoicing, on the other hand, might well suggest that Newfoundlanders were not overly excited at becoming Canada's newest citizens, though Paul Bridle, the former acting high commissioner, reported from the provincial capital that 'spontaneous celebrations were held in many widely scattered parts of the island.'[1] Neither the Commission of Government nor the Government of Canada had wanted to give the public an opportunity to express its joy – or to vent its anger – at union. Charles J. Burchell, the Canadian high commissioner to Newfoundland, had informed Ottawa in January 1949 that he and the Newfoundland commissioner of justice and defence, Sir Albert Walsh, both feared that rioting was a 'real possibility' if Canada sponsored a formal celebration on 1 April.[2] Happily, their fears came to naught. As events on that day were to show, they had greatly exaggerated the degree of discontent with Confederation.

Nevertheless, the state ceremony at historic Government House in St John's to mark the occasion was short and solemn, with the gravity of a farewell to a dear friend rather than the jubilation of final reconciliation with a persistent suitor. The swearing in of Walsh as the province's first lieutenant-governor and the presentation to him of a certificate of Canadian citizenship on behalf of all Newfoundlanders consumed all of thirty minutes. Then the 100 or so invited guests listened to the proceedings from Ottawa before Joseph R. Smallwood and his cabinet were sworn in as the province's first government. Unlike the first Canadians, many of whom partied well into the night on 1 July eighty-two years earlier, Newfoundlanders went to bed early after their first full day as Canadians. Nothing unusual happened in St John's. 'As far as St John's was concerned,' the *Evening Telegram* observed the next day, 'Newfoundland slipped as quietly into Confederation last midnight as the grey mist which settled over the Capital early this morning.'

The celebrations at the base of the Peace Tower on Parliament Hill in Ottawa, however, showed more enthusiasm for Newfoundland's constitutional baptism. The bells of the carillon reverberated to the tune of 'The Squid Jiggin' Ground,' one of Newfoundland's best-loved folk songs, and a nineteen-gun salute greeted the official party as hundreds turned out to witness the historic event, although many were civil servants given an early lunch break to attend the ceremony. The atmosphere was anything but sombre; Ottawa welcomed Newfoundland to the Canadian family in grand style. Union with Canada, after all, was Newfoundland's natural destiny. Prime Minister Louis St Laurent was elated, greeting Newfoundlanders as fellow Canadians, and promising them full and equal partnership in the federation. The arch at the base of the Peace Tower, he told Canada's newest citizens listening on radio, had one extra shield for the day that Newfoundland would join the union. 'This day has come,' he exulted, as he cut the first line of the Newfoundland coat of arms in the blank shield.

F. Gordon Bradley, who was sworn in just minutes before as secretary of state and the first minister from Newfoundland in the federal cabinet, praised his province's entry into Confederation as the fulfilment of the dream held by the earlier Fathers of Confederation. The Canadian dream of uniting all British possessions in North America within one nation had finally been realized. He extolled Canada as a great nation and told his fellow Newfoundlanders that they were all Canadians now and that together they could fulfil Laurier's promise of making the twentieth century Canada's. The governor general, Viscount Alexander of Tunis, welcomed the new province and conveyed greetings from His Royal Majesty the King. Patriotic anthems, including the 'Ode to Newfoundland' and 'O Canada,' closed out the celebrations. Newfoundlanders were impressed with the ceremony; perhaps the editor of the women's page of the St John's *Evening Telegram* summed it up best: 'Quietly, yet in so dignified a way that must have won hardened doubters, we were welcomed ... to the big family of Canadian Provinces ... It was a true Newfoundland welcome. No greater compliment can be paid.'[3]

Paul Bridle wrote to Ottawa a few days later that a friend of his, a correspondent in St John's to cover the union for an important British newspaper, had remarked that Confederation 'had come to Newfoundland in a pair of soft-soled shoes.' He was right, and Bridle reminded Ottawa that 'this was our minimum objective: and if we did something better, well and good.'[4] In fact, Canada had walked lightly along Newfoundland's road to Confederation. Canada and Newfoundland were never alone on that journey, as the United Kingdom was always nearby, sometimes cajoling, always manoeuvring to make the trek towards union possible. Although the Canadians and the British could limit and influence the choices to be made in the long summer of 1948, Newfoundlanders alone decided their constitutional future.

I

The issue of Confederation had not lain dormant after Newfoundland first rejected it in 1869. On no less than five separate occasions between 1880 and 1933 the two nations had discussed the possibility of union. Confederation had little chance of success, however, because each Canadian government that had to deal with Newfoundland knew that it could not be too generous without creating problems with some of the other provincial governments. And Newfoundland was not interested in union unless Canada offered an attractive package. When the issue arose in 1933, for instance, Prime Minister R.B. Bennett, though sympathetic towards union, decided that Ottawa could not offer a package acceptable to Newfoundland without alienating many Depression-weary Canadians. In the decade after 1939, however, a mixture of Canadian self-interest and sentimentality combined to make Newfoundland extremely attractive. Because of its geographical position, Newfoundland seemed destined to occupy an important place in the growing and profitable world of civil aviation. Already a pioneer in the field, Canada stood to benefit handsomely if it controlled Gander which later gained the title 'Crossroads of the World,' an indication of its importance to air travel. Likewise, union would simplify Canadian defence matters in Newfoundland and prevent Washington from assuming even greater control on the island. Moreover, union promised to add considerable mineral and forest resources, especially from Labrador, and give Canada title to the rich fishing grounds off the east coast It would, above all, complete the union of all British North America into one dominion that the Fathers of Confederation had envisaged.[5] And now Prime Minister William Lyon Mackenzie King, nearing the end of his career, saw union as his crowning achievement.

After the outbreak of the Second World War in 1939, Canada rekindled the interest in Newfoundland that had dwindled during the Great Depression. King realized from then on that Canada could not afford to lose the island that guarded the approach to the St Lawrence. Canada's interest was largely strategic – so much so that, two days before Canada declared war with Germany, King told the House of Commons that Newfoundland would be included in Canada's defence preparations.[6] After the fall of France in June 1940, Canada assumed much of the responsibility for the defence of Newfoundland. Troops were dispatched to the island, and control of Gander airport passed to the Canadian government. Yet Canada remained without a policy on Newfoundland, and as the Leased Bases Agreement of 1941 between the United States and Great Britain demonstrated, its position in Newfoundland was far from secure. Before Great Britain and the United States consummated a deal, King reminded London that Canada had a long-standing interest in Newfoundland and that he wished to be consulted on matters pertaining to it.[7] Britain's hands were tied, however, as it desperately needed the American destroyers. The Canadians were awarded mere observer status at the negotiations. When the Leased Bases Agreement was signed on 27 March 1941, the American military became firmly entrenched in Newfoundland.[8] It was given extensive powers to defend the bases, and it had complete jurisdiction within the leased area. All was not lost, however, as a protocol attached to the agreement recognized Canada's special relationship with Newfoundland. The protocol was no victory for Canadian diplomacy. In a recent book, David MacKenzie concludes that the Canadian government was slow to act to safeguard its interests in Newfoundland. Consequently, 'the negotiations produced a degree of resentment and bitterness [at their government] in some Canadians such as Lester Pearson [then assistant under-secretary of state for external affairs], but it also forced the Canadian government to take a more determined and creative role in its future relations with Newfoundland.'[9]

Already officials at the Department of External Affairs were thinking of uniting Newfoundland with Canada. The prescient under-secretary of state for external affairs, O.D. Skelton, reminded King that if the Americans leased territory there it might create a problem for Canada if Newfoundland ever decided to join.[10] In the meantime, Canada had forged its own Airbases Agreement with Newfoundland, though without the wide-ranging powers given to the Americans. Canada merely provided defence during the war, and its military privileges were secure only so long as the war should last. If it hoped some day to bring Newfoundland into the union, Canada has to maintain a profile there comparable with those of the British and the Americans. To do so, Ottawa dispatched Nova Scotian Charles J. Burchell as Canada's first high commissioner to Newfoundland in September 1941.[11] When King appointed Burchell, he reminded him of Canada's military, strategic, and long-term interests in the dominion and told him to 'emphasize Canada's special relationship with Newfoundland.'[12] The establishment of the High Commission reflected Canada's continuing interest in its eastern neighbour.[13] 'Moreover, it was a recognition of past failures in Canadian policy,' MacKenzie concludes, 'and a symbol of Canada's determination not to repeat the same mistakes.'[14] American strategic interest in Newfoundland in 1940 prompted Ottawa to reassess its policy and shocked Canada into action. The Canadian government finally realized that if it wanted Newfoundland, it would have to develop in the future more specific policies towards the island than it had in the past. Newfoundland would not simply fall into its lap: it had to be courted or, at the very least, Canada had to work more assiduously for union.

This view was most prevalent among a small cadre of senior bureaucrats within the Department of External Affairs who, J.L. Granatstein has argued, 'presided over the change in Canada from a timid Dominion to a sometimes aggressive and nationalistic middle power.'[15] To Norman Robertson, under-secretary of state for external affairs after O.D. Skelton's death, Lester B. Pearson, Canada's ambassador to the

United States, Hume Wrong, assistant under-secretary of state for external affairs, and others, Newfoundland had became too important to lose.[16] Canadian politicians eventually came to share the bureaucrats' view. Mackenzie King's first public pronouncement regarding Newfoundland came in a 1943 parliamentary exchange with Co-operative Commonwealth Federation MP J.W. Noseworthy, a former Newfoundlander then representing an Ontario riding. It offered the bureaucrats hope. The door for Newfoundlanders to join was opened, King had said, and 'should they make their decision clear and beyond all possibility of misunderstanding, Canada would give most sympathetic consideration to the proposal.'[17] Robertson continued to press the prime minister. After a conversation in 1943 with Malcolm MacDonald, the British high commissioner, who was pressuring Robertson and King for an early discussion on Newfoundland, Robertson told King that 'somehow, sometime Newfoundland should become part of the Canadian Confederation. I think that, in the long run, both political and strategic considerations make this inevitable.'[18] King's response is not recorded, but Robertson must certainly have had the Prime Minister's support[19] since he subsequently asked R.A. MacKay, his special assistant, to prepare a five-part memorandum on Newfoundland as a basis for discussion. The memo emphasized Canadian interests and stressed the need for a policy on Newfoundland.[20]

Canada's position in Newfoundland was vulnerable; unlike the United States, it had few post-war rights there, though Canada recognized the significance of the island's geographic position especially in defence and civil aviation. After his initial memo made its rounds in Ottawa and at the High Commission in St John's, MacKay prepared another for Robertson on 21 March 1944. After still further discussion, Robertson presented MacKay's proposal to the cabinet War Committee on 12 April. The committee agreed that Newfoundland should remain a high priority, but did not consider the time propitious for actively pursuing union. With the pressing matters of war, the issue disappeared from the War Committee's agenda. Nevertheless, a marked change had occurred in Canadian thinking towards Newfoundland. The subsequent appointment of Hugh Keenleyside, the assistant under-secretary of state for external affairs, as acting high commissioner in St John's from January to April 1944 reflected the realization that the time had finally come for Ottawa to have a clearer policy on Newfoundland. Gone was the notion that the initiative for union must come solely from Newfoundland.[21]

The British government sought even the smallest signal that Canada was interested in Newfoundland. At the outset of the war, the United Kingdom had jealously guarded its position in Newfoundland, but as the focus of the war shifted from the Atlantic to Europe with the mastering of the German U-boat threat in 1943, Newfoundland's strategic value diminished for the British. Moreover, Britain felt secure in Newfoundland as it had guaranteed itself a role in post-war civilian use of Newfoundland's airfields and access to St John's harbour.[22] As London turned its attention to post-war reconstruction, Newfoundland threatened to become a financial liability, especially after the Commission of Government presented a ten-year reconstruction plan in September 1944, estimated to cost the British $100 million. Britain could scarcely keep itself solvent; it could not afford scarce dollars to rehabilitate Newfoundland.[23] The best solution would be union between Canada and Newfoundland.

The cautious and politically conscious King was certainly interested, but he feared that some of the provinces would not fancy taking on a potential financial liability such as Newfoundland. Moreover, he felt that if Canada made its objective known to Newfoundland, the people there might resent Canadian interference and destroy all hope of union. The initiative, King maintained publicly, must be left entirely to Newfoundland. In fact, Ottawa never gave an official commitment, but it expressed just enough interest for Britain to seize the initiative. P.A. Clutterbuck, assistant under-secretary of state for dominion affairs, wrote to the Newfoundland governor that Keenleyside's appointment showed that Canadians were 'now taking Newfoundland much more seriously than they have in the past'[24] In June 1945 at the United Nations conference in San Francisco, Hume Wrong approached Lord Cranborne, secretary of state for dominion affairs, about Newfoundland; Cranborne came away convinced that Canada wanted Newfoundland and wanted Westminster to withhold financial assistance that might encourage the island to shun union with Canada. The British pursued the matter on two separate occasions later that fall. Although the Canadians held their cards close to their chest, the Dominions Office concluded that King, too, welcomed union – provided, of course, that Newfoundland was not coerced.[25] Clutterbuck visited Ottawa in September 1945 to discuss informally with Canadian officials the prospects for Newfoundland. Although he informed London that he found an almost complete absence of interest in Newfoundland, Canadian officials again suggested that London should withhold financial assistance to 'assist Newfoundlanders to turn their thoughts to Canada.'[26] Meanwhile, King had informed MacDonald that 'it would never do to compel Newfoundland to come into Confederation or to show a desire to have them come in. On the other hand, we should let them know we would be willing to have them consider favourably their coming into Confederation at any time.'[27] King had said much the same to Lord Addison. Newfoundland was a financial liability, he reminded the secretary of state for dominion affairs in the Attlee government, but strategic concerns made union desirable.[28] This was enough for the United Kingdom. Addison then told the British cabinet that it should regard union with Canada as its objective for Newfoundland. 'It would, of course,' he warned, 'be fatal to take any overt steps to encourage Newfoundlanders in this direction, or even to let it become known that this is the solution we envisage. On the other hand, we must take care to say and do nothing which would be inconsistent with this objective or make it harder to achieve.'[29] Canada adopted a similar policy, and King had indicated privately that he would welcome union and do his best to offer Newfoundland generous terms. Ottawa wanted Confederation, but it still refused to court Newfoundland publicly. Nevertheless, Canada had demonstrated enough interest to make British designs for Newfoundland possible.[30]

II

While officials in both London and Ottawa were pursuing the possibility of union, in Newfoundland itself a few rumblings were audible for a return to self-government. Since 1934 Newfoundland had been without a democratically elected government. Following the recommendations of Lord Amulree, whom Whitehall had appointed in 1933 to investigate the country's financial and economic problems, the Newfoundland legislature requested the suspension of responsible government. On 16 February 1934, Frederick C. Alderdice, the last prime minister, signed the necessary documents that provided for a Commission of Government, a six-member appointed body with at least three Newfoundlanders and chaired by the governor. It administered the country until union with Canada.[31]

On 11 December 1945, British prime minister Clement Attlee, who had earlier visited Newfoundland, announced in the British House of Commons the formation of a National Convention in Newfoundland 'to consider and discuss ... the changes that have taken place in the financial and economic situation of the Island since 1934 ... and to make recommendations to His Majesty's Government as to possible forms of future government to be put before the people in a national referendum.'[32] To prevent the affair from being dominated by the St John's professional classes, candidates for the convention had to have resided for at least a year in the districts they wished to represent. The forty-five-member National Convention, elected on 21 June 1946, convened in St John's on 11 September.

Confederation had little support in the National Convention. Smallwood was the only member elected as an avowed supporter of union with Canada. Although he attracted several converts to his cause, his group remained very much a minority. Smallwood himself had had a varied career in Newfoundland. At times, a union and cooperative organizer and a political journalist, he was best known for his immensely popular radio program, 'The Barrelman,' that promised to make 'Newfoundland better known to Newfoundlanders.' Although his voice was perhaps better recognized than any other, Smallwood was considered virtually a nonentity on the political scene prior to the convention. What he may have lacked in credibility, however, he more than compensated for in determination, courage, intelligence, and unparalleled political astuteness.[33] These qualities served him well later in the National Convention, but not so early on, as the convention rejected his first motion to send a delegation to Ottawa to explore the possibility of Confederation.

Meanwhile, on 30 October 1946 the Canadian cabinet decided that it would welcome a delegation from the National Convention to discuss the possibility of union. Senior bureaucrats had already begun to prepare memoranda on the various aspects of union. A cabinet committee of King's most influential ministers was appointed to advise the government and supervise an Interdepartmental Committee on Canada-Newfoundland Relations (ICCNR), charged with the task of preparing the terms to offer Newfoundland.[34] By December, however, when the ICCNR reported that union would cost Canada between $10 and $15 million annually, King began to vacillate. While union remained his long-term objective, he was worried that some of the provinces might demand more money from Ottawa and delay a new taxation arrangement he was hoping to complete with them.[35]

After the defeat of his first motion in the convention on 5 November 1946, Smallwood teamed up with respected St John's fish merchant R.B. Job to introduce a resolution calling for discussions with the United States, the United Kingdom, and Canada. The Commission of Government ruled discussions with a foreign power, the United States, outside the convention's jurisdiction. A delegation was in London from 24 April to 9 May, and following its return to St John's, a second group held discussions in Ottawa from 19 June to 30 September. In London, the Newfoundlanders received a chilly reception, hardly a surprise considering Britain's desire for the island's union with Canada. Lord Addison promised aid only if Newfoundland continued Commission of Government; it had to sink or swim alone if it chose a return to self-government. The British cupboard was bare, the Newfoundlanders were told.[36]

The Canadians were more accommodating. When the delegation arrived in Ottawa in June 1947, the government laid out the welcome mat.[37] Prime Minister King was more excited than anyone. He had discussed the prospects of union with Lord Addison, American president Franklin D. Roosevelt, and Attlee, but he had not played an integral role in what had transpired since the matter had first been raised. At a dinner given in honour of the delegation, and again at the opening session, he demonstrated his delight. Union was not 'a course to be undertaken lightly,' but one that merited 'serious and unhurried examination' by both parties. He stressed unequivocally that 'the question of the colony's future was one for the people of Newfoundland to decide and not a matter in which the people of Canada or the government of Canada would wish to interfere.' And he basked in the compliments he received on his remarks. 'Many of our men and others spoke of me and my speech. They seemed to think it was one of the best I ever made. I know it produced a fine effect,' he bragged to his diary. The event undoubtedly had a beneficial effect upon him. The prospect of becoming a Father of Confederation prompted him to reconsider retirement. Perhaps he should hold the reins a little longer in order to oversee Newfoundland's entry into Canada; '[i]t is a strange thing,' he wrote,

that among the many other things which now fall into my lot, I should be called upon to complete the union of all British possessions in the North American Continent ... I should not indeed be surprised if it might be that my part would help bring about the rounding out of Canada as a nation in a manner which would take in all the territory from the waters of the Atlantic to those of the Pacific. To this end I would be tempted to remain a little longer in public life than otherwise I would wish to be.[38]

King favoured union, but the political problems that it threatened to create served as a brake on him. J.W. Pickersgill, then King's special assistant, recalls that there were 'grave doubts in the minds of nearly all, well, I think all the ministers in Ottawa. Not about the desirability of having Newfoundland as a part of Canada, but about the viability of fitting Newfoundland into the federal-provincial picture in Canada.'[39] On the other hand, C.D. Howe, the minister of reconstruction and supply, thought that Canadian access to the untapped deposits of high-grade iron ores on the Newfoundland side of the Quebec-Labrador boundary would more than compensate for the initial problems of incorporating the province into the federal system. Jules R. Timmins, a mining promoter, had told Howe much earlier about the mineral resources of Labrador, and the minister realized their importance to Canadian and American industrial development.[40]

Ottawa was particularly worried over how the Maritimes would view Confederation. King, the consummate politician, learned from New Brunswick premier John McNair that if he offered Newfoundland better terms than the Maritime provinces were then getting he would stir up a hornet's nest that might weaken Liberal support in the region. He also feared retaliation in Quebec, the bastion of Liberal support. Premier Maurice Duplessis and many Québécois, still smarting over the 1927 ruling of the Judicial Committee of the Privy Council that had awarded resource-rich Labrador to Newfoundland, saw union as a 'plot to bring three hundred thousand more Britishers into Canada.' Duplessis demanded to be consulted, but King knew that the premier would never agree to admitting Labrador into Confederation as a part of Newfoundland.[41] Quebec and the Maritimes could prove to be the fly in the ointment, but King and St Laurent knew that if Canada allowed Newfoundland to slip away, the Americans would surely improve their position there. Neither wanted an Alaska on the east coast.

Despite such concerns at Ottawa, the two sides hammered out an agreement for the 'Proposed Arrangements for the Entry of Newfoundland into Confederation,' which King dispatched to the dominion's governor on 29 October 1947.[42] Although the Newfoundland delegation had left Ottawa a month earlier, King had refused to release the proposed terms while his party was fighting a by-election in New Brunswick to replace that province's sole representative in the cabinet. Much of the proposal was based on poor statistics and much of it was mere guesswork, but it did serve as a blueprint for union. Canada promised to provide the same public services available to the other provinces, take over the services normally provided by Ottawa including the Newfoundland railway and the Gander airport, assume the Newfoundland sterling debt, and provide the normal statutory subsidies as well as a special transitional subsidy.[43]

For twenty-four days the National Convention debated the Canadian proposals clause by clause. Each day Smallwood led the debate, trumpeting the advantages of Confederation and educating the people over the public airwaves. As a small nation Newfoundland could not survive on its own, he told them. Canada promised security, democratic responsible government, and an improved standard of living. The whole process gave the proponents of union a jump on those who favoured a return to responsible government and made Smallwood even better known. Nonetheless, the National Convention voted twenty-nine to sixteen to keep Confederation with Canada out of the referendum that the British government had promised. Wisely, the British had given the convention authority only to recommend constitutional options to be decided in a referendum; they had reserved the final say for themselves, and their mind was already made up: Newfoundlanders would be given the opportunity to vote for union with Canada. For Whitehall to include Confederation on the referendum ballot after the National Convention had refused to do so, however, might suggest that Newfoundland was being coerced into union with Canada, raise the ire of Newfoundlanders, and scuttle the British plan. Although they did not realize it at the time, Smallwood and Bradley helped Whitehall out of its predicament. Immediately following the rejection of Confederation in the convention, they mounted a massive radio campaign asking people to tell the governor that they wanted union with Canada placed on the ballot. The response was overwhelming. Within days, Government House in St John's was inundated with telegrams, letters, and petitions from more than 50,000 Newfoundlanders demanding the inclusion of Confederation. The public outcry for Confederation gave the British the needed pretext for action. Even before public support could be mobilized by Smallwood and Bradley, Lord Addison had asked for Ottawa's reaction to the inclusion of Confederation on the ballot. Officially, the Canadian government informed London that the decision was Whitehall's alone to make, but unofficially, Ottawa welcomed the British decision.[44] On 2 March 1948 Philip Noel-Baker of the Commonwealth Relations Office told Newfoundlanders that they had three choices in a national referendum: responsible government as it existed in 1933, Commission of Government for an additional five years, or Confederation with Canada. 'It would not be right that the people ... be deprived of an opportunity of considering the issue at the referendum,' he concluded.[45] Now the constitutional future rested in the hands of the Newfoundland people.

III

The outline of the story is generally well known, though it is sometimes difficult to separate myth from reality in such a highly charged and partisan struggle. The urban-rural split in the voting, for instance, has been presented as a sectarian vote, with the Roman Catholics supporting a return to responsible government and the Protestants voting for Confederation. This has been mistaken for a geographical cleavage among the electorate: the Protestants were dominant in the rural areas and Catholics in the urban, but each religious group had strong representation throughout the country. In his brief study of the Responsible Government League (RGL), Jeff A. Webb demonstrates that sectarianism in the referenda has been overstated. He attributes the failure of the RGL to 'rural resentment of the exploitation of the metropole.' In other words, rural Newfoundlanders saw responsible government as bringing a return to the economic uncertainties and exploitation of the 1930s, and they were not about to give control back to a St John's élite.[46]

The degree to which the promise of Canadian social-welfare programs, such as family allowances, was responsible for winning the referenda for the Confederate Party has also been greatly exaggerated. If social-welfare programs were the main attraction, why was not the vote for Confederation greater? Surely the people on the Avalon Peninsula – who voted slightly better than 67 per cent in favour of responsible government – would have benefited from the various social programs. The promise of Canadian largesse was particularly appealing in the many rural areas where the people were largely without newspapers and cut off from the discussions that the Avalon Peninsula enjoyed. A better explanation is to be found in the appeal of the Responsible Government League. The RGL had a powerful weapon in Newfoundlanders' nationalism and independence, but it was not well enough organized to wield that weapon effectively throughout the country. The Avalon Peninsula certainly had a greater sense of national identity than the rest of the island. Its proximity to the seat of power and the mechanisms of government undoubtedly fostered a greater sense of nation than existed in the isolated outports, but the whole population dearly loved their country. Voters in and around the capital were familar with the different constitutional options through partisan tabloids – *The Confederate* and *The Independent* – and the two St John's dailies, and many responded to the appeals of nationalism and voted for a return to responsible government and national independence. The material in the RGL newspaper, *The Independent*, appealed to this nationalism and sense of independence. The epithet that appeared on each issue was a phrase from the national anthem: 'Where once our Fathers stood we stand.' A slogan directed to young Newfoundlanders asked, 'Are you going to admit to the rest of the world we're not fit to govern ourselves?' – powerful words indeed.[47] Although it was poorly organized, the RGL carried its message to the area around St John's, where it concentrated its campaign and won substantial support. By largely ignoring the rural areas, the RGL defaulted to the Confederates, who campaigned vigorously in the areas outside St John's.

Others who supported responsible government generally believed that it was the best choice for Newfoundland or that it would be a transitional stage to precede Confederation or some other arrangement. During the National Convention debates, Chesley Crosbie, later leader of the Party for Economic Union with the United States (PEU), and others, including Smallwood, claimed that Newfoundland could not go it alone: it had to link up with a larger trading bloc. They agreed, maintains Donald Jamieson, PEU campaign manager, that 'a reconstituted, independent government would be free to explore a variety of options, including Confederation and even a closer union with the United States.' Though he rejected Confederation himself, Jamieson realized that 'What was needed ... was some form of insurance, an anchor to add stability to the Newfoundland economy under self-rule.' People like Crosbie never objected to Confederation on ideological grounds, but 'saw distinct advantages in acquiring the leverage a potential deal with the United States would provide in talks with Ottawa. As he saw it, the choice of Responsible Government closed no doors.'[48]

Crosbie was not alone in this view. Others agreed that an elected government could get a better deal out of Canada, a view expressed in countless letters to both St John's dailies in the days leading up to the final vote. In fact, the common thread running through *The Inde-*

pendent, as its title suggests, was Newfoundland's independence. The inaugural issue on 22 March 1948 emphasized 'its strong conviction that the people of Newfoundland should not be asked to vote on the question of Confederation until the terms have been negotiated on their behalf by a sovereign Government of their own choosing.' As Peter Cashin, the fiery former Newfoundland minister of finance and ardent opponent of the Commission of Government, long considered the leading anti-Confederate and an important member of the RGL, told a group of Canadian historians in 1967, 'I was not against Confederation so much as against the methods which brought it about.'[49] Others have supported his contention. Michael Harrington, a member of the National Convention, recalls that eleven or twelve members of the National Convention were truly Confederates, but they objected to union with Canada before the restoration of responsible government; many who supported responsible government, he remembers, were very interested in Confederation, but they firmly believed that an independent Newfoundland would get better terms.[50] Grace Sparkes, then a columnist and political activist, shares Harrington's view: Newfoundland entered union through the back door, hardly an honourable entry for such a proud people, she laments. While many were willing to discuss Confederation, they refused it under the circumstances presented in 1948.[51] Commenting in 1949, Isaac Newell, another member of the convention, claimed that many who were dissatisfied with the outcome directed their criticism at the means by which the end was accomplished rather than the end itself. M.O. Morgan, a Newfoundland Rhodes Scholar and later president of Memorial University, made a similar claim shortly after the second vote: 'many voted against Confederation, though agreeing with it in principle because they disapproved of the procedure.'[52]

The labels of Confederate and anti-Confederate are generally used to describe the factions in the referenda campaigns. The view persists that those who supported a return to responsible government simply opposed union with Canada and did not have a strategy apart from this. In fact, nothing could be farther from the truth: many of those who saw a course for Newfoundland other than immediate union with Canada did not rule out eventual Confederation. They held that union remained an option, but they believed that Newfoundland would be able to extract better terms if it could pursue negotiations either in Washington or in Ottawa as an independent, sovereign dominion. Hence, they were not simply anti-Confederates. Simply to see the nearly 48 per cent of Newfoundlanders who voted for responsible government as anti-Confederates is to overlook the nuances of an emotionally charged constitutional campaign.

Two referenda were needed to decide the issue. On the first, neither option polled the majority necessary, though support for responsible government came close at nearly 45 per cent. Confederation garnered 41 per cent. The Commission of Government won 14 per cent of the vote even though its supporters refused to campaign, perhaps a vindication of competent if uninspired government. This set the stage for a run-off vote between the two most popular choices, as British legislation had decreed. In the second vote – on 22 July 1948 – Confederation emerged with 52.34 per cent of the total, not quite the victory King had hoped for. Even so, if King failed to complete union, it might destroy forever the vision of Canada held by the original Fathers of Confederation.[53]

Faced with a dilemma, he dispatched R.A. MacKay, head of the British Commonwealth Division at the Department of External Affairs, to Newfoundland from 24 to 28 July 1948 to survey the post-referendum state of opinion. MacKay's first impression was that the public, including many people who had supported the return to responsible government, accepted the outcome, and his report prompted King to act swiftly and in a positive manner. After conversations with John T. Cheeseman, RGL vice-president, Malcolm Hollett, W.L. Collins, A.M. Fraser, R.B. Job, Gordon F. Higgins, and other RGL supporters, MacKay concluded that a 'large number of those who voted for Responsible Government were not against Confederation as such, although they preferred Confederation by negotiation.'[54] Bridle, again acting high commissioner in Newfoundland, reported to Ottawa in early September 1948 that 'it is clear that none of the more responsible men who advocated Responsible Government during the referendum campaign wish to be associated with the League's present activities [continuing the fight against union].'[55] Higgins, for instance, a prominent St John's lawyer and member of the 1947 delegation to Ottawa, accepted the verdict and was ready to work within union; he subsequently ran as a Conservative in the 1949 federal election.[56]

The actions of several other prominent RGL members seemed to reinforce MacKay's findings. F.M. O'Leary tendered his resignation as president on 13 August 1948, claiming 'that any further action at this time [by the RGL] would not be in the best interests of the League or the country. As I understand that it is the intention of the League to continue to oppose the decision of the people,' O'Leary lamented to Collins, 'I view with alarm any measures which may result in keeping our people divided ... I cannot in honesty, play any further part in its activities.'[57] Chesley Crosbie shared O'Leary's sentiments. When Governor Sir Gordon Macdonald asked him to join the Ottawa delegation to complete the final negotiations for union, he accepted. 'In the best interests of Newfoundland,' he informed MacDonald after consulting with supporters throughout the island, 'it is my duty to accept Your Excellency's request ... The most urgent necessity for us all is to act in what will be the best interest of the people of Newfoundland so that we will be able to work and live together as a united people, whatever the future may hold for us.'[58] A small group within the RGL was determined to fight for the return of responsible government to the bitter end; one could hardly have expected otherwise, considering the high-spirited campaigns waged by both groups.[59] Nevertheless, MacKay must have been accurate in his assessment. If 48 per cent of the voters remained vehemently opposed to union with Canada, the events after 22 July would not have been so peaceful; after all, much of the opposition was concentrated in and around the dominion's capital.

The editorial comment in the two St John's dailies also accepted the people's decision. Even the ardently pro-responsible government *Daily News* editorialized: 'We are not fighting against a union which is clearly inevitable. It would be political suicide for a Canadian parliament to reject the opportunity of rounding off the Dominion by the inclusion of Newfoundland and Labrador. We are in, even if it takes many months to make the deal official.' The *News*, however, remained doubtful that Newfoundland could expect proper terms with Canada without a duly elected government representing Newfoundland's interests.[60] The rival *Evening Telegram* chastised those who continued to fight against union; a few days before the Newfoundland delegation departed for Ottawa, it wrote that 'this is not the time for a display of rank partisanship. It is a time when all should be working with all honesty and sincerity of purpose for the welfare of the State.'[61] The *Sunday Herald*, the champion of the PEU, also acquiesced. Similarly, Lewis Ayre, president of the Newfoundland Board of Trade, reflected the mood of most Newfoundlanders when he warned in the year-end edition of the *News* that 'there will be little room for dissension among us and anyone attempting to divide the country for political or selfish reasons will be guilty of a great injustice to his fellow New-foundlanders.'[62]

When the cabinet decided on 27 July to accept Newfoundland into Confederation, it was the only logical thing to do. Newfoundland had, after all, voted to join after Canada had made its position known. Although the decision to proceed might create rumblings of discontent in the Maritimes if Newfoundland received terms considered too generous, King realized that union was the only course. For once, he ignored political considerations and did what he thought was best for Canada and himself. 'This will be completing the nation in its physical boundaries,' he recorded in his diary. In addition to nationalistic motives, King derived considerable personal pride from being a Father of Confederation:

I had never dreamt that my name would probably be linked through years to come with the bringing into Confederation of what will be the 10th and quite clearly the last. Having relation to my grandfather's part in laying the foundation of responsible government, it is interesting that it should be left to me as practically the last of the completed task before giving up Leadership of my Party, to have been the one, as Prime Minister, to announce the entry within a few month's time, of Newfoundland into Confederation. It is wholly probable that, if spared, I shall have something of significance to do with the event when it comes to pass. Might even be listed as one of the Fathers of larger Confederation.

When King announced the Canadian decision on 30 July 1948, he told the people that the plebiscite in favour of union was 'clear and beyond all possibility of misunderstanding.' He may have lied a little when he added that it was attained 'without any trace of influence or pressure from Canada.'[63] The Prime Minister then invited a delegation from Newfoundland to negotiate terms of union on the basis of the 1947 Canadian proposals to the National Convention. With the word 'negotiate,' King had opened the door to changes in the earlier proposal for union.

IV

Once the decision had been made, both the British and Canadian governments agreed that the process of union should begin immediately. With the approval of the Dominions Office, the Newfoundland gov-

ernor appointed a delegation on 5 August to negotiate the final terms
of union with Canada. The delegation alone would decide whether
the deal worked out in Ottawa was acceptable. There were no real
surprises when the delegation was named. The two leading Confederates, Smallwood and F. Gordon Bradley, were both appointed, as
well as Chesley A. Crosbie. St John's lawyer and former chairman of
the National Convention John B. McEvoy was selected, and two
prominent businessmen, Gordon A. Winter, a young St John's manufacturer and former president of the Newfoundland Board of Trade,
and Philip Gruchy, vice-president and general manager of the Anglo-
Newfoundland Development Company, one of the country's two large
pulp and paper mills, were also invited. Albert Walsh served as chair.[64]

The Newfoundland delegation convened for the first time on 25 August and spent the next six weeks planning strategy for the Ottawa
negotiations.[65] The obvious starting point was, of course, the proposed
arrangements for union submitted earlier to the National Convention.
The delegation meticulously scrutinized the document, best known
as the Grey Book (because of the colour of the covers), looking for
problems that might arise from union based on the 1947 proposal.
Government officials were paraded before the delegation, pointing
out potential problems with the proposed terms, and a large number
of individuals put in an appearance to express concern over particular issues or to lobby for protection from the adverse effects of union.
The delegation realized very early that under the proposed arrangements, because of the province's limited tax base, Newfoundland
would be saddled with a deficit from the beginning. When the delegation discussed asking Canada to increase the subsidy to be paid to
Newfoundland, Smallwood said that the arrangement worked out in
1947 paid more proportionately to Newfoundland than to the Maritimes and, 'to avoid repercussions in the Maritime Provinces, the
words "and in recognition of the special problems created for the Island Province of Newfoundland by geography and a sparse and scattered population" had been included in the clause.' He said that there
was 'absolutely no possibility' of having the amount of the subsidy
increased.[66] There might be some movement on the transitional grants,
Smallwood suggested, but not if the delegation based its demands on
fiscal need alone.

Smallwood was clearly the most knowledgeable on the proposed
terms and the self-proclaimed expert on the mechanisms of the Canadian federal system. More importantly, he possessed remarkable in-

sight into how Canadians – bureaucrats and politicians alike – would view the various proposals that the delegation contemplated during its preparations. Smallwood realized that the federal government could not be seen to favour Newfoundland over the existing provinces, and he continually reminded his colleagues of the constraints on the Canadian government. He tried to impress upon them that their best hope to improve the terms lay in building a convincing case based on the colony's peculiar and unique circumstances. Newfoundland had to show that it was a special case.[67] Smallwood said that Ottawa had consistently refused requests from the provinces on the basis of need. Walsh, on the other hand, thought that if the delegation could show that union would generate more revenue than Ottawa had anticipated when it compiled its estimates of revenue and expenditure in 1947, the federal government might be willing to offer better terms. Smallwood disagreed, though the other members of the delegation thought that Walsh's proposal would dispel the myth of Canada's generosity. Smallwood continued to caution the delegation that 'it was imperative that the case submitted by the delegation in favour [of additional financial assistance] should be unassailable from every angle.'[68]

Smallwood also said that if the delegation hoped to increase financial assistance, it must be shown quite clearly that the revenue raised by taxation in the new province would be quite limited because of the country's peculiar development. When the delegation had W.M. Marshall, secretary of finance, produce a draft provincial budget, it became clear that in each of the first two years of union there would be a deficit of $5 million, though by the time the delegation had completed its work, the projected deficit had doubled. Prepared without final revenue figures, the budget provided merely for the maintenance of existing services without allowing for the improvement and extension of others.[69] Consequently, finances took precedence over all other issues when the Newfoundland delegation presented its demands in Ottawa. Its memorandum to the Canadian government reflected Smallwood's view; instead of simply asking for additional revenues, it attempted to build a special case by emphasizing Newfoundland's peculiar features:

The cost of maintaining services for a small population scattered over a long coastline will impose a heavy burden on the new government. Revenue to maintain these services will have to be sought from people who are, in the main, fishermen and seasonal workers accustomed to a system of indirect taxation and traditionally opposed to any system of direct taxation. It therefore follows that the most important question for consideration is the ability of the new Province to provide public services which will remain her sole responsibility. While the standard of these services has been considerably improved within the past decade, the present standard is below that of any Province of Canada.

The delegation warned that if the financial arrangements were not improved an annual deficit of $10 million was inevitable: 'revenue from provincial sources, plus anticipated Federal grants, will be inadequate to meet the cost of those public services which remain the responsibility of the Province.' The gap could not be bridged either by increasing revenue from provincial sources or by reducing the present level of public services. 'The existence of this gap presents a problem which is more than a financial one,' the delegation warned. 'It is one the solution of which is a prerequisite to workable union. It should therefore be placed in the forefront of the discussions.'[70]

In all, the memorandum contained forty-one sections, most responding to points in the 1947 Canadian proposal. What was missing from the Newfoundland agenda is also quite revealing: that matters pertaining to the future economic development of the province were absent was a terrible blunder. In fact, the broader picture of Newfoundland's economic development was discussed neither by the delegation before it left St John's nor with the Canadians in Ottawa. Yet it was not as though the delegation would have had to start from scratch. In September 1944, the Commission of Government had presented to London an ambitious reconstruction plan costing in excess of $100 million. The plan was beyond Whitehall's financial capabilities at the time, and it received little attention during the constitutional wrangling after 1945. Nevertheless, the commission's reconstruction strategy reflected considerable planning and insight into the social and economic development of Newfoundland and shows very clearly that Newfoundlanders were looking ahead in 1948. It is regrettable that the plan was not dusted off for discussion in Ottawa. Although the first provincial government embarked upon some of the projects originally envisaged by the commission, this was more by accident than design. During the 1948 negotiations, the commission and its ideas were relegated to the sidelines.[71]

In Ottawa, preparations began within a few days of King's invitation to Newfoundland. Canadian civil servants were coached before the arrival of the delegation in the correct pronunciation of the word 'Newfoundland.' Charles J. Burchell, who had been reappointed Cana- dian high commissioner to Newfoundland, told Ottawa that 'the rule is simply to give the syllables the same emphasis as in the word "un- derstand."' They were warned against calling any resident of the is- land a 'Newfie.' The Interdepartmental Committee on Newfoundland (ICN) was reconvened 'to consider and report on urgent administra- tive problems of the interim period and matters of procedure and pol- icy relating to union.' On 10 September, the Cabinet Committee on Newfoundland was reconstituted, and Milton Gregg, minister of fish- eries, was later included, on the suggestion of the deputy minister of fisheries, Stewart Bates, that a Maritime representative should be pre- sent to ensure that Canada did not offer Newfoundland terms that might create problems in the region.[72] It was feared from the begin- ning that there might be serious differences between Newfoundland and the Maritime provinces.

Under the direction of R.A. MacKay, the ICN established five sub- committees, which reported to cabinet on 1 October. With the excep- tion of the fisheries subcommittee, the reports were very general, merely reviewing the 1947 proposals and outlining responsibilities to be assumed by Canada after union. Because the reports did not out- line strategy for the negotiations, Canada was hardly prepared to begin actual negotiations when the Newfoundland delegation arrived in Ottawa.[73] Mitchell Sharp recalls that there had been discussions on principles, but no specifics had been worked out; Ottawa had cer- tainly not staked out its final position on any issue, largely because it had to reconcile the demands of Newfoundland with what was eas- ily defensible in the Maritime provinces.[74] First, it had to hear New- foundland's demands.

Nonetheless, a definite willingness existed on the part of Canadian politicians to reach an agreement that would satisfy Newfoundland. Lester Pearson, who had not forgotten how shabbily Canada had been treated during the leased-bases negotiations, insisted that Ottawa do everything possible to complete union. Furthermore, he realized that the manner in which the negotiations were conducted would have an effect on subsequent relations between Ottawa and St John's. 'There will be a good deal of sensitiveness on the part of Newfoundlanders about the present position,' he wrote to St Laurent on 3 August, 'and I think that it would be wise to lean over backwards to avoid giving any cause for irritation, especially since such irritation would linger long after confederation is accomplished.' Moreover, to create the right atmosphere in Newfoundland, a high commissioner should be reappointed (Canada had replaced him with a junior official during the referenda to remove any suggestion of influence).[75] MacKay shared Pearson's sentiments and suggested that the government modify the 1947 terms in Newfoundland's favour. If so, he argued, it would dispel the claim of the Responsible Government League that Canada dictated the terms to Newfoundland. Furthermore, nearly 48 per cent of Newfoundlanders had voted for the return of responsible government, and if the terms were improved it would make union more acceptable. And, MacKay added, the 1947 proposals had not been criticized in Canada – not even for their special transitional grants; hence, improvements were possible without worrying about adverse political publicity.[76]

The two delegations met for the first time on 6 October. Albert Walsh spoke for the Newfoundland side, and St Laurent, then minister of justice and Liberal party leader but not yet prime minister, and Brooke Claxton, minister of national defence and deputy chairman of the Cabinet Committee on Newfoundland, shared the duty for Canada.[77] Ottawa adopted a conciliatory approach early on, a sign of its willingness to try to meet the special needs of the new province. Consequently, many issues were settled quickly. The federal government agreed in Term 46 to allow the production of oleomargarine, which was prohibited in Canada, and to enrich it and flour to compensate for dietary deficiencies throughout Newfoundland; in Term 38 it extended the benefits for Canadian veterans to Newfoundlanders, including re-establishment credits which had been refused in 1947; and Ottawa consented to Newfoundland's demand for constitutional safeguards in education. The British North America (BNA) Act provided constitutional guarantees for denominational schools by allowing appeal to the governor in council if educational rights were violated. Such a recourse had not worked. Since Newfoundland had a long history of denominational education, St Laurent allowed the delegation to write its own constitutional safeguards to improve upon the BNA Act. Under Term 17, Newfoundland maintained control over its denominational system of education, but the delegation placed the constitutional safeguard with the courts rather than with the governor in council. St Laurent later said that union was much more complex in 1949 than it had been in 1867, and the differences between

Newfoundland and Canada had to be harmonized with the fundamental basis of the Canadian constitution. Where differences existed, the terms for Newfoundland were often improved.[78]

MacKay reported to Bridle on 21 October that 'on the whole, it seems to be a rather happy family party.'[79] But families often quarrel over finances, and this was true of the 1948 negotiations when the delegation demanded that Ottawa sweeten the financial deal to alleviate the large deficit that the province would incur under the 1947 proposal. Ottawa was already worried over financial matters. Sharp had led a group of senior bureaucrats to Newfoundland in early September 1948 to make a preliminary study of the administrative problems involved, and had discovered that government officials had greatly underestimated in 1947 the revenues Canada would collect in Newfoundland. 'This is an embarrassing situation,' he wrote to the ICN, 'because it is being alleged that we purposely underestimated our revenues in order to mislead the Newfoundland public into believing that the costs to the Canadian Government were higher than they actually will be.' He added that the delegation might attempt to get better terms by showing that the costs to Canada were not as high as Canada had suggested.[80] In spite of this, when the subcommittee on finance and economic policy made its report to the cabinet, it noted that 'the basic premise underlying the Canadian offer to Newfoundland was that no special terms could be offered Newfoundland which any of the existing provinces could claim should be extended to them.' In other words, the terms were similar to those enjoyed by other provinces or were of a transitional nature, designed only for a brief period.[81] The Canadian negotiators held firmly to this position, and P.A. Clutterbuck, now British high commissioner in Ottawa, reported that the Canadian delegation was unresponsive to Newfoundland concerns over the expected annual deficit of nearly $10 million. Walsh and Smallwood had told him in separate conversations that 'unless [the] Canadian attitude becomes more responsive and sympathetic, Confederation is doomed.'[82] MacKay also recognized the problem. If the financial terms are not improved, he told Bridle, a majority of the delegation might refuse to sign. 'Although our friend W.C. Clark [the deputy minister of finance] may put up a pretty stiff fight,' he added, 'I sense some disposition at the top to improve the terms, at least a little.'[83]

Officials within the Department of Finance, however, were more reluctant to improve the terms than those at External. The financial problems were just as big an issue in Canada as they were in New-foundland. The problem in Ottawa was how much could be offered without offending and stirring up discontent in the other provinces. Consequently, much of the discussion was between various govern-ment officials over what Ottawa could afford and what Newfound-land would need. The issue often became what was the minimum the delegation would accept. There was little inducement to get New-foundland to join. In fact, face-to-face negotiations with the delega-tion were few, especially on the financial terms, though internal discussions over Newfoundland between the nationalistic Department of External Affairs and the parsimonious Department of Finance were often heated.[84]

Finance officials had resolved not to give Newfoundland more than any other province received, at least not until Canada had driven a hard bargain.[85] Sharp's subcommittee on finance and economic policy suggested that 'the Canadian replies to various financial questions raised by the Newfoundland delegation should be given at one time in order to maintain a strong bargaining position.'[86] Sharp also re-minded the cabinet committee that the level of expenditure and rev-enue was a matter of provincial concern, and Newfoundland's level of taxation was pitiful; only $13 per capita from local sources com-pared with $50 per capita in New Brunswick, $49 in Nova Scotia, and $29 in Prince Edward Island. Although it would take time to tap local sources of revenue, Sharp and others at Finance insisted that New-foundland take immediate steps in that direction. If Ottawa conceded Newfoundland's demands for an increase in the transitional subsidies to alleviate the deficit without a commitment to increase the provin-cial revenues, the problem would persist. 'Too much temporary as-sistance,' Sharp wrote on 29 October, 'would probably result in a postponement of necessary provincial action to balance the budget.' Nonetheless, he realized the gravity of the situation and feared that if Canada did not accede the negotiations might break down.[87] Fail-ure at this juncture might have destroyed all future hope of union.

St Laurent also recognized the problem. In an attempt to find a so-lution, he suggested on 2 November that the two sides begin infor-mal and private consultations without making any commitment to produce a settlement to Newfoundland's budget deficit. A day later, he told the cabinet that 'unless some substantial additional assistance were forthcoming from the federal government, it was likely that ne-gotiations would have to be broken off.' While he acknowledged that

changes in the 1947 financial arrangement might create political difficulties in the Maritimes, a solution to the financial impasse had to
be found.[88] During this critical stage of negotiations, Pearson again
telegraphed to St Laurent that

I still feel that the national interest requires that Newfoundland should be
brought into federation if at all possible and that the present may be our last
opportunity to do so. I think, therefore, that we should be prepared to improve our financial position to the extent necessary on the assumption that
the Newfoundland delegation do not make impossible demands, and if this
can be done without raising difficulties with the existing provinces.[89]

C.D. Howe shared the sentiments of his cabinet colleague and asked
his trusted adviser, Alex Skelton, director general of the Research
Branch of the Department of Reconstruction and Supply, what it
would take to satisfy the Newfoundland delegation.

Skelton was blunt: unless some arrangement was made the Newfoundland delegation would be justified in refusing to sign the terms.
Although the deficit stemmed from Newfoundland's financial weakness and the low income level that limited local taxation, Newfoundlander's reputed aversion to property tax and other local
taxation was unacceptable, he said. Like Sharp, he realized that municipal taxation and property tax would take time to develop. Sales
taxes, on the other hand, should be introduced at the time of union.
If a sales tax – the most effective means of raising revenue in a relatively undeveloped and unindustrialized economy – were imposed
upon the removal of the tariff from Canadian imports, there would
be few political or economic problems, as the reduction in the cost of
living and import duties would exceed a new provincial sales tax. As
revenue increased from local sources, the deficit would progressively
diminish. Here Skelton saw a solution: the transitional grant offered
in 1947 should be doubled, but tapered off over ten years rather than
twelve. A general understanding should be reached with the delegation on the encouragement of municipal institutions, municipal services, and property taxes. MacKay supported Skelton's proposal, but
James Coyne at the Bank of Canada and Sharp at Finance thought the
grant unnecessarily high, though they, too, realized the necessity of a
modest increase. Skelton argued that the additional subsidy would
facilitate improvements to the Newfoundland public service, justify
an effective provincial tax system after union, and 'make it possible

to clear up practically all the other outstanding issues at the departmental official level and put an end to these interminable time-consuming conferences.'[90]

The Newfoundland delegation suggested that a solution might be found in Whitehall. If London absorbed half of Newfoundland's sterling debt, approximately $16.5 million, Canada would be free to provide an equivalent amount without increasing its expenditure to reduce the estimated provincial deficit. St Laurent baulked at the suggestion, as it would take considerable time to finalize even if the British agreed. Moreover, it might mean sending the Newfoundland delegation home without the signing of the terms. Newfoundlanders might interpret this as a lack of Canadian goodwill – hardly the way to begin union. Another solution had to be found. MacKay reminded Claxton that the original transitional grants recognized the special needs of Newfoundland and were only for the transitional period until the new province had adjusted its 'existing administrative and tax system to that of a province within the federal system.' A substantial increase in the grant therefore would not give any province reason to complain, as the principle remained unaltered. 'I should think also that an offer of this kind,' MacKay added, 'would tend more to strengthen the sentiment for union and to lessen the criticism against it in Newfoundland, than would an offer by the United Kingdom to assume part of the debt in order to make union possible.' Thus the cabinet committee refused to involve London, and St Laurent adopted a variation of Skelton's proposal. A supplementary grant of $16.5 million was offered in addition to the original transitional grant on a descending scale during the first eight years of union.[91] St Laurent had overruled the officials in the Department of Finance who feared that special financial concessions for Newfoundland would find all the provinces beating on Ottawa's door.

Even so, some officials lobbied for strict conditions on the supplementary grant. Above all, they insisted that Newfoundland implement taxes to reduce the prospective gap in the current account after union. If the province refused to introduce a system of taxation, then some sort of penalty should be imposed, perhaps something as severe as allowing the grants to lapse after the first year. Because Newfoundland was allowed to keep its sterling deposits and other revenues due, it would begin union with a surplus of nearly $45 million. Term 24 of the terms of union stipulated that one-third of the surplus was to be placed on deposit with the federal government for the first eight years of union to cover expenditures on current account. The remaining two-thirds were made available to Newfoundland for development of the province's resources and for improving and extending public services. 'It will be a very serious temptation to a government and legislature quite inexperienced in managing public funds,' MacKay cautioned St Laurent, to use the surplus to avoid taxation. He suggested that Newfoundland should limit withdrawals from the surplus in one year to $4 to $5 million.[92] Skelton disagreed, though he shared MacKay's concern. Newfoundland should certainly meet its share of the financial gap by raising new taxation rather than by drawing on the accumulated surplus. 'It seems clear that it would be considered an infringement of provincial autonomy to specify the provincial taxes which Newfoundland would be required to levy after Confederation,' Skelton wrote to Howe.[93] Skelton also doubted that withdrawals from the Newfoundland surplus could be limited: 'it not only smacks of loan control and tutelage which would be resented by all provinces, but seems to me unrealistic in the light of Newfoundland's probable capital requirements.' The Newfoundland delegation had been equally concerned that the surplus be used wisely. Walsh suggested early in the negotiations that no more than $2.5 million should be available in any given year to meet deficits on current accounts. At a subsequent meeting, however, he said that upon reconsideration the delegation had decided not to propose any more restrictive conditions regarding the use to be made of the accumulated financial surplus.[94]

St Laurent presented the revised proposal to the Newfoundland delegation, and 'wondered ... if this would meet the situation.' The new proposal effectively increased the transitional grant by $16.5 million to be spread over twelve years on a tapered scale, raising it from $26.25 million to $42.75 million. The chairman of the Newfoundland delegation asked for an additional $2.75 million. When St Laurent refused, Walsh chose not to push further, as the Canadians had considerably improved the 1947 proposal. Though willing to discuss the disbursement of the supplementary transitional grant, St Laurent also refused Walsh's suggestion of $2.5 million for the first year and $2 million for the next seven. 'This is scarcely in line with the idea of the transitional grant which was that Newfoundland's taxable revenue could only be developed gradually and therefore the grant should taper off,' MacKay later explained to Claxton. Such an arrangement was less defensible against provincial criticism since it departed from the tapering-off principle outlined in the 1947 proposed terms.[95] The cabinet agreed on 15 November to the increase in the transitional grant, but St Laurent, who had finally replaced King as prime minister on the same day, said 'a review of estimates of provincial expenditure made it clear that, even with this special fund, a provincial government would not be able to carry on effectively. Time would be required to develop new sources of provincial taxation.'[96] This became Term 29. Because there was no satisfactory way found of providing for the imposition of appropriate and reasonable taxation by the province at the time of union, Escott Reid, acting under-secretary of state for external affairs, told Claxton that 'it has, therefore, been concluded that the provincial government and legislature should be left full responsibility in this respect.'[97] Ottawa could not be Newfoundland's guardian.

Nevertheless, Canadian officials remained worried about Newfoundland's will to impose new taxation. After all, the delegation had decided to forgive all income and corporation taxes for the first three months of 1949. Minister of Finance D.C. Abbott warned that such action made it very difficult to justify the increased transitional grants to the new province and threatened to raise embarrassing questions in Parliament. The Newfoundland delegation held its ground, however, and maintained that it was 'necessary to remit these taxes in order to cushion the change to Newfoundland business which Confederation would entail.'[98] Canada had already agreed to extend to Newfoundland the same benefits offered to Canadians in 1943 when the exigencies of war forced the federal government to implement a pay-as-you-earn system of income-tax collection rather than having its citizens paying their previous year's taxes in a lump sum at the end of the government's fiscal year. Hence, Newfoundlanders were granted an income tax holiday for the first three months after union. Deductions began at source on 1 July 1949.[99] By contrast, Canada refused to honour various tax and customs exemptions that Newfoundland governments had granted to private companies before union.[100] This was one of the last issues to be resolved as the Newfoundland delegation pressed strongly for the recognition of such contracts, 'partly on the ground of sacredness of contract, partly on the ground that Newfoundland might be liable to the companies concerned if the Canadian Government pleaded to levy taxation in excess of those [sic] provided under the contract.'[101] Canada recognized Newfoundland's concern in Term 27, section 4, of the Terms of Union, noting that if Newfoundland signed a tax agreement with Ottawa it would not be required to 'impose on any person or corporation taxation repugnant to the provisions of any contract entered into with such person or corporation before the date of the agreement and subsisting at the date of the agreement.'[102]

By 22 November the two sides started to draft an agreement. Not until 11 December and thirteen drafts later, more than two months after the delegation arrived in Ottawa, were negotiations completed and an agreement on union reached. Including the various terms discussed above, the two sides hammered out fifty Terms of Union that admitted the island of Newfoundland and Labrador (as defined by the Judicial Committee of the Privy Council in 1927) into Canada as the province of Newfoundland. The Canadian constitution, save for the provisions contained in the Terms of Union, was to come into force in Newfoundland 'immediately before the expiration of the thirty-first day of March, 1949.' The pre-1934 constitution of Newfoundland was to become the constitution of the province subject to the Terms of Union and the British North America Acts, 1867 to 1946. A schedule attached to the terms provided for seven electoral districts, which would each return one member to the House of Commons. Six members would represent the province in the Senate. The provincial executive would follow the form in the other provinces: the governor general in council was to appoint a lieutenant-governor who would be advised by a premier and his cabinet, the executive council. All the Newfoundland laws that existed prior to union would have force, subject to the Terms of Union, unless otherwise repealed, altered or abolished by either the federal or provincial legislature. The statutes of the Canadian Parliament would take effect in Newfoundland as soon as practicable after union, but not until the proper machinery was in place. The application of Canadian criminal law, for instance, was delayed until the law enforcement agencies and the courts had time to familiarize themselves with the new Canadian regime. It was clear that Canada wanted to implement union with the minimum of disruption.

Under the terms, Canada assumed responsibility for a wide array of public services, including the Newfoundland Railway, Gander airport, postal services, and aid to marine navigation. The federal government was required to maintain a freight and passenger steamship service between North Sydney and Port aux Basques. Newfoundland retained its natural resources, but as later events were to show, the province's jurisdiction did not extend to the offshore resources. The terms also provided for federal technical employees and agencies to assist in an economic survey of the province to determine what resources and industries might be developed or expanded. As well, Canada extended to Newfoundland 'on the same basis and subject to the same terms and conditions as in the case of other provinces of Canada, the welfare and other public services provided from time to time by Canada for the people of Canada generally.' This was the most immediate and visible sign of union, as Newfoundlanders now received Canada's unemployment insurance, family allowances, veterans' benefits, and old-age pension, and the province qualified for health grants, housing assistance, and a number of other programs. Most of these programs were immediately beneficial to the province.

Clutterbuck wrote from Ottawa that the terms were more favourable to Newfoundland in matters about which the delegation had expressed the greatest concern – finances and fisheries.[103] Crosbie, though, refused to sign, claiming that the financial position of Newfoundland was far from secure. It was courting chaos, he claimed, to use the accumulated surplus to cover the budgetary deficit, even for the short term. He pointed out that the secondary industries were very vulnerable after Confederation. 'It is impossible to adapt [the] Canadian economy to this country over-night,' he charged, 'without causing chaos and distress in many places, particularly when for centuries we have had our own economy peculiar to this country. I feel therefore that much unemployment will follow such a drastic move.'[104]

Time has proven Crosbie accurate in his assessment of the inadequacies of the terms. That they did not provide for Newfoundland's financial security was equally clear to Smallwood and the other members, but they believed that the terms were not etched in stone and that Ottawa would prove responsive later on if the province encountered financial difficulty. Even so, the delegation had won substantial revisions to the 1947 financial proposal, and Term 29 provided for a royal commission to review the province's financial position within eight years of union and, if necessary, to recommend additional assistance if required. The delegation failed to realize, however, that governments change; and as the events of 1959 were to show, the Conservative government of John Diefenbaker was not as responsive to the financial needs of the province as the Liberal government of 1948.

The delegation won important concessions in 1948 by emphasizing Newfoundland's uniqueness. Ottawa had been equally anxious to meet Newfoundland concerns; however, the federal government had to weigh each demand from the Newfoundland delegation against the constraints placed on it by the other members of the federation. In other words, federal officials and politicians had to balance the terms offered to Newfoundland with what they perceived to be the reaction to such an offer in other provincial capitals. During the negotiations the Newfoundlanders had their first taste of the limitations and constraints of Canadian federalism.

High Commissioner Burchell reported from St John's that the Terms of Union had been favourably received, especially in the outports. 'Even among the opponents of Confederation in St John's the Terms have made a rather deep impression,' he declared, 'and while some of them continue to grumble, they are finding it rather difficult, at this stage at least, to criticize their substance with any measure of success.' Reports from the outports appearing in the *Evening Telegram* used such words as 'seemingly very considerate,' 'splendid work,' and 'very generous' to describe the terms. The *Newfoundland Journal of Commerce*, the official organ of the Newfoundland Board of Trade, said that it was satisfied with the terms and credited the delegation with obtaining substantially better terms than those offered in 1947. Not surprisingly, it continued to worry that Newfoundland businesses were not adequately protected from the new conditions that might develop as a result of union.[105] Ardent supporters of responsible government, however, remained critical of the terms.[106]

The Newfoundland Bill, giving legislative approval to the Terms of Union, passed Parliament quickly, with all parties supporting the union of Newfoundland with Canada. When Prime Minister St Laurent introduced the address to the king to give approval to the act of union, George Drew, leader of the Progressive Conservatives, hoped to score political points with provincial-rights' advocates, especially in Quebec, where Premier Duplessis continued to protest that the premiers were not consulted. Drew introduced an amendment calling for consultation with the provinces. To put the Conservatives on the spot, Liberal backbencher Wilfred LaCroix moved an additional amendment to put some bite into Drew's motion. The shrewdly crafted Liberal amendment called for not merely consultation but provincial consent.[107] Even Drew realized that such a measure might make union impossible. If he insisted on provincial consent, he might kill union. When he joined with the Liberals to kill the LaCroix amendment, Drew looked ridiculous, and his true motives were there for all to see.

Despite Drew's antics, the address was made to the king, and the British Parliament complied with Canada's request to authorize union. The Newfoundland delegation minimized the role played by the Commission of Government in approving the terms of union. It stayed out of constitutional matters after the referendum, but approved the Terms of Union on 26 January 1949.[108]

V

By the time the British Parliament had passed its legislation, the process of extending federal services was well under way. Planning had begun in early August 1948, when Ottawa reconvened the ICN. The most important consideration for MacKay, who was coordinating the integration, was ensuring that the technical aspects involved in absorbing the existing services in Newfoundland and extending new federal services were ready by 1 April 1949. Both politicians and bureaucrats were aware of the sensitivities of Newfoundland, and officials were constantly 'warned to exercise great care against giving offence or being in any way patronizing towards Newfoundlanders or about Newfoundland conditions.'[109] When the Civil Service Commission received requests for approximately 500 additional employees in Newfoundland, cabinet was alarmed. Ottawa had feared that many federal departments and agencies would be over-zealous in extending their services to the new province. Thus coordination became extremely important, as Canada did not want a large-scale invasion of Newfoundland that might create the impression that it was merely taking over the country. Ottawa also realized that while the Newfoundland Civil Service had operated under rather austere circumstances, it had provided 'generally efficient service on a very economical basis.' If the federal government had too large a presence at the time of union, it would surely invite criticism. The cabinet subsequently ordered all government departments to limit the number of appointments to those actually needed to perform their duties at the time of union, and to increase staff only gradually thereafter.[110]

The extension of federal services fell into two categories: those to be absorbed completely by Canada, and those to be established as new services in Newfoundland. With the former, the Newfoundland personnel had to be retrained to operate in accordance with Canadian law and practice; in the second, the issue centred on whether or not a new establishment was necessary in Newfoundland, and if so, how many employees were required, the classification of each, and how much office space was necessary to begin operation. The cabinet allowed its officials tremendous independence in extending federal services to Newfoundland, but actual establishment did not begin until negotiations concluded. On 28 December the chairman of the cabinet committee authorized federal departments to begin the extension of services to Newfoundland. Within a few weeks, G.P. O'Keefe of the Civil Service Commission arrived in St John's to arrange recruitment for the federal civil service.[111]

Canada had to assume responsibility for Newfoundland civil servants whose departments were absorbed into the federal government. Under Term 39 of the Terms of Union, such employees had to be 'offered employment in these services or in similar Canadian services under the terms and conditions from time to time governing employment in those services, but without reduction in salary or loss of pension rights acquired by reason of service in Newfoundland.'[112] Salaries for Newfoundland civil servants at the lower range of $3,000 per annum were comparable with Canadian rates. The Newfoundland superannuation scheme, however, unlike the Canadian, was non-contributory. Consequently, when Newfoundland employees joined the Canadian contributory superannuation plan, a considerable reduction in pay resulted. To solve the problem, C.H. Bland, chairman of the Civil Service Commission, suggested that Ottawa apply the same policy it had adopted when it revised salaries in 1947. Newfoundland employees who received less than the minimum would proceed to the Canadian minimum, those at the maximum would proceed to the Canadian maximum, and those at intermediate rates would proceed to the Canadian equivalent. In no case, however, should the salary increase exceed $600 – unless duties and responsibilities changed – until a thorough investigation of each position had been completed. 'It would appear,' Bland concluded, 'that such a policy will have the effect of not reducing the take-home pay of the Newfoundland employees as of April 1949 and may allow some small increase.'[113] St Laurent had earlier made it quite clear that he wanted Term 39 interpreted to benefit Newfoundlanders transferring to the Canadian civil service.[114]

The administrative changeover went smoothly. Each department was individually responsible for its own administrative integration, and there were no serious disruptions. Burnham Gill, then editor of the *Western Star* of Corner Brook, remembers with affection the Canadian officials who came to Newfoundland. 'They were friends of the new province,' he recalls, 'and the greatest ambassadors of goodwill' that Ottawa could have sent. The federal officials were knowledgeable, usually high-ranking public servants who could make a decision on the spot,[115] and to them must go much of the credit for launching union on its proper course.

VI

There had been considerable discussion in Ottawa over how Newfoundland was to be governed between 1 April and the first election. Smallwood and Bradley had raised the issue of a provisional government when they attended a preliminary, though unofficial, meeting with Canadian bureaucrats in early August 1948. Sharp had suggested that the Commission of Government be retained until elections were held, though it would report to Ottawa rather than London. Such an arrangement would allow the imposition of 'certain taxes during the interim period ...'[116] The legal subcommittee of the ICN, however, pointed out that governing Newfoundland was a political not a legal question, and one for the Newfoundland authorities to decide. The Newfoundland delegation made its position clear: 'It is assumed that, after union, the Lieutenant-Governor will immediately appoint a Provincial Executive to administer the Government of the Province.'[117] St Laurent was uncertain that such a procedure would be appropriate. He wanted a 'formula which would reduce any possibility of public criticism to a minimum, yet provide the basic machinery necessary for administration during that period.'[118] He eventually decided upon the appointment of a lieutenant-governor to establish an government on 1 April 1949. Bradley and Smallwood lobbied hard for the appointment of Sir Leonard Outerbridge, an influential St John's merchant who had furthered the cause of union immensely with his public support for Confederation during the second referendum. St Laurent even asked Bradley to approach Outerbridge about becoming the province's first lieutenant-governor.

When Smallwood and Bradley went too far, however, the Prime Minister changed his mind on Outerbridge.[119] Mitchell Sharp recalls that official Ottawa was horrified when Smallwood announced in January 1949 that he would become premier and Outerbridge lieutenant-governor. The aristocratic Outerbridge was embarrassed. Smallwood had clearly overstepped himself and, as Don Jamieson recalls in his memoirs, it 'was the first hint of a rift in the relationship between Smallwood and his new friends in the Liberal Government in Ottawa.'[120] While St Laurent continued to let Smallwood and Bradley believe that their candidate was also his choice for lieutenant-governor, he personally lobbied Walsh to take the post for a short time. Pickersgill claims that St Laurent decided upon Walsh only when rumours reached Ottawa that Outerbridge refused to accept Smallwood as premier unless Ottawa so directed.[121] Unsubstantiated rumours hardly influenced such an important decision. Moreover, St Laurent despatched his parliamentary assistant, Walter Harris, to investigate the rumours only after his invitation to Walsh.[122] St Laurent used Outerbridge's reluctance to appoint Smallwood to justify his appointment of Walsh. In a memorandum to Bradley, St Laurent wrote: 'it is felt that we should accept at face value his [Outerbridge's] reluctance to make political decisions without direct instructions from the Government ...'[123]

Walsh's administrative experience helped to get responsible government 'properly launched' in Newfoundland. 'It seemed to me,' St Laurent later informed Burchell, 'that an element of continuity and stability would be provided if Walsh would act as Lieutenant Governor until after the provincial elections.'[124] He also realized that the Catholic hierarchy had opposed Confederation, and he feared that the appointment of Outerbridge, a Protestant like Bradley and Smallwood, might be interpreted among Roman Catholics as retaliation for their opposition to union.[125] Walsh, a prominent Catholic, 'would create a reassuring effect and might make such distinguished Catholics as the Archbishop [Edward Roche] and Bishop O'Neill less apprehensive.'[126]

After Sir Albert Walsh was sworn in as lieutenant governor, he followed the procedure laid down earlier by his counterparts in Alberta and Saskatchewan after they were granted provincial status in 1905. That Walsh called upon Smallwood to form a ministry was no surprise. As the widely recognized champion of union, Smallwood had led the Confederates to victory in the second referendum. Prime Minister Louis St Laurent also regarded him as the leader of the Confederate Association, though F. Gordon Bradley, a prominent Liberal politician from the pre-commission days, was nominally elected president. 'It is our feeling,' the Prime Minister wrote to Charles Burchell, Canadian high commissioner, 'that Bradley and Smallwood are the only personalities who, until elections have been held, can be considered to represent any substantial organized body of opinion.' Be-

cause Bradley shunned provincial politics, the Prime Minister concluded, 'Smallwood is the person who should be called upon to form
a provincial administration.' St Laurent maintained that he did not
wish to impose this view on the new lieutenant-governor, but in his
invitation to Walsh to become the king's representative in Newfoundland, he clearly expressed his wish to see Smallwood appointed
premier: 'From everything I hear the Lieutenant-Governor, whoever
he is, will probably feel that Mr. Smallwood should be invited to form
the provincial Executive Council pending the election.'[127] Despite his
public insistence that he did not wish to give any politician an advantage in the first provincial election, St Laurent had obviously
placed Smallwood in the driver's seat; for this, both the St John's
dailies criticized the Prime Minister, as he had bestowed upon Smallwood not only the prestige associated with the premier's office but
also the advantage of calling the first provincial election. The federal
Liberals also stood to reverse a series of by-election losses and increase their slim majority if they won the province in the first federal
vote.

On 1 April, Sir Edward Emerson, the chief justice of Newfoundland, administered the oath of allegiance and the oaths of office to
lieutenant-governor designate Sir Albert Walsh. In turn, Walsh invited
Smallwood to become the province's first premier. With the day's proceedings out of the way, Newfoundland had formally become
Canada's tenth province. The historic occasion arrived eighty-five
years after Newfoundland first considered Confederation and fifteen
years after the surrender of responsible government. The process of
making Newfoundland a Canadian province was already well under
way, though much remained to be done. Among the most important
tasks was to restore democracy.

2

Back to politics: political organization in post-Confederation Newfoundland, 1948–1951

Joseph R. Smallwood struggled to make himself heard. Amid the thunderous ovation from the eleven hundred cheering delegates gathered at St John's from 28 to 30 April 1949 to organize the federal and provincial wings of the Newfoundland Liberal party, his harsh, high-pitched voice was barely audible above the roar. 'Newfoundlanders, fellow Newfoundlanders, fellow Canadians,' he finally bellowed into the microphone. 'Here tonight for the first time in the history of Newfoundland we see the common man gathered to elect those who will represent him in an election. You have come from every cove along our coastline to say just what kind of men you want to represent you. That has heretofore been an unheard of thing in Newfoundland.' The applause grew even louder, and Smallwood paused for a few seconds to bask in the adulation. Then he continued. 'This is no hole in the corner affair where a few people meet to decide a policy or a party. This is a convention where you, the common people, have the say, the right to determine.'[1] With this stance of Lincolnesque devotion to democracy and the common man, Smallwood opened the Liberal convention and effectively formalized Newfoundland's return to party politics after a fifteen-year political hiatus of appointed government. During the convention, Smallwood announced a provincial election for 27 May 1949 to allow Newfoundlanders to elect their first provincial government. When the Liberal party triumphed at the polls, returning twenty-one members to the Progressive Conservatives' five, Smallwood's Liberals began their domination of the political landscape that would span the next two decades.

When the Tories and the Liberals solidified their ties to the two major federal parties, it was a signal of integration into the Canadian political system. Although the Conservatives campaigned for better financial terms with Ottawa, they were merely trying to squeeze more out of Confederation, a tradition that has a long history, especially in the Maritimes and the Prairie provinces. If nearly half the electorate was leery of union and wanted better terms, the Tories had a good campaign weapon. They failed, not because of their program, though the perception that they were anti-Confederates may have cost them some support, but because of the moribund state of their organization. The Liberals had a vastly superior organization extending throughout the entire province. The Conservatives had little organized support in the outports, though – like the Liberals – they fared well in the districts where they had organized. The weak, ineffective leadership that failed to convey party policy to the voters exacerbated the lack of Tory organization. To a lesser extent, late recruitment and internal squabbling contributed to the poor showing, but leadership and organization were the dominant factors in Newfoundland politics in 1949.[2] Thus, what may seem an inevitable Liberal triumph in 1949 flowing from the Confederate victory a year earlier was precisely the dividend that Smallwood deserved after he had campaigned and organized for months prior to voting day.

With the issuing of the election writs, Newfoundlanders were summoned to the polls for the third time in less than a year. It was, however, their first opportunity to elect a government since the election of 1932. In the meantime, the period of commission rule had done little to change the political values and attitudes in the country. The new political parties would operate with the 'political orientation of Newfoundlanders in the twenties and thirties,' where their success lay in 'delivering the goods.' Moreover, the denominational balance remained an important factor, as did the outport–St John's antagonism. Even after union, the people still hoped that their political leaders could deliver the El Dorado promised by earlier leaders Edward Morris and Richard Squires. It was into this political culture that the provincial political parties emerged.[3]

I

Although 1 April marked the official return to party politics, the task of political organization was already well under way. Co-operative Commonwealth Federation leader M.J. Coldwell approached Smallwood even before the second referendum, suggesting that Smallwood and the CCF were fighting the same forces that had exploited New-foundland's people for generations. Smallwood's prior association with labour unions and socialist parties made him an ideal recruit. He had left St John's in 1920 and eventually became a reporter at the New York *Call*, a prominent socialist newspaper of the time. After five years as a socialist propagandist in New York, he returned to New-foundland to organize locals of the International Brotherhood of Pulp, Sulphite and Paper Mill Workers at the Grand Falls and Corner Brook paper mills. Thereafter, he turned to organizing railway workers throughout the country before he became a broadcaster and writer.[4] Coldwell invited Smallwood and Bradley to the CCF convention in Win-nipeg in late August 1948. Coldwell also said that his party would be establishing contacts in Newfoundland as soon as possible.[5] Although Smallwood's decision not to attend obviously disappointed Coldwell, the CCF remained enthusiastic about its prospects in Newfoundland.

Following the Winnipeg convention, the CCF began its drive to or-ganize in the new province. Funds were authorized for Newfound-land, and party treasurer A.M. Nicholson visited the island from 11 to 16 December 1948.[6] Nicholson's tour proved a bitter disappoint-ment. After meeting with both labour officials and private citizens, he realized that the party lacked the support necessary to contest the provincial election.[7] His report to the national executive confirmed what party leaders already suspected: an indigenous organization had failed to develop in Newfoundland, and it looked unlikely that a CCF leader would emerge there. Moreover, a lack of money, a perennial CCF complaint, compounded the problem. Meagre financial resources could be better spent elsewhere.[8]

In fact, CCF failings in Newfoundland were no different from those elsewhere in Atlantic Canada.[9] Although the party enjoyed a little suc-cess in industrial Cape Breton, the region was largely a wasteland for Canada's socialist party. The CCF had hoped for better results in New-foundland. In 1945, a group of trade union leaders created the St John's District Labour Party to contest the municipal election sched-uled for that year. Although the party failed to capture even a single seat, it made a respectable showing, finishing second in the mayoralty race. Greater success followed when it elected two candidates to the National Convention.[10] In fact, a total of six trade unionists and sev-eral former labour activists, including Smallwood, sat in the conven-tion. Moreover, several field workers from Newfoundland's burgeoning cooperative movement were also elected. Even so, the CCF was unable to capitalize on labour's brief foray into political action in the late 1940s. The National Convention and the subsequent referenda traumatized the Newfoundland labour movement, as it splintered over support for the various constitutional options. Ronald Fahey, president of the Newfoundland Federation of Labour, supported the Responsible Government League (RGL). D.I. 'Nish' Jackman, president of the Wabana Mine Workers' Union, favoured economic union with the United States. Smallwood and his rallying cry for union, however, attracted the largest contingent from labour circles, including Harold Horwood, Irving Fogwill, Gregory Power, Charles Ballam, Sam Hefferton, Bill Frampton, Billy Bond Taylor, and Charles Horwood.[11] Similarly, cooperative workers gravitated to him. Hence, Smallwood effectively attracted much of the political left, and during the weeks leading up to the first provincial vote and in the first month after the election, he enacted several progressive labour laws that kept labour friendly for the first years of union.[12] Harold Horwood, himself a labour organizer, recalls that though Smallwood's sympathies lay with the CCF, he realized that it could not finance an election campaign in Newfoundland. It is doubtful that he ever seriously entertained the notion of an alliance with the CCF, as his view of socialism was rather simplistic. His rudimentary style of socialism meant support for policies that improved the life of the toiling masses, as he liked to call the fishermen and lumbermen of Newfoundland.[13]

When Eamon Park, CCF member of the Ontario legislature, visited Newfoundland before the June 1949 federal election to prepare for Coldwell's visit, he found that the CCF had made a fatal mistake in not having organized earlier. 'Many of the best people from our viewpoint,' he wrote to Coldwell, 'are committed to Smallwood and this seriously reduced the number of potential candidates available to us ... On the list I received from the National Office ... several persons are either Liberal candidates or Liberal cabinet ministers.'[14] The CCF had, in fact, lost its first potential leader to Smallwood. Edward Russell, a former teacher, magistrate, and director of cooperatives with the Commission of Government, had considered leading the CCF, but accepted instead Smallwood's offer of a cabinet post.[15] Nish Jackman offered to run provincially for the CCF, but when party secretary David Lewis and the national executive failed to provide financial and administrative assistance, he ran successfully as a Conservative.[16] R.J. Fahey and Grand Falls labour leader James Pond also demonstrated interest in the party, but they, too, joined the Tories. Even then, political ideologies and allegiances in Newfoundland were fluid. Nevertheless, Park established an eight-member provisional committee to handle the initial organization and the federal campaign for CCF candidates.[17] Although labour leader Bill Gillies was the sole CCF candidate in the 1949 federal election, the party maintained interest in Newfoundland and ran at least one candidate in subsequent federal campaigns. After 1954, one or more CCF candidates contested each provincial election, but the party failed to win a seat in the legislature until then party leader Peter Fenwick won a 1984 by-election. Despite Coldwell's hope for success in Newfoundland, Atlantic Canada remained a political desert for the CCF.[18]

II

As with the CCF, the impetus for the organization of the federal and provincial wings of the Progressive Conservative party came from national headquarters in Ottawa. The party brass had thwarted an offer from within Newfoundland to organize a provincial PC party shortly after the second referendum. W.L. Collins, secretary of the RGL, offered to take the initiative in party organization in a personal capacity and not as a member of the league, but Richard A. Bell, national party director, thought that organization should await a successful conclusion to union.[19] Collins and other supporters of responsible government had realized that union was inevitable, and their approach to a major Canadian political party indicated their readiness to prepare for the political future and work within the Canadian system. The Tories were naturally worried about aligning themselves with former RGL supporters. They could, however, have used Collins and others as a launching pad into Newfoundland, and with proper direction from Ottawa they might have built an organization to attract some of the leading and most capable personalities before Smallwood siphoned them into the Liberal party. After all, as later events were to show, ideology and party allegiances mattered little in Newfoundland.

Bell had wanted to dispatch George Nowlan, an aspiring Nova Scotia Conservative, and party president J.M. Macdonnell to Newfoundland to lay the foundation for a provincial organization and to select delegates for the national leadership convention scheduled for the end of September 1948. Fearful that national officials might affiliate with the wrong people or ignore and offend future supporters unless the necessary exploratory work was completed to secure proper contacts,

Nowlan baulked at the suggestion.[20] The Tories missed valuable media coverage in Newfoundland and across Canada by not having New-foundland delegates appear at their convention as the Liberals had done. Although it passed a resolution calling for immediate action in Newfoundland, the party suspended the organizational drive, pend-ing the outcome of negotiations between the Newfoundland and Canadian delegations.[21] Whether George Drew's election as party leader figured in this decision remains a matter of conjecture,[22] but the new leader maintained that the provinces had to agree to New-foundland's entry. Nonetheless, Drew and the Tories supported the Union Bill in Parliament.

The party had had little communication with Newfoundland, and despite the combined efforts of Bell and Macdonnell, reliable contacts were scarce even when they went to the new province to organize the party in early 1949. A formidable task confronted them when they ar-rived in St John's on 19 February, armed only with a letter of intro-duction to Gordon Higgins.[23] They must have realized that many of those who had not supported Confederation might rally around a political party opposed to Smallwood and Bradley, but they soon dis-covered that very little thought had been given to joining the Con-servatives. In fact, those on the losing end in 1948 had leaned towards a nationalist, pro-Newfoundland party, but prior to the arrival of the two Canadians, Smallwood and Bradley had the political field very much to themselves.

After interviewing several likely Conservatives, Bell and Macdon-nell convened a meeting of potential supporters who established a committee to examine the possibility of creating a PC party. Most of the twenty-eight individuals invited had been associated with the fight for responsible government. However, only eight had held executive positions in the RGL, and only J.S. Currie, editor of the *Daily News*, and Collins, who had already attempted a liaison with the Tories, were members of the executive of the RGL elected after the second referen-dum to continue the struggle for responsible government. Those at the meeting were of the same mind as John T. Cheeseman, who had resigned as RGL vice-president shortly after the second referendum and vowed to make union work. In fact, many of those who figured prominently with the Conservatives had played only minor roles in the struggle for responsible government.[24] Not surprisingly, the com-mittee declared two days later that the political future could not be left to Smallwood and Bradley and recommended that a Newfoundland Conservative party would be the most effective means to stop them from controlling the provincial government. A provisional committee, established to organize the PC party in Newfoundland, agreed on the immediate appointment of two permanent organizers and a public-relations officer.[25]

Bell and Macdonnell saw leadership as a major problem for the party. The unanimous choice, they thought, was Raymond Gushue, chairman of the Newfoundland Fisheries Board, but despite considerable pressure, he refused to take the plunge into politics. They had no better luck convincing Donald Jamieson and Geoffrey Sterling, two prominent media personalities, to join the party.[26] Other possibilities, including businessman Chesley Crosbie, Harry Mews, the Newfoundland manager of North American Life Insurance Company and St John's city councillor, and Edgar Hickman, another businessman and member of the National Convention, failed to impress them.[27] Nevertheless, they left St John's reasonably satisfied. They had laid the foundation for the provincial Conservatives and had overseen the selection of two provincial organizers. Newfoundlanders themselves had to build a party that could win the federal and provincial elections expected within a few months.

Although the provisional committee moved quickly to select a headquarters and hire staff, the question of leadership divided the party. The *Evening Telegram* reported in early April that 'if they [the Conservatives] soon don't settle their differences and work as a body behind one leader, the Liberals will sweep the country.'[28] Several people wanted the leadership, but at a St John's meeting on 8 April the party finally settled on Harry Mews, an earlier supporter of responsible government. The partisan *Daily News* described that affair as being 'attended by a large number of citizens representative of all classes and opinion, including visitors from several out-of-town districts.' In fact, the leadership meeting, a cloistered affair, contrasted sharply with the Liberal convention staged later in St John's. No public announcements of a Tory leadership convention ever appeared in either of the St John's dailies, and the Tories themselves advertised their *first public* meeting a few days later.[29]

Mews promised at his nominating meeting to accept Confederation and to unify the province with sound, constructive government. 'Whatever may have been the conflict among us before the advent of Confederation, and however much a feeling of soreness may remain,' he promised in his acceptance speech, 'the fact cannot be ignored that this is still Newfoundland and this island of ours will prosper only if those who have its good at heart will unite to secure good government and a constructive public policy.'[30] Later, in his first radio address as Conservative leader, Mews explained the decision to forge an alliance with a major Canadian political party rather than create a nationalist provincial party. 'After long consultation,' he told those listening,

it was felt that the interests of Newfoundland could be served by full participation in the national life of the Dominion of which we now form a part, and that in so doing we could still preserve the things we cherish, while seeking in our new sphere a more balanced aid of the Federal Government in the development of our resources. To seek these benefits without participating fully in the affairs of the Dominion seemed to be unworthy of Newfoundland, and it was decided to affiliate with the Progressive Conservative Party of Canada, and thus do our part to establish in our country a party which we feel has much to offer our people.[31]

By throwing their weight behind a national political party, the supporters of responsible government had taken another important step towards integration with Canada. Moreover, it was a sign that the former supporters of responsible government were ready to bury the hatchet and accept union.

Because those involved in organizing the party came primarily from St John's and several had earlier links to the RGL, both federal and provincial party leaders realized that the base of the party had to be widened to include the outports. Yet, in the two months before the provincial election, the party élite did little to broaden party support, largely because of Mews's incompetence. It appointed a committee to establish contacts in the outports, but Mews missed a great opportunity to follow through on this, rally the troops, and attract new supporters when he decided against a convention. This would consume too much time, he claimed, and detract from planning for the upcoming provincial election. Neither did he tour the island to make himself and his party better known. Instead, he preferred to speak to voters over the radio.[32] Throughout the period leading to the first vote, the Newfoundland Conservatives continued to look to Bell and the national party for assistance. The national organization gave financial support and provided the provincial Tories with an organizer during the 1949 elections; to the national body must go much of the credit for what little success the provincial Tories achieved.

III

The impetus for organizing the Liberal party came from within New-foundland, not, as with both the Conservatives and the CCF, from national headquarters. In fact, the Liberals evolved from the Confederate Association, which had successfully created the perception of a mass movement, a party of the 'toiling masses' that had pitted the outports against St John's in the referenda battles. Much of the Liberal success can be attributed to the dynamic, charismatic, and capable leadership of Smallwood, who fully understood the one important reality of Newfoundland politics: sixteen of the twenty-eight members elected to the House of Assembly came from outside St John's and the Avalon Peninsula. And the party, especially Smallwood, had ample time to build a foundation and create an informal organization throughout the island. Smallwood toured the island during the winter and spring of 1949, drumming up support for himself and the party he hoped to lead.[33] After the Liberal leadership convention, he campaigned even more vigorously as the party leader.[34] He never missed an opportunity to take the Liberal message to the voters in the outports as well as to those on the Avalon Peninsula.

During the referenda campaigns Smallwood and Bradley had solidified their ties to the Liberal party of Canada. The party had avoided direct financial contributions to Newfoundland, but it supplied the Confederates with a list of loyal donors who, some have suggested, contributed nearly $250,000 to the Confederate cause.[35] After the Confederates emerged victorious from the second referendum, most followed Smallwood and Bradley into the Liberal party. Although Smallwood insists in his autobiography that he was a socialist, he did not see a future for a socialist party in Newfoundland, and opted instead for the Liberals. The pre-1933 Newfoundland Liberal party, he claimed, had traditionally been the party of reform, leading the fight for representative government, the struggle for wider suffrage and the secret ballot, and the first attempts at industrialization with the pulp-and-paper mills and railway construction. Smallwood's ties to the Liberals dated from 1928, when he had sought the party nomination in Corner Brook, only to step aside in favour of party leader Richard Squires. Smallwood then became Squires's campaign manager and editor of the party newspaper until he ran unsuccessfully as a Liberal in the 1932 election that saw all but two of the Squires Liberals defeated.[36] Bradley, too, had a long association with the Liberals, having once served as solicitor general in Squires's government. He survived the Liberal débâcle of 1932.[37]

Bradley and Smallwood attended the national Liberal convention in Ottawa in August 1948 a few days after Prime Minister King decided to accept the results of the second referendum. The Liberal party denied inviting them, and King thought it was particularly unwise to have them appear on the platform. They were well-received, however. Bradley told the cheering delegates that Newfoundland needed an alliance with a prosperous and powerful nation and, in his view, 'the only one with which to form an alliance is Canada.' To equally thunderous applause, Smallwood praised Canada and called Newfoundlanders Canadians.[38] Even King later admitted that he quite enjoyed sitting between them as he 'felt that there was something quite significant about this little feature of the evening.'[39]

Although Smallwood and Bradley were quite adamant that they would join the Liberal party, assurances of political rewards from Prime Minister St Laurent for bringing Newfoundland into Confederation were not immediate. Having been the host of a popular radio program from 1937 to 1943, Smallwood was probably one of the best-known personalities in Newfoundland before the referenda. Even so, many supporters of Confederation, especially those in St John's, turned up their noses at his populist, folksy approach, and Ottawa had remained cool until it finally realized that his efforts were largely responsible for a successful completion of Confederation.[40] Early in the fight for union, J. Scott Macdonald, then Canadian high commissioner in Newfoundland, informed Ottawa that if Bradley withdrew his support, Confederation was destined to fail. 'Mr. Smallwood, though a first-rate propagandist,' he told St Laurent, 'is hardly a substantial enough man to provide the standing and leadership required.'[41] At the outset, Bradley's involvement was crucial, but as the battle for union inched forward, Smallwood clearly emerged as commander-in-chief.

Smallwood often became uneasy about his political future during the final negotiations in Ottawa. By 18 November 1948, he could play the waiting game no longer. He approached R.A. MacKay, then chairman of the steering committee of the Interdepartmental Committee on Newfoundland, and told him that 'if he [Smallwood] and Bradley did not get control, the [Liberal] Government would lose every seat in Newfoundland.' MacKay sensed that Smallwood feared that Chesley Crosbie and John B. McEvoy, former chairman of the National

Convention and close friend of MacKay's, were conspiring to control the interim government.[42] Whatever the reason for Smallwood's anxiety, he received little comforting news on his political future until the negotiations between Newfoundland and Canada concluded on 8 December. Only then did St Laurent turn to the subject of political leadership in Newfoundland. With the constitutional side of the meetings completed, Smallwood recalls that the Prime Minister told him that 'we may turn to some less ponderous matters', and invited Bradley and him along 'for a chat.'[43] Smallwood emerged from the meeting convinced that his ambition to become premier and Bradley's desire to join St Laurent's cabinet were secure. St Laurent realized that Smallwood was the only choice for premier.[44]

Although Smallwood and Bradley quickly established personal ties with St Laurent and the Liberals, they did not rush to organize the provincial and federal wings of the Liberal party in Newfoundland. J.W. Pickersgill, special assistant to the Prime Minister, had suggested to St Laurent that, if Smallwood should be appointed premier, he should be identified as a Confederate, not as a Liberal. It would be more difficult, Pickersgill maintained, for the other parties to wage a successful campaign against the Newfoundland Confederates than against the provincial Liberals.[45] Nevertheless, Smallwood suggested at a Confederate dinner in St John's in early 1949 that the association would become the Liberal party.[46] Plans for this began three days after union when Smallwood asked Bradley to ship flags, bunting, photos, and other paraphernalia left from the Canadian Liberal convention to decorate the Church Lads' Brigade (CLB) Armoury where Newfoundland Liberals would meet to create the party. With Confederate executive members C.F. Garland (secretary treasurer), Ray Petten (chief fund raiser), and Gregory J. Power (assistant campaign manager), Smallwood organized the whole event, hoping, in his own words, 'that a slam-bang convention will go a long way in making a Provincial sweep.'[47] From across the province more than 600 delegates and 500 guests – most prominent citizens in their communities and many former Confederate vice-presidents – were invited to St John's from 28 to 30 April to organize the Liberal party. The Confederate Association absorbed most of the costs with funds that remained from the referenda campaigns. Additional money came from local contributions and from the National Liberal Federation.[48]

Smallwood promoted the Liberal convention as one of ordinary Newfoundlanders. Many of the delegates could not afford to pay their way to the convention, but Smallwood found a quick and effective solution. 'To have invited only those who could afford to come would have been undemocratic, to say the least,' he telegraphed the delegates, 'and the result would not have been a cross section of the people. We have therefore, undertaken to pay the expenses of all delegates who cannot afford to do so themselves.'[49] Needless to say, this furthered the image of the Liberal convention as a people's affair, a stark contrast to the closed Conservative leadership selection process. The image of a party of ordinary Newfoundlanders was carried into advertisements in one St John's newspaper asking for room and board: 'The delegates are plain, ordinary Newfoundlanders. They are not looking for luxury, but plain simple comfort.'[50] Yet the convention was anything but simple. A special train, displaying Union Jacks and banners proclaiming 'We are off to the Liberal Convention,' left Port aux Basques at one end, picked up delegates along the way, and arrived in St John's to be welcomed by a brass band and Smallwood, whom the *Evening Telegram* described as 'wearing an ear-to-ear smile and a very flexible elbow which received plenty of exercise in the handshake way.' Grabbing a microphone at the railway station, he assumed control, broadcasting directions to the delegates before they formed a motorcade through the streets of the capital city on their way to the convention centre.[51]

The delegates, many of them from logging and fishing communities, were impressed by the lavish decorations at the CLB Armoury. One side of the armoury exhibited the names of great Canadian Liberals such as Laurier, King, St Laurent, and Howe, while names of Newfoundland's greatest Liberals – Whiteway, Bond, Squires, Bradley, and Smallwood – were showcased on the opposite wall. Such slogans as 'There's only one Tory Government in North America [Ontario], let's keep it that way,' reminded delegates of the extent of Liberal popularity. In his opening address, which was broadcast across the province, Smallwood provided a history of Canada's political parties. He told them that Newfoundland's future was brightest in Liberal hands. After all, the party was the only one that worked for the 'toiling masses,' and the three Maritime provinces had strong Liberal governments.[52] Many prominent St John's personalities including Lady Helena Squires, wife of former Prime Minister Richard Squires, and St John's mayor Andrew Carnell graced the Liberal platform. Although Smallwood had invited the Maritime premiers, only J. Walter Jones of Prince Edward Island attended. There is no indication that members of the St Laurent cabinet were invited, though Smallwood had earlier suggested to Bradley that some 'federal men' should be present. Senator Gordon Fogo, president of the National Liberal Federation, had to cancel because of the impending federal election.[53]

A carefully orchestrated affair, the convention nonetheless presented the Liberals as a party of ordinary Newfoundlanders involved in the democratic process. Under chairman Eric Cook,[54] various committees kept the delegates busy throughout the three-day affair. Cook was elected president, a position he held for many years, and several of the Confederate Association vice-presidents assumed similar positions in the Liberal party.[55] In a session devoted to party policy, a special policy committee heard debate on a wide range of issues before the delegates ratified the party platform for the provincial election. The convention also broke into district caucuses to nominate candidates to contest the election. In some instances, four or five individuals vied for the nomination, though the Premier told the convention that wherever he sent his cabinet ministers there would be no selection by the local representatives themselves. Later, Smallwood boasted that he met with delegates from the various constituencies to 'tell them ... who their candidates were to be.'[56]

The convention was truly Smallwood's, and the Newfoundland Liberal party, both federal and provincial, was in every sense, his party. During the National Convention Smallwood had directed his message to the outport people, who had listened attentively to the debates on the radio; he had played to the same audience during the referenda. Now, as two drummers led Smallwood and his cabinet into the convention on the opening evening, the delegates erupted into a thunderous cheer to welcome the man who had led them into union with Canada. He was clearly their leader and, when nominations began, he was unopposed for the provincial leadership, as was Bradley, Newfoundland's representative in the federal cabinet, for the leadership of the federal wing of the party.[57] Bradley, who had given the drive for Confederation the credibility it so desperately needed, was no longer necessary for Smallwood's success. After his coronation at the convention, Smallwood was ready to become Newfoundland's premier politician.

IV

Smallwood's announcement of the forthcoming provincial election at the convention signalled the beginning of the official campaign. A few days later, the Prime Minister dissolved Parliament and called a general election for 27 June, in part 'to give the people of Newfoundland the earliest possible opportunity to be represented in Parliament.'[58] The overlapping campaigns worked to Liberal advantage, as Bradley had informed St Laurent before the Newfoundland convention that the provincial and federal Liberals were all one.[59] The CCF, plagued with organizational difficulties, had decided to withdraw from the provincial election and fielded only one candidate in the federal contest, leaving the battle to the Conservatives and the Liberals. The Liberals would have defeated the Conservatives simply because of their superior organization and leadership, but Smallwood had several other advantages – such as his appointment as premier, the recent referendum victory, and the federal social programs – that combined to rout the Conservatives. The Liberal party received the credit for all the benefits that flowed immediately from the federal and provincial governments, as Newfoundlanders – like many other Canadians – had not yet distinguished between the two levels of government. The federal Liberals also helped in the provincial campaign, when Paul Martin, minister of national health and welfare, and Robert Winters, minister of reconstruction and supply, made timely and highly publicized tours of Newfoundland. Martin toured several districts on the Avalon Peninsula and held rallies at Harbour Grace, Bell Island, and St John's. As well, he and Smallwood signed the federal-provincial old-age-pension agreement.[60] Winters also appeared at large rallies in Carbonear and Heart's Content.

The Conservatives failed to mount an effective campaign in the first post-Confederation election. The party, a rather loose collection of people with diverse interests and views, drawn together in part by its opposition to Smallwood and organized in late February 1949, had planned little for the election. Much of the blame can be laid at the feet of party leader Mews, who failed to recognize the importance of early recruitment and of erecting a province-wide organization. The party brass came largely from the St John's professional and mercantile élite and were not prepared to match Smallwood's forays into the outport districts. They believed that the outports shared their contempt for Smallwood and would regard him as an illegitimate leader who had to be replaced. They did not need to dirty their hands in political dogfights, as the people would, of course, come to their senses and vote Tory. R.S. Furlong, one of the party's founders, sensed this superior view and informed Bell in early April that he feared the party was not 'aware of the importance of getting suitable candidates in the field promptly.'[61] Although George Drew twice visited Newfoundland, when he arrived in St John's for the first time on 19 April, not a single candidate had been nominated for the provincial election.[62] The national leader was well received, and the party could have used him, the first prominent mainland politician to visit Newfoundland, to publicize many of its candidates. That they did not reflects again the lack of planning that characterized the party throughout its first campaign. Party organizers failed to realize the importance of an island-wide campaign. Even the widely publicized Liberal convention and Smallwood's intensive campaign through the province failed to awaken the lethargic Tories to the need to match the Liberals meeting for meeting in each of the twenty-eight districts.

As late as 26 April, the newspapers reported that the Tories were still in the throes of organizing and that, beyond the appointment of Mews as leader, they had not completed any arrangements for contesting either of the elections.[63] Shortly after Drew's first visit to St John's, Mews took to the airwaves to outline the aims and policy of his party. The decision to affiliate with the Progressive Conservative Party of Canada, he said, had been made after a careful analysis of the party's policy towards Newfoundland and Drew's commitment to improve the terms of union. Mews was quick to add that the Conservatives were looking ahead and not behind. In other words, his party was committed to the union with Canada, and he reminded voters that the referenda had been held on a constitutional issue, not a political or party one. Now, his party was worried that once the Newfoundland surplus had been spent and the transitional grants had expired, the province's financial needs might not be met. As a result, he promised that the Tories would work to improve the Terms of Union. Mews had little else to say about policy, however, as the party platform was not ready until 21 May, just six days before the election and much too late to have any effect on the outcome, though he repeated Drew's promise to increase family allowances and old-age pensions.[64]

While he was at St John's, Drew expressed his disapproval of the constitutional procedure used to secure union.[65] While his objection might not have been an auspicious first step, he made it amply clear to Newfoundlanders that his party supported union. With his promise to improve the Terms of Union, Drew certainly courted the supporters of responsible government. During the campaign, his House of

Commons speech in support of union during the debate on Newfoundland's entry into Canada was sent to every household. In it, his
party's support was unequivocal: 'Speaking on behalf of all members
of the Progressive Conservative Party in this House, I wish to welcome the introduction of such measures as will complete this union
upon terms satisfactory to the people of Newfoundland and to the
people of Canada.'[66]

More damaging to the Conservative campaign than Drew's stand
on the constitutional procedures of union was his 1944–5 opposition
to family allowances, opposition that Smallwood exploited to Liberal
advantage. A few days before the election, Smallwood reminded Newfoundlanders in a radio broadcast of Drew's position: 'He fought them
[family allowances] tooth and nail, he fought them night and day, he
fought them in every way he could think.' Smallwood reminded them
that during the August 1944 debate on family allowances, Drew had
told an Ontario radio audience, 'I assure you that the Government of
Ontario intends to do everything in its power to make sure that the
iniquitous bill does not go into effect. It is not this bill alone, but the
whole principle involved that we intend to resist.' And Smallwood
quickly pointed to the similarities between provincial Tory leader
Mews and Drew: they promised to raise family allowances, but they
had both fought hard against Liberal social programs, Drew as Ontario premier and Mews in the referenda campaigns. Newfoundlanders undoubtedly grasped the point that Smallwood hoped to make:
'the Liberals brought in those wonderful laws to help the toiling
masses, and the Tories were against every one of those laws and did
everything in their power to kill them.'[67] The Conservatives fiercely
denied Smallwood's accusations, but the damage had been done, even
though Drew had said in Newfoundland that both Liberals and Conservatives accepted the various social-security measures. Moreover,
his party promised to institute the old-age pension at age sixty-five
rather than seventy and without a means test. The message, however,
never reached the voters.

Even so, Drew's visit injected life into the Conservative campaign.
Within two weeks of the leader's appearance in St John's, the party
announced its first candidates. A giant PC rally in the capital on 3 May
introduced seventeen of the twenty-eight candidates, but J.S. Currie
wrote to Bell at the beginning of May that the party was 'having a
desperate time trying to get candidates and there was no enthusiasm.'
Unfortunately, the party did not complete its slate until a few days

before nominations closed on 17 May. On 14 May, less than two weeks prior to the election, an *Evening Telegram* correspondent reported from Grand Bank that the townspeople 'have not heard of the PC candidate'.[68] Internal squabbling also harmed the Conservatives. The immensely popular, but fiercely independent Peter Cashin – the proverbial loose cannon and a bitter opponent of Smallwood's – was virtually assured of success in any eastern Newfoundland constituency. He initially agreed to carry the Conservative banner in the federal riding of St John's West, but when party organizers tried to keep him on the sidelines during the provincial election, he bolted the Tories to run as an Independent in the provincial district of Ferryland, a district held formerly by his father, Sir Michael Cashin, and one that would have returned any Conservative that Cashin supported.[69] Yet he remained close to the party, appearing with Drew at a St John's rally where, with his great oratorical skill, he stole the limelight and upstaged Drew on his first Newfoundland visit.[70] And in the dying days of the campaign, Cashin lambasted the Tories in a province-wide radio address for kicking him out of the party, claiming that the party was run by a clique out solely for personal gain.[71]

What little energy the provincial Tories mustered came largely from the national executive. Despite the appointment of a provincial organizer, Mews pleaded with Bell to send a 'political organizer down here with all possible speed. We are,' he continued, 'all very amateurish and feel the guidance of a Provincial Organizer would be of great service.'[72] Within a few days, Allister Grosart arrived from the national office and things started to hum at Conservative headquarters. Conservative press releases flooded the newspapers and radio stations, and the party appeared to be gathering momentum for the first time in the provincial campaign.[73]

Drew failed to capitalize on the momentum during his second tour of Newfoundland from 11 to 13 May. Although he travelled across the island with Mews, the campaign swing did little for the party. Drew's reception was cool, perhaps because his speeches paled in comparison to Smallwood's and much of his policy seemed to further existing Liberal policy. An *Evening Telegram* correspondent described the Corner Brook rally as 'dull and ponderous.'[74] While Smallwood promised a fair deal in the outports, Drew promised audiences in central Newfoundland that he could get tough with Communists. He lectured the 2,500 attending a St John's rally on the difficulties of Canadian trade and promised – without details – immediate negotiations to remove the suspension of sterling convertibility to help fish exports to Europe. Even when Drew discussed social programs and economic development, he echoed promises such as development of the province's natural resources that Smallwood had already made, or he promised increases to programs that Liberal candidates told voters he had earlier opposed. Such rhetoric from Drew made him an easy target for the Liberals to ridicule.[75]

Although Mews toured some of the communities along the railway with Drew, it was only his second tour outside St John's; earlier in April he had visited Bell Island, a mere nine miles from the capital.[76] He later toured some of the northeast coast constituencies, but he remained largely an unknown quantity off the Avalon Peninsula. Most of the political commentators, as well as many Conservatives themselves, realized from the outset that the party was handicapped with him, but they had hoped he could rise to the occasion. He did not, as he was not leadership material. He neglected to insist upon a provincial organization, and his failure to campaign vigorously in the coastal ridings to make himself and his party better known caused the inevitable collapse of Tory fortunes. The PC campaign was very much left in the hands of local candidates, many of whom were local merchants and largely unknown outside their community. There had been no convention to rally the supporters, and unlike Smallwood, Mews had made no personal contact with local élites. The exception, of course, was in the two St John's districts where local committees had been organized. Elsewhere, local Tory candidates slogged through the campaign alone. George Rowsell of Pushthrough recalls that the Tory candidate in Fortune-Hermitage, Douglas Pinsent, made only a whirlwind tour of the district before the election, but his Liberal opponent, John R. Courage, was already well known throughout the district.[77] When Colonel Alfred J. Brooks, a prominent New Brunswick Conservative, campaigned with provincial candidates, he too restricted his efforts to the eastern parts of the province where organization was strongest.[78] The Tories should have realized that they had to win outside eastern Newfoundland to form the government.

The Liberals benefited from the organization established by the Confederate Association, the only real organization in the referendum campaigns, according to A.B. Perlin, a columnist with the *Daily News*.[79] When Smallwood announced his cabinet on 1 April 1949, the ties with the Confederate Association were glaringly obvious. Of the nine appointees, seven had actively supported Confederation and only one had opposed it. Moreover, the appointees were fairly high-profile men in Newfoundland.[80] Smallwood also informed St Laurent that his cabinet contained three Roman Catholics, three Anglicans, and three Nonconformists to reflect the denominational composition of Newfoundland. Although he made no mention of the religious balance when he introduced the cabinet to the Newfoundland people, Smallwood emphasized that it represented 'the various geographical and ideological interests of the Island.' As well, he stressed that his cabinet was 'an average group of Newfoundlanders who [were] determined to discharge their duties faithfully and, while respecting minorities, to do their utmost to promote the welfare of the mass of the people,' a theme promoted throughout the Confederation debate and one he continued to emphasize during the election.[81]

The Confederate Victory Dinner in St John's in early January 1949 signalled the beginning of Smallwood's campaign. He spent much of his time before the Liberal convention solidifying and strengthening his support. His purpose, he told the *Evening Telegram*, was to 'line up his outport Liberals, and prepare them for the fight which is to come.'[82] The first leg of his tour took him on an extended trip to Corner Brook and the west coast, followed by a two-week triumphant tour of the south coast. In the prosperous fishing towns of Grand Bank and Fortune, he promised that the south coast would be well represented at the upcoming Liberal convention and that the region would receive better attention than it had in the past. Then he boarded the s.s. *Burgeo* and visited many of the isolated communities on the coastal route to Port aux Basques.[83] Smallwood continued to make himself visible before the campaign officially began, attending a number of functions with his cabinet ministers throughout the island.[84] Even Bradley took to the hustings before the election, helping to launch a Liberal Association in the Corner Brook area.[85]

During the four-week campaign, Smallwood spent most of his time in the outports, a fact that accounts for much of his success. Rupert Jackson, columnist for the *Evening Telegram*, remarked during the campaign that if anyone wants to cover the entire island, 'just latch on to Joseph R. Smallwood.'[86] After a Liberal rally in St John's on 9 May, the premier campaigned in Bonavista North and spent three days in his own riding of Bonavista South, two days in St George's, and two days in St Barbe, from which he flew to White Bay, Twillingate, Fogo, back to Bonavista South, and then to the two Trinity Bay districts.[87] Many of the delegates at the Liberal convention returned home and organized local committees to work for the party in the elections.[88] In the final days of the campaign, Smallwood maintained the torrid pace he had set earlier: in the final four days he delivered 150 speeches – nearly 40 a day – in the various settlements on the Avalon.[89] Moreover, at no time throughout the campaign had the Liberals neglected the districts in St John's.

Smallwood also attracted a competent group of men to his party. Many Liberal candidates were high-profile people who had generally distinguished themselves in public affairs in such areas as labour unions, cooperatives, social services, and teaching. Linked to their constituencies through either birth or employment, they had their finger on the pulse of the district, knowing key people and the major issues in the areas they hoped to represent. Courage, principal of the Adult Education Centre for Newfoundland, for instance, elected in his native Fortune-Hermitage, informed Smallwood of the key individuals – often businessmen, sea captains, teachers, or clergymen, and generally former Confederate vice-presidents – to contact when he visited each community. Courage suggested that 'Fortune-Hermitage needs better health and communication services. This is what we must give them ... Use my name whenever you can, this will identify you with me and will help me in my campaign.'[90] Aware of his popularity, Smallwood waged a very personal and leadership-oriented campaign, and Liberal candidates like Courage realized that Smallwood was their ticket to victory. Smallwood also knew that the candidates needed him more than he needed them. When he mentioned Liberal candidates he always described them as 'my Liberal candidates.'[91] Towards the end of the campaign, Liberal advertisements focused primarily on Smallwood, describing him as the 'People's Leader,' and asking voters to 'Let "Joe" Finish the Job.'

In addition to attracting a number of high-profile candidates to his party, Smallwood won the support of some prominent businessmen. None were more important than the Crosbie clan. Chesley, an ardent supporter of Responsible Government, who had refused to sign the Terms of Union, threw his support behind the Liberal party, perhaps because he realized it had the better chance of winning. Speculation was rampant that he would run for the Liberals, but poor health allegedly prevented him from doing so.[92] Even so, he spoke in a Liberal radio broadcast in the final days of the campaign, and the influential Crosbie family supported Smallwood, as did several other Water Street merchants including the Monroes and the Lakes.[93]

On matters of policy, the Liberals and the Conservatives were barely distinguishable. Both advocated economic development, greater social security, fishery development, improved educational services, and expanded medical and health services. Both courted the various interest groups, such as civil servants, teachers, and labour, but while Mews refused to meet the Newfoundland Federation of Labour's legislative committee to discuss its agenda before the election, Smallwood consented to do so.[94] The Liberals had two clear advantages over the Conservatives: Smallwood's appointment as premier, and the Liberal government in Ottawa. Although the federal government began the process of integration immediately after it became clear that Newfoundland would become the tenth province, Smallwood and the Liberals received the credit for the immediate benefits of Confederation. In a radio speech a few days before the election, Smallwood emphasized this point. 'Do you know what these two great Liberal Laws [family allowances and old-age-pension laws] will put into the pockets of our Newfoundland people?' he asked. A brief pause brought listeners to attention. 'Nearly fifteen million dollars a year ... Just think of it,' he told Newfoundlanders whose average annual income barely exceeded $500, 'nearly fifteen million dollars a year, and getting bigger year after year.' As if he had not already convinced them of the magnitude of federal contributions, he added, 'in other words ... Family Allowances and Old Age Pensions are now worth more to Newfoundland than all our fisheries.'[95]

Conservative broadcasts were quite different. Where Smallwood attacked and vilified the merchants and what he described as the millionaire class, even though a large number of this group supported him because they stood to benefit handsomely from the increase in provincial purchasing power after union, the Conservatives defended the merits of the capitalist class, telling Newfoundlanders that entrepreneurs were necessary to develop the province's resources. 'The world must have merchant adventurers who are willing to risk their money,' John Higgins, a prominent St John's Tory, told the voters. 'Must this class – call them merchant or millionaire class if you wish – be consistently lined up to be vilified or like sheep to be sheared?'[96] Such political rhetoric won the Conservatives scant support anywhere.

Before Newfoundlanders cast their first ballots, unemployment insurance benefits and family-allowance cheques had arrived, giving ample proof that the Liberals' campaign slogan, 'The party of deeds – not promises,' was unimpeachable. Such concrete benefits also enhanced Smallwood's credibility.[97] He tried to pry the federal doors open wider, but St Laurent refused to allow him to abuse federal favours. During the provincial campaign, Smallwood asked the Prime Minister to help a private company acquire the necessary licence so that it could improve communication in Newfoundland. 'Our election is on the 27th [of May],' he hastily wrote, 'and it would [sic] highly desirable that we made public announcement here of the imminence of this project.' St Laurent reminded him that proper channels had to be gone through.[98] Similarly, Bradley warned the Prime Minister shortly after his appointment to the cabinet that a 'great victory' was impossible without the appointment of Newfoundland senators. St Laurent refused, unwilling to yield to every political request of Bradley or Smallwood.[99] On the other hand, both St Laurent and Smallwood knew that the Liberals would receive the credit for the benefits that flowed from union.

By contrast, Smallwood turned the government, even though it was merely an interim administration, to political advantage. He expected the price of consumer items to drop immediately after union as Canadian products arrived duty-free. When some merchants failed to reduce prices, he instituted a program of price control to ensure that consumers enjoyed the benefits of Confederation. Merchants who failed to comply were prosecuted, further solidifying Smallwood's image as a man of the people. Lieutenant Governor Albert J. Walsh informed the Prime Minister that 'prices of a large number of commodities have dropped substantially and there is a noticeable feeling of confidence in the future.'[100] Smallwood undoubtedly received the credit. He also promised the Newfoundland Federation of Labour that he would enact favourable labour legislation. He assured civil servants that a cost-of-living bonus that the Commission of Government had failed to include in its final budget would continue. He also announced a major road-construction and repair program, a popular election item.[101]

When the last ballot was finally counted, Smallwood and his Liberals had captured 65.5 per cent of the popular vote and twenty-one seats. In a radio broadcast following his victory, he emphasized his party's wide-spread support. Once again, he returned to his familiar theme of the workers. 'If it never happened before in Newfoundland,' he told his listeners, who were glued to their radios, 'for the next four years the government in every decision it makes, everything it does, is going to put the toiling masses first.'[102] Smallwood had directed his campaign towards ordinary Newfoundlanders both in the outports and in St John's. According to Walter Harris, parliamentary assistant to St Laurent, however, Bradley and Smallwood believed that it was 'impossible to bridge the gap between the rest of the Island and St John's and therefore, it ... [was] ... easier to fight St John's and carry the rest of the Island.'[103] Smallwood did not ignore St John's, however, and Liberal support came from all over Newfoundland. Even in the nine Avalon constituencies where the supporters of responsible government were thought to be in the majority, the Liberals received 52.6 per cent of the popular vote and six of a possible twelve seats,[104] largely as a result of good Liberal organization. Only in the dual district of Harbour Main-Bell Island did the Conservatives poll 60 per cent of the vote; in the other districts that they won, they only narrowly edged out the Liberals.

Despite their strong showing in St John's and throughout much of the Avalon Peninsula, the Conservatives failed miserably in their first electoral contest, winning only five seats with 32.9 per cent of the vote.[105] Even Mews was defeated, in a close St John's race. The Conservatives proved competitive in the districts where the party had organized and campaigned effectively. Strong Tory performances on the Avalon can be attributed largely to their organization and their effective campaign and not to a Catholic population that continued to harbour anti-Confederate sentiments.[106] In the areas of the province that Mews ignored and left to the devices of the local Tory candidate, the party paid the price. It had organized and campaigned little off the Avalon Peninsula. In those districts, the Tories proved unable to compete with the Liberals.

While a lack of organization was undoubtedly the key to the Tory débâcle, the party was also encumbered by several intangibles that its leadership failed to counter. Simply because the Liberal party was the offspring of the victorious Confederate Association, the Tories were automatically perceived as anti-confederates. While some supporters of responsible government gravitated to the Tories, nothing in Mews's speeches or in the party's campaign literature lends credence to the perception of the party as an anti-Confederate one. Nonetheless, the perception may have lingered largely because of the party's ineffectual campaign. Moreover, the Conservatives were also perceived in some sections of the province as the revival of the old St John's-dominated Tory party.[107]

The *Evening Telegram* declared the outcome a Liberal landslide and suggested that Newfoundlanders had once again voted in favour of union. 'The insinuation that those who voted Liberal were bought by two million dollars of federal funds distributed in April and May,' the lead editorial ran, 'is a base allegation and an affront to the voters' integrity and intelligence ... The triumph ... is due, not to the support of any one particular class, but to the votes recorded by every class in the community.'[108] Perlin, a *Daily News* columnist, said that the referenda line did not hold, and the supporters of responsible government did not support the Conservatives. He claimed that Newfoundlanders had been bought by federal cheques from Ottawa: 'the wave which ... engulfed the Progressive Conservative party had its origins in about two million dollars of federal funds distributed during April and May in the form of social security and veteran benefits.' The lead editorial in the *Daily News* made a similar claim.[109] If Newfoundlanders had voted on this basis, more should have voted for the Conservatives who had promised to open the federal treasury even wider. Even if most Newfoundlanders did, in fact, believe that the Liberals would get a better deal from Ottawa than the Tories, Smallwood and his followers had nonetheless reaped the benefits of a superior organization.

The results of the more low-key federal campaign were predictable. The Conservatives captured the two St John's seats by narrow margins, and the Liberals, led by Premier Smallwood and assisted by visits from political heavyweights D.C. Abbott, C.D. Howe, and the Prime Minister, captured the five outport constituencies with nearly 72 per cent of the popular vote.[110] The campaign was uneventful until Smallwood embarrassed Gregory Power, the Liberal candidate in St John's West, during a campaign swing through the provincial district of Ferryland that made up a part of the federal riding. There Smallwood warned voters that if they did not vote for his man, 'not one cent will you get from the Government during the next four years ... I'm sitting on top of the public chest,' he reminded them, 'and not one red cent will come out of it for Ferryland district unless Greg Power is elected.' The result was a prolonged court battle that was eventually dropped by the successful Conservative candidate, W.J. Browne, who had accused Smallwood of voter intimidation. Even so, Power polled nearly 49 per cent of the vote, although Smallwood's prestige suffered. The Liberal party withdrew its invitation for him to appear as guest speaker at a large rally in Toronto on 21 June and at several other locations throughout Canada.[111]

Resounding defeats in both elections demoralized the Conservatives, and a sullen, defeatist attitude soon permeated the party. A.B. Butt, provincial Conservative organizer, captured the party's mood when he wrote to W.H. Kidd, the national secretary, in 1950 that the Conservative party in Newfoundland was worse than 'rock-bottom' and that 'it would be in our best interests not to try any formal organization for some time.' He said loyalty to the Conservatives did not exist, and many adopted the attitude that the best strategy was to 'give Joey [Smallwood] all the rope you can now in the hope that he will hang himself.'[112] Although the Tories made an attempt to organize in 1950, Butt reported that 'the result has been most depressing so far.'[113] John T. Cheeseman, selected party president, later ran as a Liberal. The federal picture was just as bleak. Gordon Higgins, one of the two Conservative MPs, informed Kidd on 1 August 1952 'that the most we can hope for in the next federal election are the two seats we presently have.'[114] The party was unable to mount any effective opposition to Smallwood, either provincial or federal, until the late 1960s.

Some Liberals in Ottawa were also worried about the weak opposition to Smallwood. When Brooke Claxton visited Newfoundland in July 1949, he appeared indignant that Smallwood had 'no intention of introducing effective municipal institutions with local taxes and school taxes.' After his return to Ottawa, Claxton gave the Prime Minister St Laurent his assessment of the wily premier:

He knows exactly how to appeal to [the people] and he does not hesitate to pull out all the stops. He is a person of tremendous ambition. The fact that he is already thinking of becoming Prime Minister of Canada may keep him lined up with us but my own feeling is that he will find that it will pay to attack the federal government for not satisfying his rapacious demands and he may find in the long run that it will be better to do this as a member of the CCF or some other left wing group than as a member of the Liberal Party. Like everyone else, I view the future of his administration with extreme alarm and it is small satisfaction for us to observe that it was inevitable.[115]

Neither Claxton nor anyone in Ottawa could dictate to Smallwood, although the national executive tried to keep a watchful eye on him. In 1952, National Liberal Federation secretary H.E. Kidd approached the Newfoundland party president about the lack of party organization. 'There is no great point, in between elections, as far as Newfoundland is concerned,' Eric Cook told him, 'in doing more than keeping the Provincial Liberal Association in existence in a skeleton form.'[116] A year later, Kidd again asked party secretary-treasurer Garland when the party had held its last annual meeting and the scheduled date of the next. Garland replied that 'we haven't had a meeting for some considerable time, [but] Smallwood told him Convention contemplated for the winter.'[117] It was not held until 1968. Gregory Power, Smallwood's special assistant and confidant, claimed that in the early years the Liberal party was a 'dictatorship, but it was a great team.' He said that Smallwood and he had created the Liberal bandwagon, and they wanted to maintain control over both wings of the party. A president and an executive were necessary to make the party look democratic.[118]

While it is true that Smallwood played an important role in federal campaigns, it is doubtful that he controlled the first Newfoundland MPs at Ottawa. According to Chesley W. Carter, one of the Liberals sent to the House of Commons in 1949, Bradley was their undisputed leader, and the five members caucused weekly when Parliament was in session. Though Smallwood attempted to exert his influence over the members, he later bypassed the Newfoundland MPs and went directly to the federal cabinet, often using Newfoundland Senator Ray Petten as his Ottawa contact until J.W. Pickersgill became the Newfoundland representative in the federal cabinet.[119] An uneasy relationship existed between the federal Liberals and Smallwood. He frequently embarrassed the party with his crude political antics, such as threatening to withdraw financial support from the St John's Rotary Club if it allowed federal minister of justice Donald Fleming to speak during the 1962 campaign and, more seriously, decertifying the International Woodworkers of America during the 1959 loggers' strike. Yet Smallwood's political strategy paid dividends. He kept the province Liberal for twenty-three years, delivering at least five of the seven federal seats in each election until 1968. With such success, the federal Liberals tolerated him and allowed him to control federal patronage in the province.

Neither the Conservatives nor the CCF were able to mount any opposition to him. The Tories accepted Smallwood's invincibility as early as 1951 when they openly campaigned to form not the government but only a viable opposition. Smallwood's support came from all over the province, but especially from the outports where his following remained the strongest, and his position was never threatened until the voters turned against him in the late 1960s.

3

Sharing the wealth: Canadian social programs come to Newfoundland

'The social security payments which the government of Canada has been and is making each month to so many of our people ... are so numerous and so varied,' Minister of Finance Herman W. Quinton said in his first budget speech to the House of Assembly on 30 November 1949, 'that there are today very few families in Newfoundland who are not sharing directly in them, and none at all who are not benefiting indirectly from them ... It is,' he continued, 'unpleasant to contemplate the position of Newfoundland as it would be if those payments were not being received each month by thousands of families.'[1] To a society were poverty, hardship, and deprivation were the norm, social welfare programs from Ottawa came like manna from heaven. During the first months of union, millions of federal dollars poured into Newfoundland homes. Such munificence, even to those who had been less than enamoured of union, ensured that Confederation was off to a good start.

Family allowances, old-age pensions, unemployment insurance, and other federal benefits came to Newfoundland immediately after Confederation as the legitimate right of all Canadian citizens. The Terms of Union promised that after 31 March 1949 Newfoundlanders were to share immediately in the social-security benefits provided by the Canadian government. Ottawa could not wait until 1 April – the first full day of union – to begin preparations for the disbursement of its social programs. If it had, its citizens in the newest province would not have enjoyed the same benefits as those residing in the other nine provinces until a much later date. Because of the rush to have these programs operational in the first month of union, the impression had been mistakenly created that social security measures started so early after union for purely partisan political advantage. Harold Horwood, one of Joey Smallwood's right-hand men during the fight for Confederation, has helped to perpetuate this myth. In a recent biography of Smallwood, he claimed that J.W. Pickersgill, special assistant to Prime Minister Louis St Laurent,

had foresight enough to realize that in January or February navigation to the far northern ports of Newfoundland and Labrador might cease, and that no mail might be delivered to some of them until May or June, whenever the drift ice decided to move. So he arranged [in December 1948] to have family allowances cheques made out months in advance, and sent in bundles to the post offices before navigation closed for the winter. The cheques were to be delivered to their owners in April and May. This ensured that most people would receive at least one month's benefits, and probably two, before it would be possible to hold a provincial election.[2]

This was clearly not the case.

R.A. MacKay, chairman of the steering committee coordinating Ottawa's negotiations with the Newfoundland delegation, had told the Interdepartmental Committee on Newfoundland (ICN) in early August 1948 that the primary role for most federal departments and agencies during the process of integration was to establish their respective services in Newfoundland.[3] Those civil servants dispatched to Newfoundland in late 1948 worked assiduously to have the highly visible and popular social-security programs ready for the first month of union. They firmly believed that the sooner Newfoundlanders shared the benefits of citizens in the other provinces, the sooner they would regard themselves as Canadians. Yet they did not tolerate any political interference or allow the regulations governing the programs to be circumvented. Their professionalism and initiative allowed Newfoundlanders to enjoy immediately the wealth that they had heard so much about during the events leading to union. Moreover, the arrival of various cheques for family allowances, unemployment insurance, and old-age pensions from Ottawa demonstrated very clearly the financial benefits of union. Those programs not only injected much needed cash into Newfoundland but also provided Premier Joseph R. Smallwood with a means of dealing with the province's jobless. In time, both Ottawa and Newfoundland came to rely on unemployment insurance as the best means to deal with the perennial problem of local unemployment.

Registration forms for family allowances were to be among the first visible evidence of Newfoundland's transition from dominion to Canadian province. The Department of National Health and Welfare, responsible for administering family allowances and delivering the cheques into the hands of Newfoundland mothers during the first month of union, realized that it could not offend proud Newfoundlanders, who had fought long and hard for self-government. Its task, however, was a special one that would give Confederation instant credibility and properly launch Newfoundland on the course of integration into Canada. None realized this more than R.B. Curry, national director of family allowances, who was charged with registering the children.[4] 'Naturally, due to the delicate situation in Newfoundland with a very considerable minority against Confederation in any case, it is felt,' he advised the minister of national health and welfare, Paul Martin, 'that we should do the best possible job in initiating Family Allowances in order, among other things, to gain and retain the goodwill of all the Newfoundland people. To do that, ample time is considered essential.'[5]

Because he had coordinated the Canadian registration in 1945, Curry recognized the importance of an expeditious and error-free registration. From the time he established an office in St John's, he needed at least three months to explain the registration procedure, to register the children, to process the claims, to prepare the necessary records, and to distribute the first cheques. All the preliminary work, including the registration and the issuing of the first cheques, could best be executed by a small group of experienced officials from throughout the Maritimes. Within two or three months a group of six to eight, working in St John's under the supervision of Paul Stehelin, the director of family allowances for Nova Scotia, would ensure a smooth initiation of the family-allowance program in Newfoundland.[6] Curry wrote to George Davidson, deputy minister of national health and welfare (welfare branch) that 'with such a group we can improve greatly on the experience that we had in setting up any of the original offices and ... avoid most of the mistakes that we made at that time.'[7] The Director wished dearly to avoid the interminable delays and errors created in 1945.

Yet Curry and his officials knew little about the support mechanisms they would find in Newfoundland. They had to familiarize themselves with such matters as the control of school attendance, child placement and family-welfare services, birth-registration records, and a number of other services essential to the administration of family allowances. Although an investigation into these conditions was needed before plans could be finalized, Curry shared the view of many of his Ottawa colleagues that they should avoid the impression that the bureaucrats were leading a Canadian invasion of New-foundland. He suggested to Martin that 'such a survey ... should probably wait conclusion of the negotiations between Canada and Newfoundland in order that no embarrassment should be caused by a feeling that we were moving in too soon.'[8] Curry and Stehelin did, however, meet discreetly with officials from the Newfoundland de-partments of Health and Welfare, Education, and Posts and Telegrams in St John's on 18 October to discuss preliminary plans for family al-lowances registration.[9]

One of the most important matters discussed was the subject of en-forcement of school attendance. The Family Allowances Act permit-ted the suspension of payment for children who failed to comply with the provincial legislation. The Newfoundland School Attendance Act enforced attendance of children between the ages of seven and four-teen. Curry informed Newfoundland authorities that his office could withhold payment only on the advice of the Department of Educa-tion in Newfoundland that a child was not regularly attending school. In other words, a clear distinction existed between federal and provin-cial jurisdiction in the area of education.[10] Curry also scouted the city for suitable office space and contacted the various officials with whom he would be working closely.[11]

Upon his return to Ottawa, Curry finalized his plans. A blanket dis-tribution of the family-allowances forms to all homes through the post office proved the most effective registration procedure, as it promised to maximize publicity and reduce omissions. Postmasters were in-formed of the main facts concerning family allowances so they could provide information to parents. To avoid the problems encountered in the initial Canadian registration, a comprehensive insert outlining the registration procedure as well as the general guidelines govern-ing family allowances accompanied each form. The department also planned a radio and press campaign to outline and encourage the proper registration of children. As well, Curry decided to use the 1945 registration forms, which permitted the registration of eleven children, as being more suitable to Newfoundland's larger families than the newer forms, which allowed for only five children.[12]

Because the Family Allowances Act stipulated that payment could be made only to children born in Canada, enabling legislation was necessary before Newfoundland children could be registered. Though residents of Canada after union, Newfoundland children would not have been born in Canada. Unless legislation cleared the way, mothers would have had to wait three years before being eligible for family allowances.[13] Similarly, new legislation, enacted at the request of the Newfoundland delegation, allowed about 40,000 Newfoundland immigrants living in Canada to qualify immediately following union.[14] An amendment to the act also allowed officials in St John's to treat applications filed prior to 1 April as having been made during the month of March. Such a provision permitted family allowances payments to commence in April, as the act specified that payment must begin the month following registration. Otherwise, Ottawa would have been liable for payments in February and March for applications received in January before Newfoundland became a part of Canada. A similar procedure had been followed when Canada adopted family allowances in 1945.[15]

In the meantime, at the request of Dr G.D.W. Cameron, deputy minister of national health and welfare (health branch), Dr L.B. Pett, chief of the Nutrition Division, became the first department official to visit Newfoundland. Pett was not impressed with what he saw, and recommended to Davidson that, except in three or four centres, the distribution of family allowances should be on the basis of credit at a store, similar to the system in use for most Native groups. Local stores, he cautioned, would find it difficult to handle large numbers of cheques, as banks were rare in the outports. Moreover, most people were unfamiliar with the use of cheques, though they were familiar with a system of getting their food on credit. Pett also suggested that Newfoundlanders be restricted in what foods they could purchase with their family-allowance cheques: evaporated or dried milk, canned tomatoes or tomato juice, canned orange or grapefruit juices, and rolled oats or oatmeal. Those foods, he claimed, were readily available, and 'they will make a better effect on the people than anything else. Believe me,' Dr Pett concluded, 'help to Newfoundland must begin at a rock-bottom level.'[16] Better tuned to the sensitivities of Newfoundland and showing a greater concern for goodwill that would help integrate the province into Canada, Curry and others in the department ignored Pett's obvious paternalism in favour of their own plans to establish family allowances on the same basis as elsewhere in Canada. The fact that Dr Pett was alone in expressing such views made ignoring him easy. In any event, Pett's concern over the lack of banking facilities never became a problem, as local merchants and mail orders from Eaton's and Simpson's proved more than capable of handling the family allowance cheques. If parents wished to save their payments, the practice of making bank deposits through the post office was well established. Furthermore, official reports from Newfoundland suggested that mothers spent their family allowances wisely.[17]

The appropriate registration forms and envelopes were quickly prepared, and Stehelin was ready to lead a small, well-trained, and experienced contingent from the Maritime region into Newfoundland by 15 November. Confident that everything had then been considered, Curry informed External Affairs that his officials were ready to begin their task. 'In order to do a thoroughly good job and to cover a number of the phases of our work that it was not possible to cover during initial registration in Canada in 1945,' he said, 'it will take all the time at their disposal from then [15 November] until March for this work.' The family-allowance registration forms had to be processed for the first payment in April 1949, and Curry saw no room for delay or error. His superior, Davidson, worked on Paul Martin. 'We feel,' he told the minister, 'that it will have a good psychological effect on the population of Newfoundland if we get our family allowance forms into their hands fairly soon.'[18] They wanted most of the applicants registered by 1 March, so that the Newfoundland staff could be recruited and fully capable of running the office from the beginning of April.[19] The registration process had to be flawless; anything less was tantamount to failure.

During the negotiations in Ottawa with the Newfoundland delegation, MacKay advised the Cabinet Committee on Newfoundland that certain federal departments and agencies would have to be established at an early date if they hoped to be operative by April. Although the cabinet refused to grant permission to establish offices in Newfoundland until the negotiations had reached a stage where such actions would be reasonably justified, MacKay interpreted this to mean that it 'does not prevent us from proceeding with the plans to create these establishments.'[20] The cabinet later approved the method proposed for registration of family allowances in Newfoundland and authorized the rental of office space and the recruitment of staff. It stipulated, however, that there should be 'no overt move in connection with either the actual registration or the broadcast [in which

Curry planned to announce the registration] until the agreement [the Terms of Union] has been actually signed.'[21] With the approval of Paul Martin in November 1948, a full month before the cabinet authorized other departments to do so, Stehelin quietly established an office in St John's.

When Curry arrived in the Newfoundland capital on 2 December, Stehelin and his staff had nearly completed the preliminary work necessary for the release of the registration forms. The Commission of Government had been kept abreast of Health and Welfare's activities, and on 16 December gave its approval for the distribution of registration forms through the Post Office. Paul Bridle, the acting high commissioner, reported from St John's that the forms would be in the hands of a majority of outport residents before the end of the month.[22]

Newfoundlanders received the first official word about family allowances in Curry's radio broadcast on 17 December, six days after the signing of the Terms of Union. The registration forms had been sent to every household to ensure the inclusion of every child under sixteen years of age. Each package contained a notice explaining how family allowances worked, how the children were to be registered, and how the money was to be used. Curry informed householders that mothers would receive five dollars for each child under six years of age, six dollars for those between six and ten, seven dollars for children between ten and thirteen, and eight dollars for children over fourteen. As well, the registration packages contained a stamped, addressed envelope for returning the forms.[23] Curry must have been pleased that the extension of family allowances to Newfoundland was unfolding as he had planned. His was the first Canadian voice that Newfoundlanders heard giving concrete evidence that as Canadians they would share in the wealth that they had been promised.[24] And Curry's announcement was well received. St John's *Daily News*, columnist Albert Perlin said that Ottawa's decision to register children for family allowances might be politically motivated, but 'it is just as well for those who need the family allowances to have their payments started at once.'[25] An editorial in the *Evening Telegram* praised the registration and criticized those who regarded family allowances as a form of political patronage.[26]

Before the end of January, a little more than a month after the forms were dropped in the mail, 68 per cent of all families had been registered. Because of the intense information campaign, errors were relatively few. The registration forms were then promptly processed and approved.[27] The operation flowed so smoothly largely because both Curry and Davidson adopted measures to avoid problems that they had encountered in the initial Canadian registration. At that time, the inability to verify all births of children on the applications had resulted in numerous errors. Overpayments were common, and suspensions and recovery left a bitter taste in the mouths of many mothers. Department officials avoided a similar situation in Newfoundland because the Dominion Bureau of Statistics had microfilmed the Newfoundland birth-registration records well in advance.[28] By the time registration began, records were available to verify most of the births and to avoid the problems and adverse publicity that recovery from overpayment created.[29] In the few cases where births had not been registered with vital statistics, the chief treasury officer at National Health and Welfare, T.F. Philips, proved quite accommodating. Although he refused to accept a statutory declaration of age by an older member of the family, he considered secondary evidence such as a letter from the clergy or a school teacher as sufficient. 'Whilst this may not conform with requirements of Vital Statistics Division,' he wrote to G.J. Rice,[30] district treasury officer in Newfoundland, 'I feel that we are on safe ground in accepting this for Family Allowances purposes after other means of verification have been exhausted.'[31]

Ottawa had wanted things to go smoothly in Newfoundland, and it was not disappointed. 'The work in respect to Newfoundland has gone even better than could have been hoped for last fall,' a jubilant Curry wrote to E.F. Hoganson, district treasury officer for Nova Scotia. 'The registration, as you know,' he continued, 'has exceeded our expectation in volume, the processing of the forms has gone forward rapidly and the vast majority of the cheques will be ready for distribution shortly.'[32] On 20 April, the first family-allowance cheques were delivered to St John's and deposited with the Post Office for delivery throughout the new province. The cheques had an immediate and tremendous impact, as they placed cash into the hands of people, creating a feeling of optimism across the province. In a society where cash was limited, family allowances were universally praised. A *Fishermen's Advocate* editorial exemplified the mood:

There is considerably more cash in circulation at Bonavista, monthly, than before the advent of confederation. This is owing to the number of regular monthly family allowance cheques received. It is notable that some little children have shoes to wear, the first time since their birth, and the ever-present cast of hopelessness on the countenances of the very poor, who could not give the little one even a piece of ribbon, is now being received by the mellowness of hope. Even a little, to those who hath not spells, in the final analysis, the difference between abject despair and a future tinged with reborn hope.[33]

A similar note of optimism came from the province's isolated northeast coast. An *Evening Telegram* correspondent from Joe Batt's Arm showered praise upon the program:

What a blessing these Family Allowances are to residents here! The April cheques arrived at a time when a bit of money was so sorely needed by a great many families. The differences can already be noticed in the new shoes, etc. worn by little children and by the extra cans of milk one sees being passed across the counter in the stores. Family allowances are a God-send. Long Live Family Allowances![34]

Although officials administering family allowances were the first to commence work in Newfoundland, there is no indication that the decision was politically motivated. Both provincial political parties made numerous references to family allowances during the 1949 elections, but J.G. Parsons, regional director for Newfoundland, informed Ottawa that they sought only information about the program. 'The politicians in the field have not been as tormenting as we thought they might be,' he told Curry. Even in cases where people approached Smallwood about family allowances, he 'referred the matter to us with the understanding that we would reply directly to the parents.'[35] Politicians had no reason to be involved. After all, family allowances fell within the exclusive jurisdiction of the Canadian government and Ottawa had made it clear that payment would begin with union. One can only imagine the criticism that would have reverberated throughout the new province had not the cheques been prepared for the first month of union. Canada had little choice but to initiate family allowances from the beginning. Officials from the Department of National Health and Welfare responsible for inaugurating the program firmly believed that family allowances were necessary to make union acceptable, and they executed their task with perfection and without political interference. In the end, though, Liberal politicians reaped some of the reward for the bureaucrats' splendid effort as they emphasized the benefits of union in their first provincial and federal electoral sweeps.[36]

Within the first year, 50,051 mothers received more than $9.7 million in family allowances, and by the end of fiscal 1955, more than $65 million had come to Newfoundland from this source.[37] Moreover, family allowances contributed to an increase in school attendance. 'Many children who were unable to attend school for lack of clothing,' the *Daily News* reported, 'started school on Monday morning [25 April] and will, we believe, attend regularly in future.'[38] When Brooke Claxton, minister of national defence, visited Newfoundland a few months after union, he reported to the Prime Minister that he found 'people reconciled to Union in greater degree than I had thought possible.' The positive signs of integration stemmed from the equitable and fair terms and the 'quiet and thoroughly efficient way in which the transfer has been carried out as well as by Family Allowance payments ... People were somehow surprised at the size of the cheques and the frequency with which the months roll around.'[39]

Another injection of federal funds into Newfoundland came from unemployment insurance. During the 1947 and 1948 negotiations between Newfoundland and Canada, both sides had agreed that union would bring some economic dislocation. Each Newfoundland delegation to Ottawa was anxious to alleviate any distress that might occur if union adversely affected the employment rate. Humphrey Mitchell, the minister of labour, reminded Albert J. Walsh in 1948 that relief from distress brought on through unemployment was not a federal responsibility unless workers had paid into the unemployment insurance program.[40] As of 1 April, of course, Newfoundlanders had not made the contributions necessary to qualify for unemployment-insurance benefits, though both sides agreed that there had to be some provision for workers who became unemployed as a consequence of union. Ottawa's answer was a temporary unemployment-assistance program that operated on similar lines to regular unemployment-insurance benefits. Those who had worked for three months in insurable employment, as determined by the Unemployment Insurance Act, and lost their employment during the six months prior to union and were still unemployed when union took effect, or lost their jobs within two years of 31 March 1949, qualified for unemployment assistance. The assistance, however, was to last for only six months, and Mitchell was emphatic that the special arrangement was to exist for only two years. That was sufficient time, he believed, to allow Newfoundlanders to qualify for regular unemployment-insurance benefits.[41]

Several officers from the Department of Labour and the Unemployment Insurance Commission (UIC) made a preliminary survey in Newfoundland in October 1948, after which the strategy for establishing offices in the island was outlined. Overseeing the process were E.P. Laberge, director of technical services at the UIC, and L.J. (Leo) Curry, the assistant regional superintendent for the Maritime Region. (Some Newfoundlanders must have wondered if there was only one super bureaucrat wearing two hats, but the UIC Curry and the family-allowances Curry were, indeed, two different people.) Laberge and Curry hoped that, because the personnel of the Newfoundland Employment Service (an agency established in 1945 for the placement of veterans) could be easily absorbed into the federal service, their task would be easier in Newfoundland. Because of pressure from MacKay, staff requirements were pared from the initial estimate of 150 to about 50 prior to union, with only 12 to 15 being transferred from Canada, primarily for training local recruits. And, instead of blanketing the new province, as was initially proposed, Ottawa opened offices in St John's, Corner Brook, and Grand Falls. Curiously enough, the personnel required to operate the Newfoundland offices was determined by using the number required to maintain the Ottawa office, while allowing for additional staff to compensate for difficulties involved in 'original organization and other difficulties not met in the city of Ottawa.' The Subcommittee on the Organization of Administrative Services also authorized Laberge to prepare for the distribution and sale of insurance stamps before union through the Post Office, a procedure followed in Canada in 1940.[42]

Because of limited industrial activity and scarce employment opportunities in insurable employment, Ottawa considered exempting certain inaccessible areas of the province from coverage under the Unemployment Insurance Act. Officials within both the Department of Labour and the Unemployment Insurance Commission foresaw difficulties with transportation and communication in remote areas. Moreover, the major economic activities in these towns and outports – fishing and sawmilling – were not covered under the act. The main reason for the recommendation, though, was financial. The cost of maintaining contact with employees and employers in those areas was considered prohibitive. 'In view of the certain risks of a drain on the Unemployment Insurance fund and also because of administrative costs,' C.R. McCord, director of administrative services in the Department of Labour, informed Arthur MacNamara, the deputy minister of labour, 'it is felt that the Unemployment Insurance Commission cannot at present cover the island.'[43] A provision in the act permitted exemptions where insufficient employment did not warrant employment insurance. In fact, the commission had previously contemplated excluding parts of the north shore of Quebec, so Newfoundland would not have been the only province affected.[44] Although this idea was mooted within the Department of Labour and the Unemployment Insurance Commission, the government decided to extend unemployment-insurance benefits to the whole province. This is hardly surprising considering that most of the Ottawa mandarins and politicians did what they could to accelerate the acceptance of Confederation in Newfoundland.

In the meantime, UIC officials had estimated the funds necessary for unemployment assistance. After their initial survey, they had determined the gainfully employed workforce to be about 100,000, though their calculations were made without reliable and up-to-date statistics. Of the total, 40,000 were considered insurable. They reached that number by subtracting those engaged in activities not insurable under the act – fishing, logging, and agriculture – together with those working without regular wages and those who, owing to transportation problems and other difficulties, were classed as 'unavailable'. To determine the funds necessary to cover insurable workers, 'the percentage of benefit recipients to the insured population of Canada was doubled and then applied to the 40,000 insured population of Newfoundland,' giving about 5,000 potential claimants. An amount of $2 million was determined by multiplying 5,000 by the 'number of compensable days possible in a six-month period (150) and then by an average daily benefit of $2.75.'[45]

Within a few weeks of receiving official authorization to extend federal services to Newfoundland, UIC officials were ready to begin.[46] As intended, L.J. Curry was charged with introducing the services. The island portion of Newfoundland fell within the Maritime Region, headquartered in Moncton, while the Quebec Region assumed responsibility for Labrador because of transportation ties with Montreal.[47] Curry had two distinct functions to perform: to establish the machinery necessary for unemployment insurance, and to prepare for unemployment assistance. The transfer of experienced staff from Canada to operate the three offices until Newfoundland personnel had been recruited and trained made his task much easier. Before the Canadians left for Newfoundland, however, they had been briefed in Moncton 'with regard to the manner in which the Newfoundland government officials and other individuals in Newfoundland [were] to be approached.' Under no circumstances were the Canadians to act in a superior manner. The Commission of Government, they were reminded, had provided good service with limited staff, and they were to do likewise.[48]

UIC offices were quickly established. Registering employers and workers and educating them about the use of employment booklets and stamps proved relatively easy. R.H. Sims, who organized the Corner Brook office, reported to Laberge on 31 March 1949 that the Newfoundland staff had been sufficiently trained to begin their duties. Curry had been particularly alert to secure competent employees for the offices, as advertisements for managers had appeared in Newfoundland newspapers towards the end of February.[49] 'There will undoubtedly be many problems to solve as soon as the public commence to use the office,' Sims noted, 'but all here are confident that they can meet any situation that arises.'[50] In addition to training the staff and preparing for the implementation of unemployment insurance, the Canadians had waged a publicity campaign. For instance, Sims had explained the UI system not only to local employers who assured him of their assistance and cooperation, but also to the various clergy and union representatives on the west coast. He did his part to make the task of the Newfoundland recruits who were preparing to assume control a little easier, while endeavouring at the same time to educate the public about unemployment insurance. R.J. Coy, the travelling supervisor of the Maritime Region, paid his first visit to Newfoundland in late February. He reported to R.P. Hartley, the regional superintendent, that the training staff was working diligently and enthusiastically 'to sell the National Employment and Unemployment Insurance Service to the Newfoundland public.'[51]

Curry feared that there might be considerable delays and disqualifications for unemployment assistance, which had to be inaugurated by 1 April. He knew that it was practically impossible to verify immediately the work history of applicants for unemployment assistance because most employers had had no reason to maintain accurate employment records prior to union. The problem could have been avoided if a flat rate of pay had been acceptable. Wages varied considerably, however, and moreover such a policy contravened the Terms of Union. Furthermore, UIC officials feared that it might provoke severe criticism from within Newfoundland.[52] Instead, Curry recommended that the claimant's daily rate on his last day of work be used to calculate benefits. Hence, the employer had to furnish only the first and last days of employment. 'These recommendations are made in view of the situation and the desirability to make the burden of introduction into Confederation as light as possible for the employer group,' Curry informed Ottawa. Moreover, he added, Ottawa should bear in mind 'that every reason for delay of payment to claimants should be eliminated if we are to establish our relations with labour groups.'[53] A meeting between UIC and the Department of Finance subsequently approved Curry's recommendation. Ottawa also authorized UIC officials to accept statements presented by claimants regarding their wage earnings as acceptable for the purposes of determining compensation, with the records being checked where possible.[54] Once again, Ottawa's rules and regulations had proven flexible for Newfoundland.

As soon as Ottawa made a decision on the work history of potential applicants, UIC officials coasted to 1 April. Appropriate forms for unemployment assistance and the accompanying brochures had been prepared and dispatched to the post offices around the island and throughout Labrador. Although applications failed to reach many communities by 1 April, provisions had been made to date the first applications from the time of union.[55] As well, the UIC had undertaken an advertising campaign to familiarize the people with the nature of the unemployment-insurance plan. Chief Commissioner J.G. Bisson explained in a radio broadcast the general operation of the program and its major provisions. Subsequent broadcasts explained in greater detail various aspects of UI, and informed both employers and employees, as well as the general public, 'what was expected of them in order that the plan might be carried forward.' Also, information regarding contributions and benefits appeared in the province's newspapers.[56]

The unemployment-assistance program was an immediate success for Newfoundland. Before he left St John's, Curry had warned Ottawa that the 'employment situation [is] the most unfavourable since 1940 and there is not any visible sign of any pick-up in the labour market.'[57] The loss of international markets for many of Newfoundland's exports made the situation particularly bleak. Layoffs at the pulp and paper mills and at the iron mines on Bell Island resulted in 6,000 fewer jobs. The American military bases employed 600 fewer workers than the previous year, the number employed in manufacturing dropped, and depressed markets for salt cod kept a large number of fishermen ashore.[58] Within four days of union, 2,000 persons had visited the St John's office alone, of which 1,000 claims were accepted and registered. By the end of the first month, nearly 3,000 claims had been processed. For the month of April, $19,467 was paid to 1,300 claimants from the St John's office, and the Grand Falls office reported making 800 payments for a total of $13,000. By 6 May, 3,450 applicants had registered for unemployment assistance. An additional 1,000 claimants were anticipated for May. Officials quickly realized that the appropriation for fiscal 1949–50 would be insufficient. R.P Hartley advised Ottawa to allocate an additional $750,000 'to be on the safe side.'[59] By the end of the first year of union, the federal government had spent $3.2 million on unemployment assistance, 60 per cent over the original estimate.[60]

Such expenditure became necessary when Premier Smallwood took advantage of federal laws. He had told Newfoundlanders during the referenda debates and again during the 1949 elections that there was untold treasure in Ottawa, and he wasted little time in getting his hands on it. To deal with the unemployment crisis the Smallwood government initiated an ambitious public-works project to reduce the numbers on able-bodied relief and transfer them to the federal rolls. As a result, unemployment-assistance costs soared, and Smallwood quickly established himself as a shrewd operator in the eyes of some Ottawa bureaucrats and politicians. He had an uncanny ability to make the federal system work for his province. He had regarded union with Canada as the best insurance against the economic uncertainties of Newfoundland, and in the first months of union Confederation paid handsome dividends. Smallwood proved himself quite adept at reducing provincial expenditure on relief by making Ottawa responsible for the province's unemployed, but at no time did he take any initiative to solicit federal help to wean the province from its dependence on foreign markets and the problems of regular unemployment.

The unemployment-assistance program had excluded fishermen, loggers, trappers, and agricultural workers. But Smallwood's public-works project – a scheme whereby a local community contributed half the labour and the province paid wages at fifty-five cents per hour for the other half (a person worked sixteen hours for eight hours' pay) – enabled the unemployed to qualify for unemployment assistance by placing them on road work (insurable employment).[61] 'We estimated carefully,' Smallwood recalls in his autobiography, 'how many days' work each man would need to qualify for the special unemployment insurance that Ottawa was offering us in that first year or two of Confederation'.[62] After they received the required number of 'stamps', or contributions, they were laid off and transferred to unemployment assistance at federal expense. From 1 November 1949 until the program ended on 15 March 1950, nearly 5,000 men had qualified. Smallwood used the system to Newfoundland's advantage. When it earmarked $150,000 for unemployment assistance in 1950–1, the federal government had not realized that the province would take direct action to transfer responsibility for the unemployed to Ottawa. Because of Smallwood's initiative on public works, Ottawa spent far more than it had anticipated. Over $4.8 million was eventually allotted for unemployment assistance, though only $3.3 million was actually spent during 1950–1.[63]

Labour minister Humphrey Mitchell recognized the severity of the unemployment situation in Newfoundland and in March 1950 initiated cabinet discussion to address it.[64] The cabinet agreed that the assistance program was costly: nearly $9.5 million by 31 October 1951, including regular UI benefits, but $6,840,788 on unemployment assistance alone. Yet its response did little to find a permanent solution to the problem. Instead, it recommended that all federal departments commence immediately any public works planned for the province to reduce the number on unemployment insurance. It made no greater attempt to solve the problem of chronic unemployment in Newfoundland than had Smallwood. Nevertheless, federal expenditure, coupled with an improvement in the international markets, put many of the unemployed back to work and kept 1951–2 expenditure for unemployment assistance to $368,281. The program expired in September 1951. After spending $1.7 million on its vast relief works, the provincial government discontinued its public-works program as too expensive for its limited resources, a decision that prevented most fishermen from joining the UI rolls until Ottawa changed the act to accommodate them in 1957.[65] Even so, his temporary use of the public-works expedient was a clear indication of Smallwood's ability to use the federal system to his province's advantage.

Unemployment assistance helped many families over rough times and, combined with regular benefits cheques, was another visible sign that the Canadian government now played an integral role in Newfoundland life. By the end of April 1955, six years after UIC offices opened their doors, more than 225,000 applicants had qualified, resulting in the payment of $26.6 million to Newfoundland's unemployed.[66] Only a few considered the consequences of such a reliance on the social-security programs, however, or saw UI benefits as an inauspicious beginning. In 1955, Herbert Pottle cautioned Milton Gregg, then minister of labour, when the federal government considered changes to the UI Act to include fishermen. There was a 'very widespread misconception of the purpose of unemployment insurance' in Newfoundland, Pottle said. 'It is coming to the point where far too many people believe that all they have to do is to get the necessary number of stamps,' he wrote, 'and unemployment insurance must follow as a matter of right.'[67] Ironically, several Newfoundland businessmen had warned federal officials before union that Canada could expect problems with UI because many Newfoundlanders had a tendency to work until they had enough money to carry on, only to return when the money ran out. Perhaps Confederation provided more workers in Newfoundland with the opportunity to practise and perfect the work habits usually associated with a pre-industrial economy. Or it might mean that Smallwood devised a system that the other provinces would copy and Ottawa itself eventually encourage. If the social-security benefits threatened the work ethic of Newfoundlanders, the province's politicians in the post-Confederation era must share the blame with Ottawa. As Smallwood demonstrated in 1949–50, if any government was to support the unemployed, it would have to be Ottawa. With an unemployment rate that often approached 20 per cent, Newfoundland workers certainly enjoyed the income supplied by unemployment insurance.

Arrangements for the payment of old-age pensions did not flow as smoothly as those for family allowances and unemployment insurance. While the latter fell within the exclusive domain of the federal government, old-age pensions were a dominion-provincial program that required special provincial legislation. Even so, George F. Davidson attached the same importance to having old age pension cheques in the hands of qualified Newfoundlanders as he had to ensuring the payment of family allowances. 'All the information I have received,' he warned Paul Martin in mid-October 1948, 'indicates that Newfoundlanders generally, and old-age pensioners in particular, expect their pensions to go up automatically in April of next year to $30 a month, the same as for the rest of Canada. Unless this situation is handled with care, disappointment is bound to result.'[68] Despite Davidson's warning, little consideration was given during the negotiations to having Ottawa share in Newfoundland pensions during the first month of union. When the federal government finally made the decision to introduce old-age pensions, federal bureaucrats stepped in to prevent it from becoming a political gimmick.

Although Newfoundland had instituted old-age pensions in 1911, its plan was far less generous than the Canadian one. For example, the qualifying age was seventy-five, except for women who were sixty-five at the time of their husband's death, and the yearly amount, paid quarterly, was paltry: $72 for a single person, and $120 for a person maintaining a wife.[69] Canadians, on the other hand, qualified at age seventy and received monthly cheques of $30.[70] Davidson realized that if Newfoundland had first to elect a government, convene the provincial assembly, and then negotiate an agreement with Ottawa, six to nine months could elapse before Newfoundland pensioners would be treated the same as those in the rest of Canada. Such a delay 'would be highly unfortunate and would not leave a good taste in the mouths of the people of the new Province,' he warned. He suggested in October 1948 that the Commission of Government be asked to pass a new Old Age Pensions Act for Newfoundland. It need only 'authorize the Newfoundland Government to pay old age pensions on the basis laid down in the Dominion Act and Regulations, and to authorize the negotiation of an appropriate agreement to this effect between the Government of Newfoundland and the Government of Canada,' he advised. The legislation could be in place, subject to proclamation on 1 April. In the meantime, the necessary agreement could be drawn up, ready for immediate ratification by both governments on the first day of union.[71]

Neither Martin nor the cabinet committee negotiating with Newfoundland seriously considered Davidson's advice. In the final days of the negotiations, the Newfoundland delegation had asked to have an arrangement in either the Terms of Union or the companion supplementary memorandum to permit an old-age-pension agreement with the federal government immediately following union, should the Commission of Government enact suitable old age pension legislation. Ottawa refused, claiming that it could not act until an agreement had been reached between the provincial legislature and the Canadian government.[72] Such a stance was consistent with St Laurent's policy not to interfere in Newfoundland. He said later, however, that the Commission of Government had refused to enact any legislation to provide old age pensions at union.[73]

During the debate on the Newfoundland Bill, both major opposition parties vehemently criticized St Laurent for failing to provide for old-age pensions immediately after union.[74] The cabinet then agreed that, if the opposition persisted, it would 'indicate its willingness to enter, without delay, into an old age pension agreement with any Newfoundland government legally empowered so to do.'[75] Although the Prime Minister wanted to avoid the impression that Ottawa was moving too quickly into Newfoundland, he wanted more to avoid criticism from the Conservatives and the CCF that his government was not doing everything possible to have Newfoundlanders enjoy immediately all the benefits of Confederation. When the matter surfaced again in Parliament on 17 February, Martin then said that he was anxious to reach an agreement with Newfoundland as soon as it was legally possible to do so.[76] The Commission of Government also had a sudden change of heart. It had previously maintained that an agreement on old-age pensions would commit succeeding governments to such expenditure that it wished to leave the matter to an elected legislature. When Ottawa approached it in February it adopted a new attitude. Albert Walsh, who had become 'the dominant Newfoundland member of the Commission' by 1946,[77] had returned from Ottawa where he had served as chair of the Newfoundland delegation to influence the commission. Moreover, by the end of the Commission's tenure, two other Newfoundland commissioners, Herbert Pottle and H.W. Quinton, had obvious political aspirations, and an early agreement on old-age pensions might improve their fortunes in the political arena. As well, Newfoundland governor Gordon Macdonald, a sympathetic supporter of union, welcomed any measure to accelerate Newfoundland's integration with Canada. The commission agreed to prepare the way for old-age pensions in April.[78]

After he joined Smallwood's government as minister of public welfare, Herbert Pottle informed Davidson that he was coming to Ottawa to sign the old-age-pension agreement.[79] He proposed to expedite the registration process and place money in the hands of pensioners during May by having applicants apply by telegraph, to be followed later by formal application when it became available at local post offices. The proposal impressed Smallwood, and he immediately received Martin's permission to proceed as Pottle had suggested.[80] E.R. Swettenham, who was in St John's to oversee the establishment of an Old Age Pensions Board and help with the registration of new applicants, was appalled at such tactics. He reported to J.W. MacFarlane, the director of old-age pensions, that while he was in Smallwood's office, Smallwood had given Pottle permission to proceed with the plan. The Premier 'quite loudly' explained to Pottle – perhaps to impress Swettenham – that they had to 'cut the red tape' because 'cheques must be in the hands of pensioners before May.' The career civil servant Swettenham was shocked that Martin had authorized such an unorthodox procedure, considering that the board had not been appointed and the necessary applications were still on the drafting table. When MacFarlane alerted Davidson to the peculiar arrangement proposed for Newfoundland, the latter acted swiftly. The regulation could not be circumvented, he reminded Martin. Later the same day, the minister cancelled the arrangement he had authorized for Newfoundland in favour of an alternate plan. The 3,000 persons in receipt of pensions prior to union and eligible under the new regulations would receive federal old-age pensions as of 1 April 1949. Moreover, applications received before 31 May were deemed to have been received and approved on 30 April so that pensions could begin in May.[81]

Smallwood and Martin, who was in the province on a whirlwind election tour, officially signed the Old Age Pensions Agreement between Ottawa and Newfoundland in the historic Colonial Building on 19 May. Smallwood had also had the agreement initialled a month earlier, however, on the eve of the Liberal convention when he, Herman Quinton, the minister of health, and Pottle affixed their signatures for the province, and H.S. Farquhar, chairman of the Nova Scotia Old Age Pension Board, and Swettenham represented Ottawa. The agreement lowered the qualifying age to seventy from seventy-five, and raised the annual pension from $120 to $360. The federal government contributed 75 per cent of the cost, which meant a saving of 30 per cent to the Newfoundland government for pensioners already in its pay, though the province assumed the cost of administering the program.[82]

Plans for establishing the old-age-pension apparatus moved rather slowly. Swettenham and his two assistants had arrived in St John's on 25 April from Ottawa. They found the procedure used for payment of Newfoundland pensions in a deplorable condition, operating without much systematic control and with cheques issued even though applications were not on file. To exasperate the Canadian officials further, the Newfoundland government did not hurry to appoint the Old Age Pensions Board or to acquire the machinery for printing the cheques. But, to be fair, Smallwood had called a provincial election for 27 May, and for much of the time that Canadian officials were busy organizing old-age pensions in Newfoundland, the cabinet ministers were on the hustings. In fact, board members were not appointed, nor were staff members recruited, until Swettenham bluntly warned the government that delays would make it difficult to have the necessary arrangements completed to allow for payment of pensions as expected. As well, Swettenham had to ask the provincial Department of Finance to order the machinery required to imprint the cheques and the pay-lists.[83]

In all, Swettenham was justifiably critical of the situation he encountered in Newfoundland, calling it `primitive' and wondering how some departments operated at all. He told Ottawa, however, that it must share some of the blame for the incompetence in the provincial bureaucracy, as the Civil Service Commission had recruited many of the best people from the Newfoundland government for its numerous positions in the new province. The creaming off of the best Newfoundland bureaucrats started early. Ottawa required approximately 500 new employees for Newfoundland, although about half would be transferred from Newfoundland departments taken over by the federal government. The Department of Education alone lost nine senior officials. In his annual report for 1949, Dr G.A. Frecker, the deputy minister of education, lamented that 'such a loss of experienced, trained staff cannot but adversely affect the efficiency of the Department. The lack of continuity in thought and action itself constitutes a serious problem.' An experienced, competent civil service would have been extremely important to the inexperienced provincial government. As it was, Swettenham confided to his superior that 'the provincial departments are now severely handicapped by the lack of competent help.'[84]

Once the board had been established and the personnel recruited, things went smoothly, at least at first. Swettenham and his team had gone through most of the existing files before new applications arrived, and they hoped to have applicants registered and cheques issued by mid-May.[85] Applications had been placed in the mail on 2 May and, within days, nearly 9,000 applications[86] had been completed and returned to St John's. The board and the staff had been sufficiently trained and, assisted by two examiners from Ottawa, they worked quickly through the new applications. After more than a month in St John's, Swettenham felt reasonably confident that his task was complete. MacFarlane, however, did not wish to leave Newfoundland on its own until everyone was satisfied that the system could operate perfectly. He did not want problems in the second month that would prevent the issuing of cheques at the normal time, an occurrence that would reflect badly on his officials.[87] The first old-age-pension cheques – 12,000 in all – were issued on 24 May to the people who were already on the Newfoundland rolls and to those who had met the regulations established by the new act. Swettenham informed Ottawa that though the old-age-pension officials were not operating at peak efficiency, he thought that they could handle the job on their own.[88]

He was wrong. The second cheques were issued without a hitch, but the Newfoundland government and the Newfoundland Pension Board soon found themselves in trouble with Ottawa. Several hundred applicants, including many pensioners on the Newfoundland pay-list prior to 1 April, could not provide sufficient documentation, primarily proof of age, to verify their claims. Because of the considerable numbers affected, the provincial government authorized a monthly allowance of $25 for persons who had not qualified for a full pension because of their inability to produce proof of age.[89] Moreover, the province issued relief to applicants awaiting birth verification or those whose pension was delayed for other reasons. When the board finally issued pension cheques, the federal government made its contributions retroactive to the date of the application, thus covering the period when the province had sustained the pensioner. The provincial government reclaimed from federal contributions the amount it had disbursed for relief and its own pensions.[90]

MacFarlane informed the Newfoundland Pension Board that diverting retroactive old-age-pension payments to the Department of Public Welfare for relief or any other purpose contravened the act. 'No pension shall be subject to alienation or transfer by the pensioner, or to seizure in satisfaction of any claim against him,' he wrote to the board. The pensioner was legally entitled to the amount awarded by the Canadian government and the board was bound by law to pay it. If the province wished to reclaim money paid for relief, it was a matter between the provincial authorities and the pensioner, not one for the federal government. Moreover, it seemed suspicious to MacFarlane that the board paid pensions retroactively in cases where the province had already provided relief. MacFarlane also pointed out that the money would have to be repaid or the amount deducted from future federal contributions.[91]

The province had a feeble excuse for its actions and, as this episode demonstrates, it had much to learn about the mechanisms of federalism. Provincial officials pointed to pencilled notations by Swettenham in May, one each on an analysis form and a pay-list, as a directive to deduct relief payments from federal funds. The board also claimed that Swettenham was aware of the plan to recover relief payments, but he denied any knowledge of it. He recalled discussing the question of relief, but he maintained that a definite policy had not been decided upon. MacFarlane was not impressed, and he remained unconvinced that Swettenham 'told them anything which could be construed as a definite assurance that the province could recover relief out of old age pension payment.' Even if a federal official had given them such assurances, the board must have understood that pensions had to be paid in accordance with the law. Exasperated, MacFarlane told the board chairman that '[n]o such procedure has been followed in any other province and I do not think that any other pension authority would expect Federal payments to be made under such conditions.'[92] In other words, the Newfoundland Pension Board had exceeded its authority.

Both the board and Pottle claimed that the recovery had not cost the federal government any additional money. If pension cheques had gone directly to the pensioner, or to the Department of Public Welfare as recovery for relief to the elderly to avoid undue hardship while the applicant awaited his pension, the expense would have been the same. The Newfoundland logic did not impress Ottawa. Despite Ottawa's insistence that the actions of the board were unacceptable, the province only reluctantly relented in May 1950, several months after MacFarlane made it aware of its impropriety.[93] There could be no deviation from the letter of agreements in formal dominion-provincial cost-sharing arrangements.

After discussions in Ottawa between Pottle and old-age-pension authorities, Newfoundland repaid the money that it had diverted to the Department of Public Welfare. 'It is unfortunate that the difficulty has arisen,' a sympathetic Davidson wrote to Pottle, 'but I am sure you will understand that we are dealing with pensions in all parts of Canada and, as far as possible, must endeavour to maintain reasonable uniformity in the administration.'[94] The federal authorities had made special arrangements to make pensions retroactive in Newfoundland, pending proof of age, an arrangement not extended to the other provinces. Davidson never hesitated to remind Pottle that Ottawa 'accepted it [retroactivity] in Newfoundland only because we recognized the difficulties which you were facing in the transition period.'[95] Certainly Davidson did not want to create problems for Newfoundland's old-age pensioners, but neither did he wish to see the system abused, not even in the newest province where he believed that the program was having a good effect upon the people and the union. He was relieved when Newfoundland fell in line with the other provinces.

During the final year of commission rule, the government paid $374,000 in old-age pensions; by the end of 1950 almost 12,000 people over seventy years of age were receiving monthly cheques, an injection of more than $5.3 million annually into the Newfoundland economy. Combined with family allowances and unemployment assistance and insurance, more than $24 million flowed annually from Ottawa to Newfoundland families. Those social-security programs came as the right of Newfoundlanders when the dominion officially joined Canada. It is clear that those involved in extending Canadian benefits to Newfoundland believed that they were fulfilling their mission to launch Confederation on a proper course. Using their experience from implementing family allowances and unemployment insurance to the rest of Canada earlier in the 1940s, they achieved their goals, and during April and May of 1949, Canada's newest citizens in even the remotest reaches of the province received the first visible signs that they were now Canadians. Shortly thereafter, Premier Smallwood tapped the financial resources of Ottawa and began a process that would allow Newfoundlanders to improve their standard of living and help sustain the province for decades. To a large extent, the monthly cheques from Ottawa dramatically increased the purchasing power in Newfoundland, and in the early period of union helped to sustain the province's indigenous manufacturing sector as it struggled to adjust to the new conditions of union and Canadian competition. Above all, the federal social programs were the most recognized feature of union with Canada, and they gave the process instant credibility. Over time, federal monies contributed greatly to the social and economic revolution that swept Newfoundland after 1949.

4

Going it alone: the federal government and secondary manufacturing in Newfoundland, 1948–1953

After union with Newfoundland, Canada had to deal with two problems concerning the province's manufacturing sector, both of which had their origins in the peculiar economic conditions of Newfoundland. Unlike Canada, which had encouraged its fledgling industries after 1879 under a national policy, Newfoundland had used its tariff primarily as a source of revenue. In 1933–4, for instance, the tariff produced 82 per cent of the dominion's revenue and 54 per cent as late as 1947.[1] Although the tariff was not erected to foster a process of industrialization, at the time of union nearly 130 firms,[2] employing about 4,000 workers, had been established, primarily in St John's, to meet some of the needs of the small domestic market of 325,000 inhabitants, though the dominion had relied heavily on imports. With a few exceptions, the industries were relatively small and content to produce for local consumption behind the high tariff wall.[3] A rapid reduction in import duties after union flooded the local market with cheaper Canadian products and threatened the small secondary-manufacturing industries.

The second problem revolved around special tax concessions that the Newfoundland governments had awarded to foreign companies to develop the dominion's natural resources, particularly forest products and minerals. The federal government refused to recognize these agreements after Confederation, and a dispute between Ottawa and the Bowater pulp-and-paper mill of Corner Brook, the firm most affected by the Canadian decision, landed in the Supreme Court of Canada.

I

Confederation threatened to destroy Newfoundland's manufacturing sector when union opened the local market to free trade with the rest of Canada. Not unexpectedly, manufacturers were extremely anxious about their fate.[4] John B. Angel, president of the Associated Newfoundland Industries Limited (ANI), an association of manufacturers, warned Albert J. Walsh, chair of the delegation to Ottawa, that 'Confederation will have an extremely serious effect on manufacturing in Newfoundland.'[5] The ANI simply conceded that Newfoundland industries had not been established to compete with the larger and more highly specialized Canadian firms. If duties were suddenly withdrawn without some form of special assistance to allow for a period of economic realignment, disaster was imminent. A collapse, the ANI suggested, would be catastrophic, as secondary industries employed about 3,500 to 4,500 workers on a full-time basis, and an additional 5,000 to 7,000 in auxiliary functions. In all, the ANI liberally estimated that 'a total of 25,000 to 30,000 people are directly or indirectly wholly or partially supported by the secondary manufacturing industries.' Furthermore, secondary industry provided continuous skilled or semi-skilled employment, a rarity in Newfoundland, where work was frequently unskilled and seasonal.[6]

The ANI and the Newfoundland Board of Trade both insisted that the impact of Confederation on local industries had to be 'cushioned' in the first years of union. In other words, the commercial effects of union had to be tempered to permit Newfoundland industries the opportunity to adjust to the new conditions.[7] What the ANI proposed to Walsh was unprecedented for a Canadian province, and would certainly prove unacceptable even for a new partner. It advocated an exemption from federal sales tax on all articles manufactured in Newfoundland, a gradual reduction in tariffs on Canadian goods similar to those manufactured in Newfoundland, the free entry of American raw materials, the establishment of a board of appeals for local manufacturers against Canadian firms dumping their products to undercut local industries, the full use of labels and containers marked 'Product of Newfoundland,' and the establishment of preferential freight rates not only to protect locally manufactured products but also to permit Newfoundland industries access, at competitive rates, to markets in the Maritime provinces. The cost to the federal government for these proposals, estimated at nearly $3 million, was to diminish annually by one-eighth during the first eight years. The ANI also demanded a special board of representatives, from industry and the federal government, to administer the subsidy scheme.[8] The Board of Trade expressed similar concerns. Though its submission to the delegation reflected its broader economic interests, it too warned of the severe effects of Confederation on the Newfoundland economy if Ottawa failed to provide assistance during a transitional period.[9]

The Newfoundland delegation assured both organizations that it 'was prepared, during their negotiations in Ottawa, to make every reasonable effort to safeguard their interests.' It failed, however, to uphold its end of the bargain. Its memorandum to the Canadian government, outlining its proposals for the consummation of union, refused to adopt a firm position on assistance for local industry during the transitional period. In fact, the delegation did not know what it wanted for secondary manufacturers. It seemed to doubt the warnings of impending disaster, and it asked the Canadian government to appoint three specialists to investigate the impact of union on local industry,[10] clearly a mistake. By placing the issue in the hands of a Canadian committee, without any Newfoundland representation, the delegation effectively removed the issue from the Ottawa discussions. Later, whenever Walsh mentioned the subject, the Canadians refused to discuss it, claiming that they had to wait until their team of experts had presented its report.[11] The delegation was caught in a web of its own making.

Representatives from the Department of Trade and Commerce left for Newfoundland on 5 November under the supervision of W.F. Bull, director of the Allotment Permit Division of the Import Control Branch, to survey the probable effects of Confederation on secondary industries in Newfoundland and to appraise the island's potential for industrial development. Only J.C. Britton, formerly Canadian trade commissioner to Newfoundland, knew the island particularly well. Nonetheless, after consultations with local businessmen, the officials provided C.D. Howe, the minister of trade and commerce, with a comprehensive overview of secondary manufacturing and outlined potential problems for the various industries. Some industries were more susceptible to Canadian competition than others, they told him. The outlook for the boot-and-shoe industry and the clothing factories was bleak, but the cordage industry had little to fear from union. The team largely confirmed the warnings of the Board of Trade and the ANI: 'unless some measure of assistance is granted,' it warned, 'it is probable that a number of Newfoundland's secondary industries will be faced with severe dislocation and financial loss causing possible retrenchment in production and consequent unemployment.'[12]

Bull had worked with Howe long enough to realize that the minister would summarily dismiss many of the ANI's earlier recommendations. Financial assistance for the faltering industries was a matter for the new provincial government, Bull told his minister. Still, some measure of assistance was clearly necessary to avert a disaster, and he submitted several recommendations for Howe's consideration: both the federal and provincial governments should consider delaying sales tax for products produced for consumption in Newfoundland; Canada should place contracts for war materials with Newfoundland firms in need of assistance; industries should be granted a reduction in duties and an extension of most favourable freight rates on raw materials; and a board should be established 'to review continuously Newfoundland's problem of development and adjustment.'[13]

Montreal lawyer-economist H. Carl Goldenberg, whom the ANI had retained as special counsel to travel with the Canadians, went one step farther. In his memorandum to the Canadian government, he warned that any reduction in employment because of the closure of secondary industries after Confederation would create a 'pocket of ill-will and dissatisfaction. If secondary industries are not given an opportunity to adjust to the new economic conditions,' he warned, 'it appears inevitable that the entry of Newfoundland into the Canadian Confederation will lead to unemployment, with its accompanying social and political problems, in the city of St John's and its vicinity.' He reminded Howe that Ottawa had already accepted the principle of special assistance during the transitional period in its proposal to offer additional subsidies, provide unemployment assistance, and permit the manufacture and sale of oleomargarine. Like Bull, Goldenberg called upon the minister to recognize the tenuous position of Newfoundland's manufacturing sector and offer special assistance during the transitional period.[14]

But C.D. Howe had already decided that Canada would provide little assistance to Newfoundland industries. Neither Goldenberg, the Board of Trade, the ANI, the feeble entreaties of the Newfoundland delegation, nor the team of experts he himself had appointed would change his mind. He reminded Prime Minister St Laurent as the negotiations were winding down that 'the welfare of industries in that province is the primary concern of the provincial government.' There could be no relief from the application of sales or excise taxes, as this would amount to tax discrimination in favour of Newfoundland against the rest of the dominion. A day after receiving the Bull report, which, incidentally, Howe advised keeping from the Newfoundland delegation, he left Ottawa for a nine-day trip to western Canada. No decision was made on special assistance for Newfoundland industries in his absence.[15] However, by 8 December, three days after Howe's return and three days before the Terms of Union were signed, the Department of Trade and Commerce produced a memorandum on Newfoundland's secondary industries. While it recognized the necessity of readjustment after union, it concluded that 'it does not appear that there are any overall measures which will meet the problems.' Nevertheless, the department suggested that the Canadian government and the armed forces make as many purchases as possible in Newfoundland, especially for local needs. It also urged the government to make available to Newfoundland industry items such as pig iron, nail rods, and steel, which were in critically short supply throughout North America as factories returned to domestic production.[16] Moreover, it proposed the establishment of a small interdepartmental committee of senior officials under the chairmanship of W.F. Bull 'to hear and deal with the problems of individual Newfoundland industries.' The memorandum also reflected Howe's view that direct financial assistance to secondary manufacturing was the sole responsibility of the provincial government.[17] Thus, the success or failure of secondary manufacturing in the post-Confederation period was thrown upon the shoulders of the provincial government and local entrepreneurs. The federal government saw a very limited role for itself. As was the case in other matters, the Canadian negotiators, including Prime Minister St Laurent, took the view: 'We're sorry but we have to treat all provinces alike.'[18]

The reference to the small industries contained in the 'Statements on Questions Raised by the Newfoundland Delegation' attached to the Terms of Union reflected the tenor of the Howe memorandum. It claimed that dislocation, though inevitable, was difficult to measure, as it depended upon the response of management and owners to the problems that arose after Confederation. Still, the Canadian government promised assistance:

The Canadian Government will do all that it can to assist secondary industries in Newfoundland in their efforts to meet such problems as may arise. The extensive facilities of the Department of Trade and Commerce will be available to assist in procurement of raw materials from other parts of Canada or from abroad. The Department will continue to maintain an office in St John's for at least two or three years, and longer if necessary. The Canadian

Commercial Corporation, which carries the responsibility of purchasing for the Armed Services, will maintain a representative in Newfoundland, and every effort will be made to ensure that an appropriate volume of purchases for Government account will be made locally. Further, the Department of Trade and Commerce will establish at Ottawa a committee of senior officials to work as a team to ensure that special enquiries and problems of Newfoundland receive as prompt and effective attention as possible.[19]

The assistance promised to the Newfoundland industries was a far cry from what was needed, largely because of Howe's tough bargaining. He had insisted that Ottawa avoid making special arrangements for Newfoundland manufacturers. Moreover, he had procrastinated as long as possible. When Walsh brought the issue to the bargaining table on 26 November, Howe claimed that he had not received the Bull report, which had been presented to him at least three days earlier.[20] When the issue was finally discussed a day or two before the end of negotiations, Newfoundland demanded little: merely a recognition that Confederation would necessitate a readjustment for local manufacturers, an understanding that Canada would cooperate during the transitional period (but nothing specific was demanded), and the appointment by Canada of a senior officer from the Department of Trade and Commerce to consider problems submitted by Newfoundland manufacturers and make recommendations for their solution.[21] Considering the ineffective bargaining tactics and the weak demands of the delegation, Newfoundland secondary industries could hardly have expected more. The Trade and Commerce memorandum on 8 December declared that 'the Newfoundland delegation must, in the last analysis, rely on the undoubted interest of the Canadian Government to see these problems [readjustment in secondary manufacturing] eased and the impact of Confederation minimized.'[22] The Newfoundland delegation obviously did.

Chesley Crosbie, however, did not place as much faith in the ability or will of the Canadians to protect the interests of secondary manufacturers as did his six colleagues. He refused to sign the Terms of Union, citing, among other reasons, the failure of the Canadian government to provide a period of readjustment to allow secondary industries to become acclimatized to the new conditions. Despite the submissions made by Goldenberg and the delegation, the cabinet committee refused to concede that it could minimize the disruption expected in the Newfoundland economy. In his minority report to the governor of Newfoundland, Crosbie warned that '[i]t is impossible to adapt the Canadian economy to this country overnight without causing chaos and distress in many places, particularly when for centuries we have had our own economy peculiar to this country.'[23]

Why, then, did the other members of the delegation take such a weak position on secondary industries while negotiating so tenaciously for Canadian concessions on other issues? The answer may lie, in part, in the value of manufacturing to the Newfoundland economy. In discussions between the ANI and the delegation, Smallwood had reminded Angel that 'the degree to which the delegation would be successful in any negotiations which it might undertake in Ottawa on behalf of local industries depended entirely on the value of these industries to the economy of Newfoundland.'[24] The delegation certainly realized that secondary industries did not contribute enough to the economy of Newfoundland to make it a sticking point in the negotiations, and were certainly not important enough to demand the measures that the ANI had insisted upon. This was primarily a St John's issue, and perhaps the three Confederates on the delegation continued to harbour a dislike for the business community. Throughout the referenda struggles, they held the economic interests of St John's responsible for Newfoundland's social and economic ills. The Confederates had charged that the business community had stood in the way of union and a better standard of living. Moreover, Smallwood had been a proponent of free trade since the 1920s, arguing that bringing down the tariff barriers would significantly lower the cost of living of working people and the costs of production in the fishery. The local manufacturers were the only ones who benefited from protection, along with a few of their employees. Under the circumstances, then, F. Gordon Bradley and Smallwood refused to put up a determined fight for local manufacturers. And, in the end, Canada had its way with the delegation on the issue of secondary manufacturers.

The first casualty of Canadian competition was the Parker and Monroe Shoe Factory. The plant announced its closure after an 'exhaustive study' concluded that its shoes would cost considerably more per pair than the equivalent Canadian shoes landed in Newfoundland. The firm had investigated the possibility of linking up with a Montreal distributor, but R. Campbell Smith, Canadian trade commissioner in Newfoundland, reported that this initiative proved unproductive. Thus, it came as no surprise on 22 January that company president John J. Parker announced that the plant was closing, putting its sixty-five employees out of work. He had made it clear to both the Bull team and the Newfoundland delegation that he could not compete with Canadian footwear immediately following Confederation. Smith reported that Parker and Monroe felt that the Terms of Union offered no inducement to small industries to maintain production. Government contracts, especially those for the armed services, were useless unless firms manufactured the required products. It made little business sense to instal new machinery on the basis of a few government contracts. 'This company [Parker and Monroe] continues in the belief that the only hope for survival lay in the exemption of sales tax on production,' Smith concluded.[25] Even so, Parker and Monroe had decided as early as November 1948 that it would expand its more lucrative wholesale and retail trade. It had, by then, sought Canadian supplies of low-priced footwear to replace its manufactured lines.[26]

When Howe travelled to St John's to address the fortieth annual meeting of the Newfoundland Board of Trade in February 1949, he met with the owner of Parker and Monroe, who wanted to discuss what incentives Ottawa would give if the company reopened its factory. 'I told him,' an irritated Howe wrote to Bull following his return to Ottawa, 'that we were not interested in opening a plant that had already closed.'[27] Howe's message was clear: once a plant closed its doors, it could forget about government assistance. He despised – and perhaps rightly so – Parker's attitude, and he had said as much to the Newfoundland delegation at its final meeting with the cabinet committee. He told them then that Canada 'could not be unduly concerned by a manufacturer who would give up before trying to adjust his production to fit the new conditions which will exist after Confederation.' He saw Parker and Monroe as quitters. He looked more favourably on Newfoundland's other shoe manufacturer, the Newfoundland Boot and Shoe Company, which, Bull had reported, proposed to expand its production of workboots to break into the Maritime market. However, Howe had failed to realize that because Newfoundland Boot and Shoe specialized in the production of workboots, it had already streamlined operations and had a better economy of scale, making it more efficient and better able to meet Canadian competition than Parker and Monroe, which produced the same lines of shoes as its Canadian competitors.[28]

When Howe spoke to the Board of Trade, he continued the line he had adopted during the negotiations. He told the businessmen that some of them would find the competition with Canadian products ex-

tremely difficult, but that the federal government intended to purchase the items needed to establish federal offices in Newfoundland.
Moreover, he frankly reminded the board, the Canadian government
could not guarantee the future of every manufacturing firm in Newfoundland. 'You will not expect this,' he told the businessmen,
shrewdly quoting Board of Trade president Lewis M. Ayre, who had
written in the New Year issue of the *Daily News* that 'in the future as
in the past our problems will be largely our own and their resolution
will rest, as it always has, upon ourselves.' Howe made the federal
position clear:

The Federal Government cannot help those who will not help themselves, but
it can be of assistance to those willing and anxious to hold and improve their
position in a territory and amongst a population with which they have the
advantage of past contacts and accumulated goodwill ... We appreciate that
there will be problems of adjustment, and the most sympathetic and careful
consideration will be given to all special circumstances.[29]

Although Ayre agreed with Howe that the outcome of the readjustment period rested to some extent on the shoulders of Newfoundlanders themselves, he took the opportunity to remind him that
secondary industry had developed under Newfoundland's peculiar
system, and it could not hope to compete unless it was eased into the
Canadian sphere. 'We are disappointed,' he told Howe, 'that no direct method of assistance has yet been offered to help industry over
the transitional period. We hope the door is still open.'[30]
    The door was not only closed, it was locked and the key thrown
away. Once again the ANI Limited pressed for tax and excise relief,
but Howe merely promised to consult the Department of Finance
about the issue. Given that the cabinet had already rejected such measures as unfair and inequitable to the other provinces, it came as no
surprise that Ottawa again turned down the request. Yet, after discussions with Howe, the ANI finally realized where it stood with him.
'We do not feel our problems are any the less evident because of our
talk,' President John B. Angel wrote to him, 'but we do know where
we stand and feel that we can count on your sympathetic consideration of individual cases as they arise and are presented to the Committee of Senior Officials at Ottawa.'[31] In other words, there would be
no wholesale assistance for island manufacturers, but if individual
firms came with cap in hand and a good case, Ottawa might listen.

Union removed immediately the protection that Newfoundland goods had enjoyed for decades against Canadian imports, and overnight Canadian goods became much cheaper. On 31 March 1949, clothing manufacturers, for instance, enjoyed a 35 to 40 per cent protection. The following day witnessed the removal of all tariffs, and the situation became truly a case of the little boat and the mighty storm. Sources of supply also changed. Prior to union, manufacturers could purchase materials from the cheapest suppliers in either North America or Europe. When Canadian import controls – which had been in effect since November 1947 to stem the loss of exchange reserves[32] – and the Canadian tariff schedule took effect in Newfoundland on 1 April, manufacturers had to buy from Canadian suppliers, often at greater cost. Within three months of union, the volume of freight to Newfoundland from Canada had increased by 75 per cent, and by 1952, the dramatic increase forced Canadian National to divide the province into zones to facilitate freight movement.[33] Moreover, manufacturers had to alter their accounting system to adjust to Canadian taxation. Not only were some taxes higher following union, but manufacturers had to adapt to new forms of taxation such as the deductions for pay-as-you-go income tax and unemployment insurance.[34] Finally, manufacturers complained that high freight rates on imported raw materials made their products less competitive.[35] Ottawa never addressed any of these problems to help Newfoundland manufacturers adjust to the new conditions.

Instead, the Canadian government adopted a simple and largely ineffective policy to assist secondary industries in the new province. It encouraged manufacturers to tender on federal contracts. On 13 January 1949, the cabinet told its departments and agencies in Newfoundland to purchase equipment, supplies, and other necessities from local producers provided prices were reasonable during the transition period. It also appointed an Interdepartmental Sub-Committee on Newfoundland Secondary Industries and Purchasing (ISNSIP) to monitor the situation. Although the sub-committee's function was clear, it was impotent and unable to fulfil its mandate because it had been given no authority to act; it could only observe. First, it compiled a list of all possible sources of supply in Newfoundland for departmental purchasing agents.[36] The subcommittee then recommended to the cabinet that Newfoundland contractors be paid a reasonable premium, where necessary, over the lowest bid in certain instances such as on supplies required in Newfoundland (though not in Labrador), and on token orders in other provinces. Still, the premium was designed only for firms that had a reasonable chance of survival in the long run.[37] In any event, government purchases were insufficient to protect local producers from lower-priced goods flowing from Canada.

Moreover, most federal departments and agencies were reluctant to use the premium, as the cabinet had not given it a per cent value.[38] The subcommittee soon realized, too, that many Newfoundland firms were reluctant to submit bids until they had become familiar with the new taxes and tariffs. Still, it saw a great urgency in inviting tenders as early as the first week of May 1949, for the publicity that it generated. In fact, it had recognized the benefit of advertising in the local newspapers the purchases made by the Canadian Commercial Corporation (CCC) and other federal departments and agencies in establishing their offices in the new province.[39] If nothing else, then, the subcommittee served as an avenue of publicity to give the impression that Ottawa cared about the fate of Newfoundland's secondary industries.

Still, some Canadian officials in charge of purchasing were hostile towards Newfoundland manufacturers. D.M. Erskine, who established the CCC there, was one such individual. He concluded that many industries did not require special assistance to survive, and that many of the small firms were doomed to failure anyway because of their exorbitant costs, which exceeded those of large Canadian manufacturers and mail-order distributors. Newfoundland entrepreneurs, he told an ISNSIP meeting in Ottawa, were more obsessed with larger profits than their mainland counterparts, but he did not bring any evidence to support his claim. Canadian businessmen, he charged, 'allowed for only a modest profit when tendering for government contracts,' but because Newfoundland businessmen had operated for so long in a well-protected market, they 'were accustomed to obtaining very large profit margins.' He warned Newfoundland businessmen that Ottawa wanted contracts from the new province but would proceed only if prices were reasonable. It is difficult to determine how Erskine arrived at his conclusions, as the CCC had received only five tenders on 597 invitations when he made his allegations to the subcommittee.[40] Moreover, he had been in St John's for only a few months when he pointed his finger at the ethos and mentality of Newfoundland manufacturers.[41] Yet, for all this, he might have been correct. A provincial royal commission investigating the cost of living after union had found that gross profits of most Newfoundland retailers and wholesalers were considerably higher than those of their Canadian counterparts.[42] About the same time, the subcommittee revised its earlier inventory of firms to separate manufacturers from distributors and to take note of firms in the 'most precarious position.'[43] An injection of funds from a federal contract might allow a firm to stagger on a little longer.

The federal policy was obviously not working. By the end of June, a mere three months after union, several industries had died or were taking their last breaths. John H. Henley's bedding factory released its ten employees and liquidated in the face of competition with Simpson's and Eaton's mail-order catalogues. The Standard Bedding Company Limited faced similar competition and was not expected to survive. In addition to the bedding and the shoe industries, R. Campbell Smith informed Ottawa, the clothing, paper bags, printing and stationery, soap manufacturing, and foundry industries were in a precarious position because of Canadian competition.[44] Even the Newfoundland Boot and Shoe Company, which Howe had earlier praised for eyeing the Maritime market, faced serious problems. Parker and Monroe, which had ceased manufacturing to concentrate on the retail trade and import cheaper Canadian products provided stiff competition.[45] With the removal of tariff protection, Newfoundland manufacturers found competition exceedingly difficult. The policy of encouraging contracts with Newfoundland firms did not help most industries. Contracts from the Canadian army, for instance, required primarily Goodyear welt shoes, but the Newfoundland Boot and Shoe Company produced only stitch-downs, cements, and staple welts.[46] What was often the case was that Newfoundland firms did not manufacture the type of products the federal government required.

Only a small number of contracts had been awarded in Newfoundland, certainly not enough to enable industries to adjust to the new conditions. Smith informed the ISNSIP on 3 August 'that to date little assistance had been given to the Newfoundland secondary industries.' Although the bottling industry benefited from the general removal of excise taxes and a nail manufacturer had received aid, some action had to be taken to prevent a complete collapse of Newfoundland's secondary industries.[47] Howe then asked for recommendations to help the struggling industries during the transitional period. In its memorandum to the cabinet on 9 August, the subcommittee concluded that the firms hardest hit by Canadian competition 'are now facing serious difficulties and have so far received little or no practical help from Federal Government Orders.' Unemployment had reached nearly 20 per cent in St John's, and the subcommittee warned that any further deterioration in the economic position of large employers such as the clothing and printing industries could further aggravate the unemployment situation. 'It is apparent that the amount of assistance being rendered to Newfoundland secondary industries,' ISNSIP secretary D.M. McDonald informed the cabinet, 'is negligible under the present government system of awarding contracts by means of competitive tenders as the Newfoundland secondary industries are not at present in a competitive position.' It advised further assistance if Ottawa wanted Newfoundland industries to adjust to meet the new conditions. The cabinet agreed, and on 17 August 1949 it authorized government departments to pay to secondary manufacturers a premium not exceeding 15 per cent of the lowest bid from producers in other provinces. The premium was to run only until 31 March 1950, when the cabinet expected Newfoundland industries to have adjusted to post-Confederation competition.[48]

Ottawa had responded only when it became concerned over rising unemployment in St John's. When the issue arose in the cabinet, the discussion centred on the growing number of unemployed; the fate of the manufacturing industries seemed of secondary concern though, certainly the two were connected. A few days after the cabinet approved the premium, Norman A. Robertson, secretary to the cabinet, suggested to Prime Minister St Laurent that the assistance given to local producers should be publicized, since it might enhance relations with the Confederation recalcitrants and create a favourable impression, though he realized the futility of the program. 'From a practical point of view,' he told the prime minister, 'this scheme will not be a very great benefit to Newfoundland producers since the latter's prices frequently exceed those prevailing in other parts of Canada by more than 100 %.'[49]

G.D. Mallory, director of the Industrial Development Division at Trade and Commerce, conducted a brief survey of secondary industries in Newfoundland in October 1949 at W.F. Bull's request. His report was mixed. He claimed that secondary manufacturing was in a much better condition than the reports from the new province suggested, and he pointed to a number of modern plants as examples. His optimism was tempered, however, by the number of firms that had curtailed production in the face of fierce competition from Canadian products and, after the devaluation of the pound, British imports.

Though he noted examples of outstanding management, Mallory saw a fatal weakness in Newfoundland entrepreneurs: 'a timidity or disinclination to strike out and fight fire with fire, to invade the mainland with specialty products, or to link up with mainland firms as Newfoundland branches.' Yet he also alluded to the higher costs in the new province created by higher freight rates, lower labour efficiency, and a lack of specialization – all largely a result of the small Newfoundland market. Mallory's grim prediction estimated that one-quarter to one-third of the existing secondary industries in Newfoundland might disappear within two years of union, displacing 1,000 to 1,250 workers. Curiously, he added that most businessmen accepted Confederation, except those whose businesses were not likely to survive![50]

When the premium was about to expire, the ANI sought its extension. It argued that since the measure had first been introduced conditions had not improved for most Newfoundland firms and the future was far from certain. The value of production in secondary manufacturing had fallen from $30 to $18 million, a clear indication of the impact of Confederation. Six firms had closed since 31 March 1949, and many others had reduced production or temporarily ceased operation. John B. Angel reminded ISNSIP that the change in Newfoundland's constitutional status had forced secondary industries both to meet many new costs, such as unemployment-insurance and income-tax deductions, federal sales taxes, and other federal and provincial responsibilities, and to respond to increased competition. These factors, he claimed, reduced the ability of secondary industries to give the required attention to tendering on federal contracts. The firms needed the premium, and since it was the 'most tangible form of assistance which had been offered to the Secondary Industries as a whole so far,' he asked Ottawa to extend it until 31 March 1951.[51] Before the subcommittee discussed the issue, Eric White, who had replaced Angel as president, promised ISNSIP secretary D.M. McDonald that all firms would pay closer attention in the future to invitations to tender on federal contracts.[52]

When the subcommittee met in late March 1950 to discuss the position of the secondary industries, representatives of several of the government departments expressed disappointment that so few Newfoundland firms had tendered on federal contracts. D.M. Erskine repeated his concerns of the previous year that many firms allowed too great a profit on government contracts and that others were too timid to bid for government contracts. However, most members of the ISNSIP agreed on the need for continued assistance.[53] 'The position of many of Newfoundland's secondary industries appears to have deteriorated seriously during the past year,' W.F. Bull wrote in his memorandum to the cabinet, 'and largely as a direct result of tariff changes which accompanied Confederation.' He cautioned that the benefit derived from the assistance would never be substantial, but the policy did provide some encouragement to several industries. In any event, costs to the federal government had been negligible, and other provincial governments had not complained about the special policy for Newfoundland.[54] The cabinet agreed to extend the premium until 1951.

At the request of the ANI, the subcommittee recommended a year later another extension of the premium. Again, the ANI contended that the secondary-manufacturing industries continued to be adversely affected by Confederation and that more plants had been forced to close, bringing the number to nine since 1 April 1949. Besides, transportation costs continued to plague the Newfoundland producer, and the ANI argued that the premium should continue until the completion in 1955 of the Newfoundland–Nova Scotia ferry. As well, many firms were adjusting to the new conditions, and a further year of assistance might help some of them succeed.[55] W.F. Bull also reminded the subcommittee 'that the Minister of Trade and Commerce had recently indicated that it was part of Government policy to pay higher prices when necessary to spread the placement of government orders.' The cost to Ottawa remained minimal, and because of the general prosperity throughout Canada, Bull assumed that there would be little objection to the preferential treatment for Newfoundland secondary industries. But more important, he reminded the cabinet, 'Newfoundland Manufacturers are getting into a position where they can derive considerably greater benefits from the government's preferential price policy than heretofore.' As a reminder to manufacturers of the temporary nature of the assistance, Ottawa reduced the premium from 15 to 10 per cent and told them that it would cease in March 1952.[56]

As the premium for contracts placed with Newfoundland secondary industries was about to expire, Premier Joseph R. Smallwood entered the picture on the manufacturers' behalf for the first time. He was concerned not so much about industries that had existed prior to union as about those that had been established under his initiative after 1949. He told Prime Minister St Laurent in early 1952 that 'the nature of Newfoundland's secondary industries has been such that this assistance had not been availed of to any appreciable extent,' but that Newfoundland plants were now in a position to benefit from it. He wanted the premium extended for an additional three years, 'to help new industries, which are in a position to tender for Government business to find a rightful place in the economy of Canada.'[57] St Laurent discussed the matter with Howe, who then served as minister of defence production as well as minister of trade and commerce. Howe reminded the Prime Minister that they had initiated the premium for a transitional period to assist industries existing at the time of Confederation. 'It was never intended to provide a form of assistance to industrial development in Newfoundland, an assistance not available to other provinces of Canada,' Howe wrote to the Prime Minister. In a letter he drafted for St Laurent to send to Smallwood, he outlined the Canadian position: 'The measure was intended to help established manufacturers, long selling in a protected market, to survive the rigours of the initial period of open competition with other Canadian producers.' The new industries could avail themselves of the new policy that promoted the principle of local purchasing to decentralize defence orders. 'We feel that the time has now come,' St Laurent acidly told Smallwood, 'for Newfoundland to participate on the same basis as other provinces in any federal assistance which may be given to provide an offset for certain regional disadvantages.'[58]

The federal government had adopted a similar attitude towards individual firms that sought special assistance. In the months before Confederation, the Department of Trade and Commerce obtained commitments from both Canadian steel manufacturers not to ship nails to Newfoundland – using Canadian shortages as an argument – to enable United Nail and Foundry to adjust to post-Confederation conditions. Howe had arranged to subsidize the shipment of nail rods imported from the United States and Europe to maintain a steady supply to Newfoundland manufacturers. Both concessions resulted from the initiative of John B. Angel, president of United Nail and Foundry, who had approached Howe before union. Angel had asked that both the Steel Company of Canada (Stelco) and Dominion Steel and Coal Corporation (Dosco) continue to supply raw materials to the Newfoundland nail producers, but that they stay out of the market in order to give local producers (i.e., Angel) a chance to survive. Howe agreed, and authorized Angel to work out an arrangement with the steel companies, which he subsequently did.[59]

In March 1950, Ottawa removed the subsidy from steel imports, but the arrangement with the Canadian steel producers continued, largely through Angel's initiative, though with Ottawa's moral support. When the private agreement expired in early 1951, Angel sought Small-wood's support to convince Howe that Canadian nail producers should be prevented from invading the Newfoundland market. Initially, the Premier had opposed the assistance Howe had given the United Nail and Foundry. In October 1949, he demanded the removal of the subsidy on nails coming into the province, claiming that the price of nails was out of line with those in the rest of Canada. Howe refused, telling Smallwood that the measure was a part of government policy to allow secondary industry in Newfoundland to adjust to new conditions after Confederation. Nevertheless, he told him that United Nail and Foundry, which benefited from the subsidy, was to reduce prices to compete with mainland wholesalers or risk losing it.[60] By the time the support for United Nail was coming to an end, Smallwood had accepted the arrangement, partly because the Newfoundland producers had successfully competed against mainland jobbers and nail prices had decreased, and partly because he wanted federal support for the new industries he had attracted to Newfoundland.[61] Howe had obviously had enough of Angel, however. 'I suggest to you,' he hastily wrote to the Premier, 'that Angel is too willing to look to Government for help and somewhat unwilling to help himself ... Surely he has now had ample time to adjust his operation to the Canadian competitive position.'[62] Smallwood then asked the two steel companies to continue the private arrangement, but, like Howe, they refused. Although he stopped short of saying that his company would ship nails to Newfoundland, H.G. Hilton, president of Stelco, informed Smallwood that his company had to compete with Dosco, which was already supplying nails to the Newfoundland market indirectly through sales by mainland jobbers.[63]

Immediately after Confederation, Premier Smallwood had placed lower consumer prices ahead of the welfare of secondary manufacturing. With little sympathy for the local manufacturer, he opposed any assistance to local industry that might prevent consumer prices from dropping throughout Newfoundland. In fact, if prices of consumer products did not fall as much or as rapidly as he wished, Smallwood blamed local businessmen and secondary manufacturers. In late 1949, he appointed Frank S. Grisdale of the Canadian Wartime Prices and Trade Board to chair a royal commission to investigate the effect of union on the cost of living. The royal commission concluded that during the period investigated – 1 January 1949 to 31 March 1950 – there was 'a substantial downward adjustment in the price of consumer goods in Newfoundland contrasted with an upward trend of price levels in other parts of Canada and in many other countries.'[64] The removal of the tariff duties on Canadian goods generally contributed to lower prices, but the report convinced Smallwood that prices would have fallen even farther if the Newfoundland businessmen had not been so greedy.

Although Smallwood allowed his name to appear on Angel's letters to Howe and the Canadian steel companies, he did not share the concerns of Newfoundland manufacturers in their battle with mainland competition. It is clear from his debates in the National Convention and in his early years as premier that he disliked Newfoundland's businessmen and regarded them as parasites who had made their fortunes on the backs of the downtrodden people. He paid little attention to pre-union industries, as he was preoccupied after May 1950 with his program of attracting Europeans, particularly Germans, to Newfoundland to create new secondary manufacturing.[65] In his memoirs, Smallwood makes no attempt to hide his contempt for Newfoundland businessmen:

It was useless to turn to the businessmen of Newfoundland. Most of them were scrambling around, like hen-hawks eyeing a chicken coop, for their share of family allowances and other cash pouring in from Ottawa. Wholesale, jobbing, retail shops, they were stocking up to the bursting point, telegraphing and telephoning urgently to the mainland for more supplies, and scouring Canada for new agencies. I didn't dare venture my life in that mob of single-minded traders. It would be useless to talk to them about investing money in new industries, so I would have to search outside, and I did.[66]

Smallwood clearly did not trust the province's future to native entrepreneurs, and his attitude towards them was no secret. When G.D. Mallory was making the second study of the impact of Confederation on Newfoundland's secondary industries, he noted the rift between the provincial government and local industry. 'It was amazing to find so little interest in the problems of the secondary industry of the province,' Mallory concluded after he attended a cocktail party given by the Newfoundland government. Though most of the cabinet ministers and other important people in the capital were present, manu-

facturers and businessmen were conspicuous by their absence. Smallwood, Mallory noted, was preoccupied with bringing down the cost
of living, and he shared the view of many in Newfoundland that secondary industries, operating behind a high tariff wall, were simply
inefficient and deserved to fail after union. Those firms had no place
in Smallwood's plan to make Newfoundland a centre of Canadian
manufacturing. Consequently, he welcomed the flood of mainland
salesmen with the hope that Canadian competition would usher in a
general price reduction. Mallory expressed surprise that Smallwood
showed 'no concern at all for the fact that from one-third to one-quarter of existing industry would probably go out of business, leaving
unemployment of over one thousand people.'[67]

Mallory was correct in his assessment. When Smallwood discussed
the need for industrial development in policy statements and in the
annual budget speech, rarely did he mention the fate of Newfoundland's struggling enterprises.[68] Even when the ANI approached Smallwood late in 1949 and asked him to dispel the general impression in
the province that he was 'not favourably disposed towards the secondary industries,' he refused to do so. A year later, in 1950, the ANI
again asked the Premier for financial assistance. It told him that the
industries were slowly adapting to the new conditions. 'Mainland
firms have continued and intensified their efforts to gain the Newfoundland markets,' Eric White wrote, 'and while Newfoundland
manufacturers are not taking this lying down and are making very
strenuous efforts to maintain trade, the disadvantages of our location,
freight rates and other problems, make the fight an uneven one.' Still,
Smallwood was unmoved. In his New Year's broadcast for 1951,
Smallwood boasted of great strides in economic development and of
his government's assistance to industry, but the pre-union secondary
industries producing for the Newfoundland market did not make the
list of those that had received assistance.[69]

Yet, they were not totally ignored. When Alfred Valdmanis, director of economic development for Newfoundland, tried to establish a
shoe factory in 1951, he approached John Parker of Parker and Monroe, only to find him uninterested in participating in the proposed
shoe industry.[70] Smallwood also refused to offer financial assistance
to firms that proposed to compete with existing industries that had
become more efficient after union. When a British firm offered to establish a cordage and wire-rope industry, the Newfoundland government refused it assistance, as the Colonial Cordage Company[71] had

'successfully weathered the changed economic conditions brought about by union, and has been able to meet competition from mainland and local imported cordage.'[72] The most effective provincial assistance came in the government's collaboration with the ANI to launch a 'Buy Newfoundland Products Campaign,' which advertised local products to help manufacturers compete with mainland items.[73]

After three years of union the situation had improved significantly for manufacturers. Most firms had weathered the bleak period immediately after union, though many had teetered on the brink of collapse.[74] Though competition from mainland products continued to pose a threat, the *Newfoundland Journal of Commerce* reported that it was a misconception to think that 'local industrialists [were] cowering behind their desks with a harried look and an air of frightened expectancy, probably awaiting one of two sounds – either a loud crash denoting the end of their enterprise, or a soft whir of a fairy godmother from Ottawa.' Secondary manufacturers finally realized the necessity of efficiency and cost-effectiveness. 'A good deal of attention was given by all industries to technical plant improvements and the further streamlining of production where possible,' Eric White wrote in his annual review for the Board of Trade. 'As a result many plants in Newfoundland are now equally as modern, if not more so than their counterparts of similar size on the mainland.'[75] The *Financial Post* saw a similar pattern. In its 1950 review of economic activity in Newfoundland, it reported that manufacturers were not standing around waiting for Ottawa to save them. Many firms had undergone a 'rigorous period of retrenchment' and had streamlined production to 'cut costs to the bone.'[76] Manufacturers of biscuits and paints, for instance, had installed modern machinery and competed successfully with mainland products. Moreover, manufacturers realized for the first time the importance of packaging. Prior to union, most food products were shipped to the outports in large crates or barrels and sold in bulk. After union, consumers preferred the Canadian products that arrived in attractive packages. When Newfoundland firms followed suit, many consumers returned to the local products that they knew best.[77]

Newfoundland's secondary industry also benefited for a few more years from the peculiar conditions from which it sprang. The province's long-term credit arrangements proved too much for many mainland distributors, who were unaccustomed to waiting months for payment from outport merchants, as was usual in Newfoundland.

Neither were Canadian distributors able to adjust quickly to the outport trade, which necessitated sending merchandise to the isolated areas months in advance. Several times goods arrived from the mainland to find that the last freight boat for the season had left for northern Newfoundland or Labrador. Thus, after a period of frenzied buying in 1949, outport merchants settled down to more regular purchasing in 1950, and in many cases they returned to their dependable (and now cheaper) suppliers in St John's.[78] Local products also benefited from the 'Buy Newfoundland' campaign. More important, however, was a general rise in personal incomes after Confederation that increased demand for most goods. Personal income per capita rose from $472 in 1949 to $632 in 1953.[79] At the same time, the American base command strengthened its policy of buying local products, a move that also helped some industries to maintain their production levels.[80] The predictions in 1948 of gloom and doom did not materialize.

The major casualties of union were the producers of shoes and boots, mattresses, clothing, and tobacco, firms whose inability to achieve the necessary economies of scale prevented them from competing with larger Canadian enterprises and the mail-order catalogues. Many of the firms producing foodstuffs and beverages lumbered on, secure in their traditional market niches. In all, only eighteen industries closed after union, throwing approximately 600 persons out of work.[81] Despite Smallwood's best efforts and success with cement, gypsum, and other industries, Newfoundland never became the major manufacturing centre he had long dreamed of, though significant progress was made in the early years of union. But neither did Confederation destroy the secondary manufacturing sector in Newfoundland as many had feared. After adjusting to the new economic conditions associated with union, most firms continued to produce for the domestic market much as they had before.[82] In fact, the value of secondary manufacturing grew in the post-confederation era. In 1957, the manufacturing sector contributed nearly 30 per cent of the net value of production in Newfoundland compared with 21 per cent in 1948. The number of small manufacturing enterprises (not including the fish-processing industry or the pulp-and-paper firms) also grew after union, accounting for 20.9 per cent of all secondary manufacturing in 1950, 24.3 per cent in 1954, and 29 per cent in 1960.[83]

II

Although the Canadian government provided a measure of assistance to Newfoundland's small secondary-manufacturing sector, it refused to honour the special tax concessions some industries had enjoyed before union. Ottawa's decision to treat Newfoundland firms no differently from similar Canadian enterprises had the greatest impact on the Bowater pulp-and-paper mill of Corner Brook. Bowater had come to Newfoundland in August 1938 when it purchased the International Power and Paper Company of Newfoundland Limited, a division of International Paper Company of New York, which had operated a mill at Corner Brook since 1927. With its purchase, Bowater inherited generous tax and import concessions awarded by successive Newfoundland administrations to International Power and its predecessors since 1915. The most beneficial was legislation limiting taxes on company income to $150,000 annually between 1932 and 1973.[84] If Bowater had been subject to Canadian tax laws in 1948, for instance, it would have had to pay taxes in the neighbourhood of $1 million on a profit of $3.6 million.[85]

During the Ottawa negotiations, the Newfoundland delegation tried unsuccessfully to have Bowater[86] exempted from Canadian taxation laws until the concessions expired. Albert Walsh proved the most determined, regarding the issue as both a constitutional matter and a moral principle. 'The edifice of union,' he protested, 'must be reared in the foundation of respect for private rights and privileges previously conferred by or under Newfoundland law.'[87] Contracts signed with companies such as Bowater, he argued, were sacred, and if Canada levied taxes in excess of those provided for under Newfoundland legislation, the provincial government might be liable for damages.[88] 'At one point, he [Walsh] was so outraged,' Paul Bridle, acting high commissioner in Newfoundland recalled, 'that he despaired of reaching an agreement on union.'[89] He demanded a formal commitment from Ottawa for consultation between provincial and federal authorities before Canadian law was extended to Newfoundland, ostensibly to ensure that Ottawa did not erase the concessions. Prime Minister St Laurent and the cabinet committee refused, claiming that such an arrangement was not only unprecedented but also administratively unworkable. Moreover, St Laurent told Walsh that there would be no special concessions for Newfoundland companies guaranteed in the Terms of Union, regardless of the privileges they had enjoyed prior to union. Consequently, the issue was one of the last to be settled, and once again the Canadians prevailed when they insisted that the problem be resolved with the provincial government and the company after union.[90]

As soon as Sir Eric Bowater, chairman of the Bowater Paper Corporation, learned of Canada's intention to repudiate the tax concessions, he immediately lobbied officials in London, St John's, and Ottawa.[91] He told Philip J. Noel-Baker, secretary of state for Commonwealth relations, that he felt 'bound to take every possible step to ensure that the fullest possible consideration is given to their every aspect before any irrevocable action is taken.' Sir Eric knew that his best hope for keeping the tax collector from his Corner Brook operation lay in Ottawa, and he wasted little time in making representation to Prime Minister St Laurent. On 24 November 1948, shortly after word leaked from the negotiations that tax concessions awarded to Bowater would not be recognized in the Terms of Union, he had H.M. Spencer Lewin, vice-president and general manager of Bowater, approach St Laurent to ask that his company be given an opportunity to present its case. Company officials subsequently met with the Prime Minister, though they came away without any commitment from him.[92] Bowater then telegraphed to St Laurent and asked for a personal interview. He left little doubt what his argument would be. 'The Company does not accept the implied suggestion,' he said, 'that the Canadian Government would intend so to have these arrangements dishonoured, and the Company seeks the confirmation of the Canadian Government that these agreements will be honoured both in the letter and in the spirit.' St Laurent was cordial in his reply, though he stopped well short of promising anything.[93]

The Commission of Government could do little to help Bowater. R.L. James, commissioner of finance and the government's director on the Bowater board, told Godfrey Morley, who had been dispatched by Sir Eric to press his case in St John's, that his hands were tied. Though the commission had appointed the delegation to Ottawa, it had no control over it. There had been no communications between the commission and the delegation, an arrangement that, James admitted, embarrassed the government, as 'we have found ourselves in a state of complete ignorance of matters about which others naturally expected us to be fully primed.' Morley then demanded that the commission refuse to ratify the Terms of Union if they adversely affected the Bowater agreement. Although sympathetic, both James and Governor Gordon Macdonald refused. If the terms were otherwise acceptable, they told Morley, it would be impossible to mount an opposition solely on the grounds that they had an adverse effect on the Bowater company.[94] With that, one door was effectively closed. Bowater then turned to London.

The British government was also in a quandary. On the one hand, it had no desire to jeopardize the union between Newfoundland and Canada that had been its avowed policy since during the Second World War. If it pushed too hard on Bowater's behalf and placed unacceptable demands on the Canadians, they might walk away and leave London responsible, once again, for Newfoundland, something Whitehall did not want. On the other hand, London had encouraged the company in the late 1930s to develop Newfoundland's resources. Since then, Bowater had invested heavily in the island's pulp and paper industry and had contributed to increased employment and prosperity. When Sir Eric promptly reminded Noel-Baker of this, the British government could hardly turn its back on him. It felt an obligation to render some assistance, but how far should it go? Sir Eric had simply demanded too much when he insisted that the U.K. demand Canadian acceptance of Newfoundland's contractual obligations awarded to Bowater before it ratified union.[95] Even if London wanted to, most senior officials realized that their success in Ottawa depended upon the willingness of the Canadians to accommodate them.

By 1 January 1949 the Commonwealth Relations Office had agreed to approach the Canadian government on the company's behalf. London had guaranteed Bowater's debenture stock, and it feared the adverse effect Canadian action might have on British shareholders. It pointed out that Canada had a moral obligation to honour any agreement that existed between previous Newfoundland governments and a private company. Under international law, Canada would be bound to honour Newfoundland's obligation. Though the British agreed to press Bowater's case, they stopped short of asking Canada to preserve the agreement. Instead, they requested Ottawa not to rescind the existing legislation until both the company and the new provincial government of Newfoundland had been consulted.[96] Even here, London later realized that it might have gone too far in intruding on dominion-provincial relations. It subsequently dropped its request that the provincial government be consulted.[97]

Meanwhile, the British high commissioner spoke to St Laurent about the matter. The situation did not look particularly encouraging, P.A. Clutterbuck informed London. St Laurent had told him 'how obnoxious it was in principle that there should be differential rates of taxation among companies engaged in the same business.' He found it 'intolerable' that Bowater should be afforded more favourable treatment, in terms of taxation, than other Canadian paper companies.[98]

When Clutterbuck pressed his government's case officially, he realized that St Laurent would not be swayed by the sanctity of the agreements. Instead, he warned him that the matter might arise during debate in the British House of Commons on the Newfoundland Bill if the Canadian government intended to act unilaterally to cancel the Bowater concessions.[99] St Laurent was resolute, though he promised that he would receive further representations if the company had anything further to add. However, there would be no commitments to Bowater, a position that was hardly surprising considering the Prime Minister's criticism of the tax arrangement. 'It is our view,' St Laurent insisted, 'that the Government and Parliament must be left free to exercise their legal and constitutional responsibility in a matter of this nature [taxation], once union had been effected.'[100]

Clutterbuck was annoyed, and he later wrote to Pearson that London regarded the Prime Minister's response as a 'severe rebuff.'[101] The Commonwealth Relations Office shared his disappointment, and London continued to press for the right to make further representation to Canadian authorities before Parliament acted on the matter. With St Laurent's approval, Clutterbuck and J.W. Pickersgill eventually reached an agreement by which Ottawa promised not to remove the concessions until every opportunity was given the company to present its case. Moreover, the Canadian government agreed 'to give consideration to any factors which the United Kingdom Government, as the Government hitherto responsible for the administration of Newfoundland, has brought to their notice.'[102] Although the British government had not received a categorical assurance that the Canadians would not carry through with their plans to repudiate Bowater's tax concessions, it believed that Ottawa would not move unilaterally on the matter. That was enough to satisfy the British. If the issue arose in the debate on the Newfoundland Bill, the government could say that Ottawa had promised not to act without first consulting the interested parties.

In his budget speech on 22 March 1949, however, the minister of finance, D.C. Abbott, presented legislation to amend the War Income Tax Act and the Income Tax Act, in part so 'that tax concessions under Statutes of Newfoundland shall not apply in respect of taxes imposed by an Act of the Parliament of Canada.' Only after Clutterbuck's intervention did Abbott agree to inform Sir Eric Bowater officially of the budget resolution and to seek representations from him.[103] Clutterbuck reminded him of St Laurent's earlier assurance that the company's representations could be considered along with those of the United Kingdom.[104] On 8 April, nearly three weeks after the budget resolution, Abbott informed Bowater officials in Montreal that the Canadian government would accept further representations if they so desired.[105] They met with the Prime Minister on 26 April, but the amendment remained unchanged. On 10 December, it became law despite Bowater's continued protest.

One possible way out of the obvious impasse was a reference to the Supreme Court of Canada. The company wished to move in this direction and had suggested to St Laurent and Abbott at the April meeting and again on 17 November 1949 that the question be referred to the court. Bowater had commissioned three legal opinions, which held that the Newfoundland legislation was safe from Canadian repeal without the consent of the provincial legislature.[106] In other words, the Canadian amendment was unconstitutional. F.P. Varcoe, the Canadian deputy minister of justice, disagreed. He told Abbott that the statutory agreements provided to Bowater related 'only to such legislation as the late Dominion of Newfoundland could have enacted. They d[id] not extend to legislation enacted by Parliament.'[107] Still, Ottawa was in no hurry to refer the matter to the justices. It had good reason to be patient. St Laurent had amended the Supreme Court Act to eliminate appeals to the Judicial Committee of the Privy Council, but legislation abolishing appeals did not take effect until 23 December 1949. Cases submitted prior to that date were subject to appeal to London, something the Canadian government wanted to avoid. Therefore, Ottawa did not refer the Bowaters question until 29 December, six days after the abolition of appeals to the Privy Council.[108]

The court proceedings began in Ottawa on 27 February 1950 with Leslie R. Curtis, Newfoundland's attorney general, and Bowater's legal counsel both arguing that the amendment to the War Income Tax Act and the Income Tax Act designed to revoke Bowaters privileges could not become effective without the consent of the province of Newfoundland. They based their arguments on Term 18 of the Terms of Union, which they claimed prevented the federal government from repealing, abolishing, or altering any of the Newfoundland laws that had existed prior to union without the consent of the provincial government.[109] Varcoe and his assistant, D.W. Mundell, argued Canada's case. They contended that the taxation exemption that Bowater enjoyed did not bind the federal government. Newfoundland statutes pertaining to Bowater ceased to have legal operation at the time of union, and if they continued in force after the union, 'they did not apply in respect of Acts of Parliament of Canada extended to Newfoundland pursuant to the union to confer tax privileges, or exemptions from duty.' The Dominion also argued that when a pre-Confederation statute fell within the jurisdiction of both the Canadian Parliament and the provincial assembly, 'Parliament had the right to override it by legislation in the subject matter within its jurisdiction.'[110]

The Supreme Court ruled in Ottawa's favour. It held that Term 18 gave the Parliament of Canada 'authority to repeal, abolish or alter any and all laws in force in Newfoundland at or immediately prior to the date of union, which deal with the subject matter in s[ection] 91 of the B.N.A. Act, 1867.' Because the taxation exemption and freedom from custom duties for Bowater fell within federal jurisdiction, the Canadian amendments were constitutional.[111] Chief Justice Thibaudeau Rinfret dismissed Bowater's argument. 'Interpreting it [subsection 3 of Term 18] as meaning that no laws of Newfoundland can be repealed, except with the consent of the Legislature of that Province,' he wrote in his judgment, 'would lead to an absurdity.' He left little doubt that the Bowater exemptions continued to apply to the province of Newfoundland. He was unequivocal, however, about Ottawa's authority: 'Under no rule of interpretation can Bowater's Newfoundland Pulp and Paper Mills, Limited, be regarded as having been given an exemption or an immunity from the taxes imposed by the Parliament of Canada. In that sense they are in no different situation from any other company in any other province of Canada.'[112] Five other justices agreed with Rinfret. Only Justice Robert Taschereau dissented. He ruled that 'the Parliament of Canada alone has no power to impose taxation upon the Company in contravention to the Terms of the agreements which have been ratified by Statutes.'[113]

Although the Supreme Court had effectively settled the issue of Bowater's tax exemption, the question remained whether the company should be taxed from 31 March 1949, when Newfoundland joined Canada, or from 10 December 1949, when Parliament ratified the tax amendments. Sir Eric later suggested to St Laurent that if the government sought taxes for the period after 10 December, it would help to re-establish the happy relationship that had existed between the company and Newfoundland's new government.[114] St Laurent agreed. After considerable discussion in the Department of Finance and the Prime Minister's Office, the cabinet passed an order-in-council on 4 October 1951 that remitted to Bowater federal taxes due prior to ratification of the amendment.[115] St Laurent understood that union stood to gain more from Canadian goodwill than from a strict enforcement of Canadian tax laws. After all, Canadian law had clearly prevailed over pre-union Newfoundland law in matters that now fell under federal jurisdiction, and Bowater was now operating under the same law as other similar Canadian companies. The Supreme Court ruling that made it so marked yet another step along the path of Newfoundland's integration with Canada.

5

Canada establishes sovereignty in Newfoundland, 1948–1952

Newfoundland had signed nearly 130 treaties with other nations before union with Canada. The Canadian government had made it clear to the world community, however, that it had no intention of honouring all of Newfoundland's international commitments. 'Our primary aim,' Secretary of State for External Affairs Lester B. Pearson wrote to the acting Canadian high commissioner in Great Britain, 'is that Canada should not be expected by the United Kingdom and the international community to honour obligations involved in Newfoundland Agreements to which Canada is not a party.'[1] Subsequently, Canada's response to Newfoundland's international obligations was quite simple: all treaties applicable to Newfoundland, other than those of a local character that conferred proprietary rights connected with Newfoundland territory, ceased at the time of union.[2] Canada honoured only three treaties after Confederation: the Leased Bases Agreement, whereby Great Britain awarded military bases to the United States, and two treaties that allowed the United States and France to retain their fishing privileges in Newfoundland territorial waters.[3] Although the question of French fishing rights lay dormant for nearly three decades, it again became a contentious issue after the late 1980s, when the depletion of fish stocks threatened the fisheries of eastern Canada, and France eyed the offshore gas and mineral resources. The matter of the American bases, however, was more immediate.

In March 1941 the United Kingdom had leased colonial territory, including parts of Newfoundland, to the United States for the construction of military bases. The Americans were given ninety-nine-year leases to bases established in three locations: an army base on the outskirts of St John's, a naval base on the south coast at Argentia, and an air base on the west coast at Stephenville. The Leased Bases Agreement gave the United States wide-ranging powers, and American authority in Newfoundland clearly exceeded the privileges that the Canadian government would have granted to a foreign power. During the Second World War, Prime Minister Mackenzie King had jealously guarded Canadian sovereignty against American encroachments. In fact, he had reluctantly undertaken to shore up defence in certain areas of the country because he was worried that if Canada were negligent in such matters, the Americans would step in and assume a larger role in the country's defence.[4] After Confederation with Newfoundland, the Canadian government had more than 5,000 American troops stationed at three separate military bases on its territory.

What was most offensive to the Canadian government was that the United States had criminal jurisdiction over foreign nationals, including British (and Canadian) subjects. The United States also had civil and criminal jurisdiction over its service personnel and American nationals on the bases and in the immediate vicinity. Moreover, the Americans were exempt from customs duties on goods consigned to service personnel and to employed nationals and their dependents. American postal facilities operated on the base areas to the exclusion of Canadian post offices. The agreement also authorized the U.S. military to operate outside the base areas in the event of war or other emergency. In fact, the command structure was not resolved until 1952.[5] Prior to this, the American military maintained that it alone was responsible for protecting Canada's east coast. Even American contractors and non-military personnel who worked on the bases avoided paying Canadian taxes.[6] In other words, the U.S. forces operated in Newfoundland as if it were American territory. This Ottawa could not allow.

The Canadian government therefore looked to eliminate the repugnant extraterritorial features of the Leased Bases Agreement without restricting U.S. military rights, as Canada required American assistance to guard the northeastern approaches to the continent. Ottawa wanted modifications to have U.S. forces in Newfoundland treated the same as those stationed in other parts of the country. The Visiting Forces Act treated American and other military forces as guests of Canada, allowing them to maintain command of their troops and be responsible for military discipline, while Canada retained the right to try them for violation of Canadian law. In other words, the sovereignty of Canada was not compromised.[7] This was not the case in Newfoundland.

The Canadian government regarded the extraterritorial rights as both an embarrassment and an impediment to Newfoundland's integration into the federation. After all, by 1949 the Americans had enjoyed a prominent position in Newfoundland for nearly a decade, and even after union the American military presence continued to overshadow that of Canada.[8] The Canadian cabinet, sensitive on the issue of sovereignty, was worried that public opinion might react adversely to further American intrusion into Canada.[9] A 1948 poll found that 42 per cent of Canadians thought that their country was becoming too dependent militarily on the United States.[10] Moreover, Lester B. Pearson, Arnold Heeney, the under-secretary of state for external affairs, and others in the government had hoped that Canada would participate more fully in international affairs and multilateral negotiations in the aftermath of the Second World War. Concomitant with these aspirations came an increased sensitivity about the inviolability of Canadian sovereignty. If the u.s. presence went unchallenged in Newfoundland it would clearly be an affront to Canadian sovereignty.

The Americans had to realize, Pearson maintained, that the rights they held there were unacceptable to the Canadian public and might 'prejudice the success of present and future defence arrangements between Canada and the United States.'[11] In the spirit of friendship that made the relationship between them special, he thought that the United States should surrender some of the rights it possessed.[12] After all, the two nations had forged a special relationship during the Second World War. Although Pearson had frequently worried over American disregard for Canada during his tenure as ambassador in Washington,[13] the two countries had collaborated on joint defence projects as neighbours without infringing on each other's sovereignty. 'The United States Government has no long-term or automatic rights at any defence site in Canada nor does it enjoy any extraterritorial rights except for purposes of discipline, as defined by the Visiting Forces Act,' he wrote to Hume Wrong, his successor in Washington. The Permanent Joint Board on Defence (PJBD) had also recommended on 20 November 1946, when it announced plans for closer cooperation between the armed forces of the two countries for more effective security of North America, that 'defence cooperation projects in either country should be agreed to by both governments, should confer no permanent rights or status upon either country, and should be without prejudice to the sovereignty of either country.'[14] Moreover, Prime Minister King and President Harry Truman issued on 12 February 1947 a joint statement promising that 'as an underlying principle, all cooperative arrangements will be without impairment to the control of either country over all activities in its territory.'[15]

Pearson, an experienced diplomat, must certainly have realized that nations had interests more than they had friends. Yet he continued to argue that Canada had strong 'quasi-legal considerations and political arguments which, if supplied with sufficient force, might convince the United States government of the desirability of modifying the Bases Agreement *without* securing from Canada a tangible *quid pro quo*.'[16] Cooperation and mutual respect for each other's territory and sovereignty had long governed defence arrangements between the two countries, and he expected the Americans to continue in this spirit. This was not mere idle rhetoric. Pearson honestly believed that the United States would respond favourably to Canada's request for renegotiations. Until it became clear that he had no alternative, he resisted all suggestions that Ottawa offer the Americans access to other Canadian military installations in exchange for altering the 1941 agreement. Despite all claims about sovereignty and territorial integrity, however, it seems that a *quid pro quo* was, indeed, necessary. Pearson offered the United States a long-term lease to the Goose Bay air base in exchange for renegotiating the Leased Bases Agreement. Even with access to the coveted Goose Bay base, Washington secured from Canada a promise that it would 'have a degree of jurisdiction comparable to that which [it]' had had prior to 1949.[17] Nonetheless, the renegotiations allowed Ottawa to save face when it claimed that the United States had respected Canadian sovereignty and had brought American military rights in Newfoundland in line with those existing elsewhere in Canada. By late 1950, at the height of the cold war, Pearson could reassure Canadians that it was in Canada's interest to have the American military stationed at Goose Bay.

The status of the u.s. bases in Newfoundland arose in discussions between American and Canadian officials shortly after Newfoundland voted to join Canada on 22 July 1948. When Brooke Claxton, the minister of national defence, said that the United States would have to modify the 1941 agreement in the event of Confederation, Julian Harrington, counsellor at the u.s. Embassy in Ottawa, informed the State Department that it should give some consideration to modifying the 1941 Bases Agreement.[18] Later, at an August meeting with the Cabinet Defence Committee in Ottawa, u.s. secretary of defense James Forrestal asked about the effect of union on the Bases Agreement.

Should he discuss the issue with Canada or the United Kingdom, he asked? Claxton promptly reminded him that after 31 March 1949 any negotiations would be with Canada, as Britain would then cease to speak for Newfoundland.[19] In October 1948, the matter surfaced again, this time in discussions between Claxton and U.S. military officials. First, Major-General C.V. Haynes, commander of the Newfoundland Base Command, and Colonel Jack C. Hodgson, U.S. Air Force attaché in Ottawa, approached him seeking permission to construct married quarters for U.S. personnel at Goose Bay.[20] Harrington later expressed his concern about the Newfoundland bases, but because the Canadian government was preoccupied with finalizing the terms of union, it had not yet paid the bases much attention.[21] However, it had become clear, if only to the Canadians, that American rights in Newfoundland were an immediate embarrassment to Canada and that the Bases Agreement had to be modified.

The cabinet then realized that its best approach was to accept the bases as a regrettable consequence of union and work for immediate modification of both the extraterritorial rights and the length of the lease. Nevertheless, when the subject first arose, cabinet flirted with the idea of assuming responsibility for the Newfoundland bases. Its delusions of grandeur were brief, though, as Claxton quickly reminded his colleagues that 'to take over the leases and operate the bases might make us [Canada] liable to do things which were really in excess of our power.' Nearly $100 million had been spent on construction alone since 1941, and American expenditure to operate the three bases exceeded $12 million annually, far beyond the resources that Canada could muster.[22] As well, the United States had its rights in Newfoundland guaranteed for another ninety-one years. It had recognized much earlier the strategic military importance of bases in Newfoundland for guarding the approaches to North America and for the defence of the Western hemisphere. Consequently, it had erected quite elaborate and permanent installations at all three bases.[23] The enormous investment in the defence facilities reflected, if nothing else, U.S. commitment and its intention to retain the Newfoundland bases. Ottawa shared the American view, and during the Second World War it too established bases in Newfoundland to secure the defence of Canada. Ottawa's only recourse, then, was to persuade Washington to relinquish its extraterritorial rights in Newfoundland.

While many officials in Ottawa shared Pearson's desire to remove the offensive features of the Bases Agreement, they doubted the efficacy of his appeal to American friendship. The United States would not be influenced by any sense of friendship or sensitivity to the political problems that the Bases Agreement might create for the Canadian government, they argued. After sounding out J.D. Hickerson at the State Department, Wrong told Ottawa that '[i]t is likely to be a tricky business to secure modifications of the 1940 Agreement which we desire, and we should be particularly careful over our initial approach.' He detected an attitude of `what we have we hold' among the senior staff of the U.S. military, and warned that unless Canada handled the matter 'very delicately' the military would be a serious obstacle. It might be advantageous to link the modification of the Bases Agreement to the conclusion of the North Atlantic Treaty, he advised Ottawa.[24]

Escott Reid, acting under-secretary of state for external affairs, shared Wrong's view, and he too recognized the necessity of offering the Americans a *quid pro quo*. Shortly after the cabinet first discussed the Bases Agreement, Reid prepared for Claxton a memorandum in which he suggested that the Americans might be willing to modify the agreement if Canada offered something significant in return.[25] By 1949, when the United States was grappling with a global air strategy, it realized that its air bases were inadequate for any large-scale operations in the European theatre.[26] Reid saw a window of opportunity here and suggested that the Americans might consider modifying the lease in return for assured rights to the use of Goose Bay, Gander, and Torbay. The Americans had access to these bases only upon the goodwill of the Canadians. The cabinet refused the suggestion, even though Pearson himself admitted that the United States might not relinquish its extraterritorial rights without demanding further military facilities such as Goose Bay.[27] Canada was trying to rectify an embarrassment it had inherited, Pearson argued, and it could not, under any circumstances initiate an agreement that might see U.S. bases erected on Canadian soil. Such an occurrence was anathema to Canadian thinking. Public opinion indicated that Canadians would not tolerate such infringements on Canadian sovereignty.[28]

Moreover, Pearson already had other designs on Gander. The Newfoundland airport was his main bargaining chip in negotiations for the United States–Canada Civil Aviation Agreement, and he reminded Wrong that even to suggest that the United States Air Force (USAF) be given rights at Gander would compromise future civil aviation negotiations.[29] Though it might be beneficial to the process of integration to remove the Americans from St John's, he realized that they would be reluctant to leave. And the government could not push too hard because it had to consider for political reasons the large number of Newfoundlanders employed at the base.[30] When Ottawa refused to offer the Americans an incentive to modify the lease, Wrong was not at all hopeful of a quick settlement. 'I think that we have to start from scratch, and it is likely to be an obstacle race,' he warned Claxton.[31]

On 19 November 1948, Wrong presented Ottawa's formal request seeking modification of the Bases Agreement to Robert A. Lovett, acting secretary of state. After emphasizing the spirit of effective cooperation that had existed between the two countries, he stressed that while the situation at the Newfoundland bases was an anomaly in Canada-u.s. defence arrangements, in no way did Ottawa wish to restrict the effective military use of the leased areas. However, changes were necessary. 'In particular,' he continued, 'the extent of the extraterritorial jurisdiction exercised by the United States authorities over non-military activities in the leased areas would, it is feared, lead to complications after the union of Newfoundland with Canada becomes a fact.' This was his main bargaining chip with the Americans: Ottawa was concerned primarily with what might happen between the two nations if the lease continued unchanged, as problems might develop over the smuggling of duty-free goods from the bases into Canadian territory and especially over problems of jurisdiction between law-enforcement officers. 'At best these complications would be embarrassing to both governments, and at worst,' the Ambassador warned, 'they might prejudice essential collaboration in other aspects of North American defence.'[32]

Wrong left no doubt in Washington that his government attached great importance to the agreement's modification. Even so, he had little hope for an expeditious and satisfactory solution. Lovett told him that Washington would have a difficult time meeting Canada's request. Recent changes in Congress had seen the appointment of a new chair of the Senate Foreign Relations Committee and the addition of five new committee members who were less amenable to State Department initiatives than their predecessors. Neither would it be an easy task for the State Department to persuade Congress that the modifications were in the American interest. Changes to the 1941 agreement, the State Department argued, would adversely affect larger defence projects, particularly the plans for the North Atlantic Treaty Organization (NATO), for which the president intended to seek congressional approval at the next session. As expected, the military establishment, especially the air force, took a hard-line stance and opposed any modification of the agreement. In fact, the military had been unsuccessfully pressing the State Department to seek additional rights in Newfoundland.[33] Wrong also informed Ottawa that James Forrestal had reminded him again that the United States had legal title to the bases for a long period and that he had to be 'convinced that they will secure definite advantages from the surrender of any existing rights.' Given Secretary Forrestal's intransigence, the attitude of the military establishment, congressional resistance, and the State Department's obvious reluctance to challenge either the military or Congress, a successful outcome to Canada's request seemed elusive indeed. Although Lovett was apparently sympathetic to Ottawa's request to limit U.S. jurisdiction in non-military matters, he warned Wrong that if Canada expressed any desire to shorten the term of the Bases Agreement, it would raise 'very serious obstacles' in the United States.[34]

Wrong was now firmly convinced that there was little likelihood of gaining U.S. agreement to Canada's demands without offering substantial concessions in return. He reminded Pearson that the Americans would certainly be reluctant to give up either Argentia or Stephenville, considering their expenditure on these bases. Yet the Americans had not chosen well in 1941 when they selected sites for their bases. Argentia was frequently fogbound, and the runways at Stephenville could not be lengthened to accommodate the larger aircraft without reclaiming land from the sea, at great expense. 'Might there not be a possibility of getting the United States forces out of St John's if we were to give them rights at some more useful place, perhaps Gander?' he asked Pearson again. He felt that some of the political difficulties would be eased if U.S. service personnel were stationed farther away from the Newfoundland capital where they would be less visible.[35] Pearson agreed that the removal of American forces from Fort Pepperrell to a more remote section of the province was highly desirable, but he continued to maintain that the extraterritorial privileges enjoyed at the Newfoundland bases had to be discussed and solved on their own merits.[36]

On 6 January 1949, Pearson produced a general statement for the United States on the modifications that Canada sought to the Bases Agreement. The government's plan was to have American forces and civilians in Newfoundland treated the same as those stationed elsewhere on Canadian soil. 'In other words,' Pearson informed Wrong, 'while the Canadian Government would not wish to restrict the effective use by the United States of the leased areas for military purposes, when Newfoundland joins Canada the United States should relinquish all those rights that it does not presently enjoy in respect of present defence cooperation projects in Canada.'[37] When Wrong discussed Pearson's statement with the State Department, the response was unequivocal. The United States, Hickerson told him, could not agree to a solution along the lines Pearson proposed. 'The National Military Establishment,' he told Wrong, 'could not agree to renounce the rights which they enjoyed under the agreement of 1941 without receiving some definite benefit in return.' To do so would be to court serious trouble with Congress and American public opinion. Hickerson believed that the best hope for a solution lay in an 'imaginative approach' such as merging the problem of American non-military jurisdiction in the bases with the larger problems of mutual defence with the aim of replacing the 1941 agreement entirely. Wrong warned that 'we shall not get anywhere by continuing to press for renunciation of non-military jurisdiction without offering some definite *quid pro quo.*'[38]

As long as Pearson refused Wrong's suggestions, there was little hope for a successful settlement. Pearson was certainly correct to consider the United States a good friend of Canada's in 1948–9. However, expecting one side to surrender guaranteed rights, as the United States was expected to do in this case, and receive nothing but intangibles in return was asking too much. The relationship between Canada and the United States was special, but not that special. When a conflict arose between them, the Americans, not surprisingly, placed their interests ahead of any concern they might have for the domestic political difficulties facing the Canadian leaders. It was hardly astonishing, therefore, that the Americans were neither persuaded nor moved by Pearson's arguments and proposals for modifications. His insistence that if changes were not made to the Bases Agreement it might adversely affect the harmonious cooperation in defence and other matters had about the same effect on the Americans as water on a duck's back. The threat simply lacked teeth. Canada was limited in how 'unfriendly' it could be towards the Americans, given their close military ties and overall Canadian surrender of defence to the United States. Their common view of the world also acted as a restraint on any show of Canadian hostility. Hence, the potential Canadian bite was not enough to induce the Americans to relinquish the rights guaranteed in Newfoundland. Wrong was frank in his report to Ottawa:

The central difficulty is that we are asking for a voluntary relinquishment of rights which have been enjoyed for eight years and have ninety more years to run. All of these rights are regarded by the services here as useful and some of them as virtually essential. We are offering nothing in return except the indirect and negative benefit arising from our conviction that unless a change is made there will be undesirable repercussions on the relations between the two countries which may prejudice harmonious co-operation in defence and in other matters. They recognize in the State Department that this is a real risk, but they also contend that what we are asking them to do in order to avoid it does not include the elements of a bargain which they can justify to the National Military Establishment, Congress, and the public.[39]

'Unless we throw something into the pot,' Wrong warned Pearson two weeks later, 'I am fairly certain that our success will be limited.'[40] Yet, Pearson continued to reject the idea of a *quid pro quo*. Nor was he willing to negotiate a new treaty with the Americans. He realized, of course, that the primary American objective was to seek permanent defence rights if, at some other point, Canada adopted either of the two solutions. 'While the permanent defence rights enjoyed by the United States in Newfoundland might be accepted in Canada as one of the obligations which we were obliged to assume,' he informed Wrong, 'an agreement, informal or otherwise, to which Canada was a party and which gave to the United States permanent rights in Canada would probably be most unacceptable to the Canadian public.' Although he realized that a new agreement might be necessary in the end, he held out hope that his initial approach would eventually bear fruit. He again reminded Wrong to impress upon the Americans the great political importance of the issue to Canada. 'For that reason and to make any further approach as effective as possible,' he later told Wrong, 'the Prime Minister will take the matter up with the President during his forthcoming visit to Washington.'[41]

Before St Laurent left for Washington, Pearson thought that he had found just the mechanism he needed to pry the Americans from their attitude of `what we have we hold, unless we get something better.' Justice officials wrestling with the legal instruments of union with Newfoundland thought that the Canadian government would have to pass implementing legislation in order to assume the obligations set out in the 1941 lease and to make the provisions of the Bases Agreement applicable under Canadian law. If so, all the provisions of the agreement would be debated in the House of Commons. Pearson saw in this a golden opportunity to win a modification without surrendering anything to the United States. This may be one of our 'strongest talking points with United States authorities and may persuade them that it would be wise for them to agree to a unilateral relinquishment of all the extra-territorial and non-military rights ... set out in my [statement] of January 6,' he hastily wrote to Wrong. Pearson felt that a parliamentary debate on the extraterritorial rights would arouse public criticism of American powers in Newfoundland and in effect prejudice the defence relationship between the two countries, a development, he believed, that some U.S. officials feared.[42]

He was right. Hickerson immediately expressed concern to the Canadian ambassador. Unfortunately, the Department of Justice burst Pearson's bubble when it decided that Newfoundland legislation implementing the Bases Agreement was sufficient, eliminating the need for additional Canadian legislation. But all was not lost. The Bases Agreement might be debated when Term 18 in the Terms of Union, providing for the continuance of Newfoundland law, was brought before the House. Wrong had already told Ottawa that the State Department did not want the Bases Agreement dragged through Parliament. Hence, External Affairs urged St Laurent to emphasize the negative reaction that the extraterritorial features of the Bases Agreement would receive. 'It would ... be safe to assume that President Truman too will be greatly exercised at the prospect of a detailed and possibly acrimonious discussion on the Bases Agreement in the House of Commons, and for this reason alone he might be impressed with the desirability of the United States waiving their extraterritorial rights under the Bases Agreement,' St Laurent was reminded in a DEA memo.[43]

Pearson did not pull any punches in his memorandum for Prime Minister St Laurent's meeting with Truman on 12 February 1949.[44] He painted the Americans as the culprits. They had refused to negotiate, even though the State Department had known Canada's objectives for several months. He was angered further by the American's refusal to relinquish their extraterritorial rights in Newfoundland unless they secured a tangible advantage for doing so. This was hardly the attitude that he had come to expect from his neighbour. He thought that the intangible benefit should be enough. Moreover, Canada's request was congruent with other initiatives in U.S. foreign policy, and he pointed to the European Recovery Programme and NATO as examples where 'benefits which are less tangible are not always less important.' He rejected the argument that the United States could not modify the Bases Agreement because it would establish an undesirable precedent. Rather, he saw American flexibility as a demonstration of sensitivity to the sovereignty and independence of other countries where the United States might wish to construct bases. The concessions that the Canadians demanded would not impair the efficient military operation of the bases for which they were originally designed. Earlier statements by the PJBD and the special arrangement existing between Canada and the United States made American action in Newfoundland different, he told the Prime Minister. The close and special bond between the two neighbours should have been enough to prompt the United States to act. 'It is felt that both quasi-legal arguments based on the Joint Statement and the important political arguments,' he informed St Laurent, 'should convince the United States Government of the expediency and, indeed, [the] necessity of relinquishing its extraterritorial and non-military rights without securing some definite *quid pro quo* in return.' Hence, he advised St Laurent to play tough in Washington. The Americans had to be warned that Canada was serious and that failure to comply with its request for the removal of extraterritorial rights in Newfoundland might seriously prejudice continued cooperation at other Canadian defence installations.[45]

Despite Pearson's pessimistic view of the situation, St Laurent flew into Washington, confident that the special relationship between Canada and the United States still counted for something. The Prime Minister told a Washington press conference that '[w]e feel that between the people of the United States and Canada it does not matter so very much what is written on paper. It is the way that people behave and we hope that the behaviour on both sides of the line [will be such] that we still will be able to feel that though we are very much smaller in size than you, we are being treated by you on the same plane of equality and that we are never being asked to do something because you force us but because we think it is something in the mutual interest of all.'[46]

Although cordially received in Washington, he did not secure any commitment from Truman when he raised the issue of the U.S. bases in Newfoundland.[47] Truman and his secretary of state, Dean Acheson,

nonetheless agreed that it was important to reach a mutually satisfactory solution to the matter and suggested that Canada present a
detailed statement of its objectives.[48] Wrong warned Pearson immediately that too much should not be read into the pleasant meeting
with the President. While Truman might have left the impression that
he wanted to reach an amicable solution, the Ambassador cautioned
Pearson, 'Hickerson continues to be very firmly of the opinion that
the United States Government would find it impossible to reduce of
its own volition the non-military rights and privileges of their forces
in the bases to the level accorded their other detachments in Canadian territory.' Pearson discovered as much himself when Laurence
A. Steinhardt, the u.s. ambassador to Canada, told him shortly after
St Laurent's return that Canada would have to make concessions if
Truman hoped to secure congressional approval for modifications to
the lease. Nevertheless, Pearson and Claxton complied with Truman's
request and handed Steinhardt an 'Oral Message' on 19 March 1949,
outlining, once again, Canada's demands. In addition to emphasizing
Canadian-American cooperation in defence matters, Ottawa claimed
that the 'prospective change in the status of Newfoundland justifie[d]
a modification of the 1941 Bases Agreement in respect of the Newfoundland Bases in order to bring that agreement into accord with the
principles which, for many years, have governed the defence relations
between Canada and the United States.'[49] As Pearson pessimistically
told St Laurent, 'I think that we will find that Mr. Truman's amiable
offers of assistance and cooperation may be somewhat difficult to implement.'[50]

In early May Pearson decided to handle the matter directly from
Ottawa. The Department of External Affairs was encouraged by reports of discussions between the State Department and the military,
though the usaf continued to resist any change in its status at the
Newfoundland bases. In the meantime, the ambassador in Ottawa had
asked External Affairs for clarification of the Canadian proposal.[51]
Pearson hoped that negotiations would soon begin. He was buoyed
by the first sign of American interest and moved immediately to
demonstrate Canadian goodwill. At the civil aviation meeting being
held in New York the Americans wanted revisions to Article II of the
Bases Agreement dealing with the commercial use of the bases.
Canada conceded, and immediately authorized civilian use of
Stephenville and Argentia to all American carriers with commercial
rights at Gander and Torbay. In the letter of agreement acknowledg-

ing the change, Ottawa said it expected the United States to reciprocate by agreeing to modify the Bases Agreement. 'In view of this important concession in relation to these bases,' Wrong wrote to
Acheson, 'the Canadian government expects that the United States
Government will give favourable consideration to the Canadian
desiderata with respect to the Bases Agreement and that the Canadian
Government's willingness to meet the United States' position in this
respect will be taken into account in discussions concerning the Bases
Agreement which should take place at an early date.'[52] Canada hoped
that the carrot would achieve a measure of success that an appeal to
a special relationship had not.

There was some movement, but not enough to satisfy Canada. The
United States might offer minor modifications, the chair of the Canadian Section of PJBD informed Ottawa. General A.G.L. McNaughton
had broached the subject of the lease with his American counterpart,
Major-General Guy V. Henry, at the PJBD meeting in late June 1949.
McNaughton penned a memorandum to Arnold Heeney telling him
that Henry was well versed on the Canadian demands. The United
States was ready to relinquish civil and criminal jurisdiction in peacetime, but it wanted assurances from the Canadian government that
the U.S. military would have the same privileges in Newfoundland as
they were given elsewhere in Canada under the Visiting Forces Act.
However, any modifications that would result in greater costs were
out of the question, effectively locking the door on an agreement over
customs and taxation. Henry felt that something might be worked out
on the postal services.[53] Still, the Americans had not issued a formal
reply to Ottawa.

Meanwhile, Claxton visited the American bases in Newfoundland
during July 1949 to survey the situation at first hand. Ottawa was
worried that the extraterritorial rights might create local incidents and
imperil Canadian-American defence collaboration. 'My trip confirmed
the view I have always had that this was a matter of the utmost urgency,' Claxton wrote to St Laurent. 'The situation is such that an in-
cident might occur any day which would seriously jeopardize
Canadian-U.S. relations as a whole.'[54] Serious trouble, even death, had
been averted before union only because, although the U.S. military police were armed, the Canadians were not. He pointed to the Evans
case as an example. In July 1948, Michael Evans, a Newfoundland customs officer who later transferred to Canadian customs, and Michael
Cahill of the Newfoundland Rangers, established a routine inspection

point outside an American base to check for smuggled goods. They stopped and searched several vehicles, including a military truck carrying a bag of U.S. Air Force mail. Although they did not search the mail bag, a military officer and two armed military policemen showed up to arrest Evans and threated to shoot Cahill if he interfered. Evans and Cahill eventually won a civil suit against the officer and the U.S. military apologized to the two, but Claxton was worried that if the American military police interfered with the RCMP in a similar manner, there was no certainty that bloodshed could be avoided.[55]

Claxton also claimed, after conversations with many Newfoundlanders, that they, too, deeply resented the rights the British had conferred upon the Americans, even though London had done so at a time of desperate need. Even in the new province, people were aware that defence cooperation between Canada and the United States had developed as successfully as it had and with relatively few troublesome incidents or friction because each country respected the other's sovereignty. Because of this special relationship, they expected to have the extraterritorial rights removed at Confederation.[56] Shortly after union, Premier Joseph R. Smallwood expressed great joy over the employment opportunities for Newfoundlanders on the American bases, although, he said, Newfoundlanders were unhappy about the loss of sovereignty. As with many other issues shortly after union, 'from now on that was the business of Ottawa as was everything connected with the bases here.'[57] Claxton's memorandum added a new dimension to the issue. It had at first appeared that the American rights had embarrassed only the Canadian government, and not the people of Newfoundland. During his Newfoundland sojourn, however, Claxton found that many Newfoundlanders shared Ottawa's concern about excessive U.S. jurisdiction in their province. Even so, it is doubtful that very many of them were willing to place sovereignty ahead of the jobs that they enjoyed at the American bases.[58]

Claxton alluded to several important matters about the bases that Ottawa had not previously considered. American employees were better paid than Canadians, sometimes receiving twice as much for similar work. The hourly rate of pay for locals was much less than that paid by some of the better Newfoundland employers such as the paper mills. Civilian employees on the bases were also prohibited from organizing labour unions. Moreover, no provision was made for unemployment insurance or workers' compensation. Claxton also noted that the Stars and Stripes alone flew at the American bases in

Newfoundland, and Canada had no presence. 'We can only imagine,' he concluded 'what the attitude of the people of the United States would be if the position were reversed.'[59]

While Claxton's report was making its rounds at the Department of External Affairs, Ottawa grew increasingly impatient for a formal response from the Americans. Nearly a year had passed since the issue was first raised, and a full eight months since Wrong officially informed the State Department of Ottawa's request to modify the agreement. Despite persistent reminders that Ottawa attributed great importance to the issue, the Americans had refused even to acknowledge officially Canada's request. R.A. MacKay, head of the Commonwealth Division at DEA and the bureaucrat charged with coordinating the transition of the federal system to Newfoundland, produced a memo suggesting that the Canadian strategy had failed to produce results. The United States had simply refused to revise the Bases Agreement or to relinquish any rights that it considered worthwhile. It was time for a new approach.

MacKay advised Heeney that before Claxton met with Louis Johnson, U.S. secretary for defense, in August 1949, Canada should consider offering the United States rights at Goose Bay. He noted that both Wrong and Reid had suggested this when the matter was first discussed. Mackay thought that the United States might be prepared to surrender Fort Pepperrell, the army base in St John's, in exchange for assured rights at Goose Bay, which, he claimed, their defence experts regarded as the most important base in the northeast region. In fact, senior U.S. military officials had coveted Goose Bay since 1945, when they initiated discussions at the PJBD for joint military action to ensure the security of North America. A few months later, the PJBD acknowledged Goose Bay as 'vital to the defence of the United States and Canada' and recommended that it 'be maintained as a military base on such a scale as to provide for the stationing of operational squadrons as required.' Even President Truman asked King about acquiring the base when the Canadian prime minister visited Washington shortly after the Second World War, a further indication of the U.S. view that Goose was 'the most important all-round strategic air base in the western hemisphere.'[60] By 1949, the air base at Goose Bay had become of paramount importance to U.S. military planners, as it was the only base in North America from which U.S. heavy bombers could strike the Soviet Union and hope to return safely.[61] Although, the Canadians were reluctant to give the Americans the authority they sought at Goose Bay, the United States persisted. The Canadian high commissioner to Newfoundland, J. Scott Macdonald, reported from St John's that the U.S. commander and his senior officials in Newfoundland 'appear really in earnest in their desire to see the United States established in Goose Bay.' Because Goose Bay was isolated, a strong American presence there would not create political difficulties for the government. It was in the national interest, MacKay suggested, to display the flag more prominently in St John's than the Canadian government had in the first months of union to accelerate the process of integration.[62]

The U.S. military knew that Canada was worried about its presence in St John's, and it hoped to make the most of the situation.[63] Julian Harrington had told Washington from the beginning that Ottawa wanted the agreement modified 'for face-saving purposes.'[64] Hence, the Americans had not simply been dragging their feet on the matter; they hoped to win a major concession from Canada for agreeing to modify the 1941 lease. It should have been obvious from the beginning. After a conversation with Hickerson, McNaughton told Ottawa that it must accept the fact that the U.S. military hoped to capitalize on its presence in St John's to win defence concessions from Canada: 'Hickerson clearly stated that until such an arrangement had been entered into the U.S. Military Authorities intended to hang on to their existing rights in the Avalon Peninsula and I gathered the impression that they saw advantage in our objections to the present arrangements as a means of pressure to induce us to enter into the new and wider undertaking the U.S. Military Authorities had in mind.'[65] McNaughton also claimed that the military was more receptive to Canadian demands than the State Department had led Ottawa to believe, and suggested that the matter be taken from the diplomatic sphere and transferred to the PJBD.[66] Pearson had made it quite clear much earlier, however, – perhaps evidence of a turf battle with the military – that the issue was a diplomatic not a military matter. Heeney also began to wonder aloud to Pearson if McNaughton was not correct: perhaps Hickerson wanted them to believe that the military was holding up the modification of the agreement. After all, Heeney had since learned that Wrong's earlier suggestion that Canada offer the Americans privileges at Gander or Goose Bay in exchange for renegotiating the Bases Agreement had come at the prompting of Hickerson, who had sounded out several senior officers in the Pentagon.[67]

In November 1949, the Americans seemed ready to deal with the bases, but they wanted the matter handled by the military through the PJBD, the avenue that Pearson wanted most to avoid. Acheson argued that the PJBD was more familiar with the Canadian-American defence relationship than any other body of equivalent rank and had successfully handled other defence problems.[68] He also knew that the Canadian military was less concerned about the question of sovereignty than the diplomats were. Pearson was reluctant to submit the matter to the military, and agreed only after Acheson promised that it would be pursued vigorously at the PJBD and that a proposal would be forthcoming shortly.[69] The government was obviously worried over the slow pace of negotiations. St Laurent had told the House in February 1949, when he introduced the Newfoundland Bill, that discussion on the bases had begun with the Americans, but no progress had been made since. Furthermore, Pearson had to deliver his statement on foreign affairs, and he anticipated tough questioning over the Newfoundland bases. If he had to admit that no progress had been made in the negotiations, despite the fact that the matter had first been raised more than a year ago, it might affect good relations with the United States.[70] Equally important was the fact that admitting failure would be highly embarrassing to the government. In the meantime, Blair Fraser, a respected journalist, had produced a scathing attack in *Maclean's* on American abuse of Canadian sovereignty in Newfoundland. External attempted to stop publication, partly because Pearson feared that the State Department might think the Canadian government had encouraged the article, partly because Fraser left little doubt that the American privileges violated the 'sovereignty and the dignity of Canada' and were a 'national shame,'[71] a view that promised to stir up public interest and criticism of the government.

Instead of finding a solution to the impasse in the PJBD, the Canadians found disappointment yet again when the United States failed to make good Acheson's promise to submit a formal proposal for modification. Both Pearson and Claxton were angry. They had been led to expect meaningful discussion through the PJBD, and they fully expected to have the matter treated with urgency. Heeney poured out Canada's frustrations to Wrong in Washington. 'If we cannot now receive assurance at a high level that serious proposals for meeting the situation will be forthcoming shortly,' he said, 'then our representations will have to be passed in language much more vigorous than in the past.' Pearson moved immediately to increase the pressure on Washington. He instructed Wrong to advise Acheson of Canada's 'serious disappointment' that the matter had gone unsettled for so long. He was further exasperated that the British had made greater progress with the Americans over the issue of jurisdiction in the West Indies than had Canada about similar problems in Newfoundland. 'For all practical purposes,' Pearson lamented, 'our earlier and urgent pleas have achieved nothing.'[72] Like Pearson, Wrong must have realized that the American refusal to negotiate was, in large part, a reflection of Canada's impotence in dealing with the United States. Once again, Wrong reminded Acheson of Canada's dissatisfaction with the way the matter was being handled and asked that the matter be settled promptly. The American response should not have surprised him. There was yet another hurdle to be cleared in the United States, he was told. Modifying the Newfoundland lease might establish an undesirable precedent. 'The United States now had base rights in various parts of the world and was seeking further rights,' Assistant Secretary Dean Rusk, who was also present during the discussions with Acheson, reminded him, 'and the situation in Newfoundland bases had to be considered from the point of view of its possible effects on United States forces elsewhere.' Complications might develop over other bases if the United States altered its agreement with Newfoundland.[73]

At the same time, the u.s. Embassy in Ottawa warned Acheson that the Canadians were extremely frustrated that American authorities had not responded to repeated Canadian requests. Further delay might cool relations with Canada.[74] Later, both Acheson and Rusk acknowledged that the United States had dragged its feet on the bases issue. Rusk admitted that the u.s. State Department had been remiss in not giving some written statement in reply to Canada's representations, and Acheson finally became concerned that Ottawa felt its requests were ignored.[75] They agreed that the matter had been handled at too low a level, and vowed to take the matter up with the 'top people in the Pentagon.' They both promised to take a greater interest in the negotiations, but warned Ambassador Wrong that 'it would take time to reach a settlement.' They anticipated difficulties with the military services, which refused to relinquish privileges on the bases, but promised to find some accommodation at the next meeting of the u.s. Section of PJBD. The intervention of Acheson and Rusk might, at last, produce a satisfactory settlement, Wrong wrote to Pearson.[76] But Ottawa was growing increasingly weary of American posturing. Heeney best summed up the attitude when he wrote to Claxton that '[t]he impression is growing here [at the Department of External Affairs] that we have been given the well-known "run-around" over the whole matter.'[77]

Ottawa was subsequently informed that the U.S. Section had met on 28 November 1949 and proposed a full meeting of the board for either late December or early January to discuss customs exemptions, tax exemptions, postal facilities, and 'to explore' the subject of jurisdiction in the hope that 'the problem could be further clarified.' But cracks had already started to show in Canada's resolve. Repeated refusals, American reticence, and general Canadian frustration over the lack of progress forced a reconsideration of strategy. Hence, Ottawa told the United States that it was willing to postpone discussion of other issues to settle the jurisdictional problem, which threatened to create political difficulties in light of the *Maclean's* article. But the United States was not interested in a piecemeal approach.[78]

On 23 December 1949, Claxton, Pearson, MacKay and their officials met in Pearson's office to discuss the issues coming before the PJBD. Because the United States had not given a response to Canada's earlier submissions, the ministers told the Canadian Section that the discussions were 'exploratory and not binding on either party, and that any proposals made by either side should be reported back to the two governments.' Because the Canadian government had no idea how the Americans would respond to its request, it prepared a series of memoranda, outlining Canada's objectives as well as its bottom line. If, for example, the United States refused to allow Canadian post offices to operate on the bases, the Canadian Section should agree with the existing postal service for the transmission of money between the bases and the United States. Other postal services that did not question Canadian sovereignty or involve the sale of U.S. postage in Newfoundland could also be allowed.[79] Likewise, if the United States refused to curtail civilian use of post exchanges on the bases, then Canada should retreat from its original demand and accept an assurance that the United States would adopt strict administrative provisions to prevent abuses, especially the resale of duty-free goods that Canada found particularly objectionable.[80]

At the January 1950 meeting of the PJBD the Canadian Section presented its demands. The Americans flatly refused to relinquish their post offices, on 'grounds of security, speed and scope of service and morale.' Because the non-military personnel were not permitted to use the post offices, the Canadians saw little point in pushing for further modification. Canada had greater success on the other issues. Because the two countries had recently agreed to a revised Double Taxation Convention, U.S. service personnel and civilians employed by the U.S. government in Canada were exempt from Canadian taxes. The military surrendered tax exemptions for both U.S. civilians employed by contractors and the contractors themselves. Similarly, the United States removed custom-excise exemptions on contractor-owned equipment. The Americans refused to abandon the post exchanges, and the Canadians realized the futility of pressing the issue.[81]

The United States wished to retain its wide-ranging powers and refused to move on the important issue of jurisdiction. Canada then demanded that American 'priority of jurisdiction' be replaced with 'concurrent jurisdiction' between U.S. service courts and Canadian civil courts. This would allow members of U.S. forces stationed in Canada to be tried for violation of Canadian law as provided for in the Visiting Forces Act. The Americans saw a number of problems with the Canadian position: they lost priority of jurisdiction over their service personnel; there was no provision for compulsory attendance of witnesses before U.S. service courts; U.S. service courts had no jurisdiction over U.S. civilian personnel; and the act did not provide for jurisdiction over security offences (spying, espionage, etc.) committed by non-U.S. citizens. The Canadian Section recommended that an amendment to the act might accommodate American concerns. A solution was within grasp but, as Heeney wrote to Pearson on 13 January, this 'certainly resulted in no Canadian victory.'[82]

As early as March 1949 Pearson had admitted to the cabinet that it should explore the possibility of offering the Americans some *quid pro quo* if all else failed.[83] In January 1950, when all hope for having the matter settled on its own merits vanished, Pearson finally realized the futility of his efforts. Together with Claxton and Heeney, he saw that Ottawa would have to tie the renegotiation of the Leased Bases Agreement to the Goose Bay access that the Americans desperately wanted.[84] In a meeting with Pearson and F. Gordon Bradley, Newfoundland's representative in the federal cabinet, on 25 March, just five days before the full PJBD convened, Claxton finally authorized McNaughton to offer the United States a twenty-year agreement covering American activities at Goose Bay if they agreed to Canada's demands for revising the 1941 agreement.[85] Pearson, it seems, had finally accepted that the Americans would agree to renegotiate only in return for expanded use of the RCAF base at Goose Bay in Labrador.[86]

On 30 March 1950 the two sides finally reached an agreement on the modifications. After the PJBD meetings Guy Henry, the chief negotiator for the United States, wrote triumphantly in his diary that 'we obtained an option for a long term lease at Goose Bay Air Base, Labrador, provided the U.S. Government accepted the Board's recommendation [on the changes to the Leased Bases Agreement].'[87] The sometimes cryptic Claxton[88] later told the cabinet that the United States had asked for and received an expansion of their facilities at Goose Bay. Moreover, he said that '[i]n negotiating adjustments in the Newfoundland Leased Bases Agreements with the United States, it had been agreed, with Cabinet approval, that in consideration of the United States giving up certain rights in the bases under lease to them, we would give the United States a 20-year lease to part of the Goose Bay base for the construction of additional accommodation.'[89] He also told Gordon Higgins, a Newfoundland Tory MP, that the United States had asked for and received permission to use Goose Bay in exchange for American concessions to the Bases Agreement.[90] Later, M.H. Wershof, head of the Defence Liaison Division at External, wrote to Dana Wilgress, the new under-secretary of state for external affairs, that '[o]ne condition of the bargain, not expressly stated but implied, was the granting of a twenty-year lease to an area or areas with the Goose Bay Air Base ...'[91] Hence, a special relationship might have existed between the United States and Canada in matters of defence but, as the Canadians had sadly learned, American interests came ahead of friendship.[92]

Even so, Canada was able to save face. It achieved much of what it had wanted, and it could claim that Canadian sovereignty in Newfoundland was no longer compromised. American postal services were limited to mail destined for the United States or other bases, and the United States promised not to establish normal civilian postal services on the bases. On the issues of taxation, customs, and excise, the United States acceded to Canada's requests, except on relinquishing the post exchanges. The United States surrendered jurisdiction over Canadian citizens, other British subjects, and aliens who were not U.S. citizens connected with the bases, and suspended for a five-year trial period jurisdiction over U.S. civilians working on the bases. The federal government needed the agreement of the Newfoundland government (other provinces had the same agreement) that its courts would not exercise jurisdiction over U.S. service personnel, especially if Canadian persons or property were not involved. Canada also agreed to amend the Visiting Forces (U.S.A.) Act to provide for compulsory attendance of witnesses at U.S. service courts.[93]

Although the letter of the Bases Agreement may have been altered somewhat, the spirit of the original lease remained basically unchanged. The recommendation on jurisdiction was 'conditional on the Canadian Government giving satisfactory assurances that the United States officials in Newfoundland will, after the United States has waived some of its rights and suspended others pursuant to the Recommendations, have a degree of jurisdiction comparable to that which they now in fact exercise.'[94] In an exchange of letters between Stuart Garson, the Canadian minister of justice, and Leslie Curtis, the Newfoundland attorney general, the two governments agreed to the condition. Ottawa also asked the Newfoundland government to leave to the U.S. service courts incidents such as those prejudicial to the discipline of the U.S. Armed Forces, those committed within the leased areas, or those involving only U.S. property.[95] Ottawa had, however, effectively removed the most 'objectionable' feature of the Bases Agreement, namely, the right of jurisdiction by U.S. courts over Canadian citizens.[96] Even so, Pearson and his colleagues continued to express serious concern over the immense U.S. defence effort in Newfoundland, as the Americans continued to expand their military operations during the early 1950s. Throughout the decade, the American military presence in Newfoundland (and Labrador) was far greater than anywhere else in Canada.[97]

On 2 May 1952, nearly four years after Canada first raised the issue of modifying the Bases Agreement, the whole matter came to an end with an exchange of notes. Before the matter was officially finished and despite the cold war fears, Prime Minister St Laurent made it clear to the Americans through the PJBD that although Canada would continue to cooperate with them in matters of defence, no more long-term leases would be given them for defence purposes.[98] The difficulties Canada encountered over securing modifications to the Bases Agreement demonstrated, as Pearson had emphasized nearly a year earlier in a speech to the Empire Club of Canada, that 'we need not try to deceive ourselves that these close relations with our great neighbour will always be smooth and easy ... There will be difficulties and frictions.'[99] He encountered a rougher ride than he had anticipated over the Newfoundland bases.

By mid-1950, following the first Soviet test of the atomic bomb and the Communist invasion of Korea, the Canadian government could justify more easily its decision to lease Goose Bay in the interests of continental security. Canada's failure to renegotiate the Leased Bases Agreement of 1941 without surrendering additional military bases to the United States underlines the fact that the Canadian-American partnership was not one of equals. Moreover, at the end of 1952, the U.S. military presence in Newfoundland was greater than it had been before union with Canada.

6

The problem of Newfoundland:
Ottawa and the fisheries, 1948–1957

Life for those who laboured in poverty and deprivation in the isolated outports and bays of Newfoundland in 1949 had changed little since their ancestors first arrived from the British Isles to catch, salt, and dry codfish. Since its inception, the traditional inshore fishery had had unpredictable markets, low productivity, low prices, and low returns, and had provided a bare subsistence living for thousands of fishermen and their families. When Ottawa began to share responsibility for the Newfoundland fishery, the average per-capita income in the new province was $475, 49.5 per cent of the Canadian average, and considerably less than the Maritime average of $689. With incomes ranging between $200 and $400, the fishermen of Newfoundland were considerably worse off than other workers.[1]

The fishermen were living in the twentieth century, but they were not a part of it. During the bright days of summer, Newfoundland had hundreds of scenic, seemingly idyllic, fishing villages. In the midst of a strong midwinter nor'easter, though, when a child, mother, or father lay dying for lack of medical attention and the heavy seas kept the small boats from seeking help at the nearest medical station, the serene picturesque beauty of an isolated fishing community quickly became marred by destitution, despair, and death. After joining Canada, a nation whose standard of living rivalled that of the United States, many Newfoundlanders realized that their living conditions had to improve. Most Canadian communities had their own teachers, doctors, and clergy. Elsewhere, such services were normal amenities along with electricity, water, and sewage, but they were the exception in most of Newfoundland's scattered and isolated settlements. Newfoundlanders were no longer content to live in poverty and under primitive and wretched conditions. Fishery policy after union with Canada, therefore, had to consider more than the catching, curing, processing, and marketing of fish; it involved changing a whole way of life. If the people demanded a dramatic improvement in their standard of living, then the fishery had to change dramatically.

The task ahead for Ottawa and St John's after 1949 was more than mere fishery development. If the governments had been concerned only with economics, they might have been able to provide a strong support to a threatened industry. The fresh-frozen fishery was seen as the hope of the future, and Ottawa and St John's sought to direct production in that direction and away from dependence on a salt-cod fishery that still relied on methods used in Cabot's time. Several commissions and investigations confirmed that changes were necessary. If the governments had pursued the policies recommended by these inquiries, they would have created a small corps of fishermen concentrated in a smaller number of communities engaged in both the salt and the fresh-frozen fisheries from modern boats and trawlers with greatly increased capacity. In the case of saltfish, the curing would have been done by mechanical dryers, or at centralized drying flakes or wharves. But governments had to consider more than the bottom line on a balance sheet. It had become clear to Ottawa by 1954 that there was no other work for the thousands of fishermen who might be displaced. From that point on, Ottawa realized that there was little hope of rationalizing the fishery. The best that it could hope to achieve was a small measure of centralization, and an improved standard of living for fishermen through various income-support programs. This eventually became Ottawa's objective. Premier Joseph R. Smallwood initially hoped that the new industries he was promoting would absorb any labour from the fishery. When he had accepted the failure of this part of his plans for economic development, he turned his fury on the federal government, blaming it for the destruction of the fishery. But Smallwood must share the blame, for he had little interest in fishery reform. On the other hand, although Ottawa recognized the severe problems the fishery had, it saw modernization with a reduction in the number of fishermen as the only solution. It did not seek alternatives when it realized this could not work. Neither did the provincial government push for alternatives. Political considerations in the Maritime provinces also hampered Ottawa in its approach to solving the problem. It could not be seen by the other

provinces to be favouring Newfoundland. Consequently, with Smallwood's acquiescence, Ottawa merely propped up the industry and allowed it to stagger along from crisis to crisis.

I

Before union there had been considerable talk about the necessity of
reforming the Newfoundland fishery, but few changes had been made.
When Lord Amulree, chairman of the British royal commission investigating the condition of Newfoundland, recommended in 1933 the
surrender of responsible government, he tied economic recovery and
the restoration of democracy to a reformed and improved fishery.[2] A
decade later, P.D.H. Dunn, commissioner for natural resources in the
Commission of Government, argued that the salt-cod fishery alone
could not provide fishermen with a reasonable standard of living. In
his view, production per man had to be increased in a fresh and frozen
fish sector geared to American markets.[3] Raymond Gushue, chairman
of the Newfoundland Fisheries Board (NFB), saw a similar future for
the Newfoundland fishery.[4] Moreover, the Fisheries Committee of the
National Convention reported in October 1946 that it too saw a new
course for the fishery. It predicted that the markets for saltfish would
decline as living standards improved and refrigeration became more
widespread. The future lay with the American market, and the government, whatever form it might take, must continue to encourage
greater development of the fresh-frozen industry.[5] Yet for all this, the
transition from salt to fresh and frozen production, already well under
way in New England and Nova Scotia, made before 1949 only minor
gains in Newfoundland,[6] as most fishermen continued to rely on the
production of saltfish.

The Commission of Government recognized many of the problems
confronting the fishery. In fact, during its tenure it considered many
of the policies subsequently adopted after union. But it followed a
conservative approach, linking improvements in the fishery to the improved marketing of salt cod, and ignored the low productivity of individual fishermen, which was the most serious problem. A
commission of inquiry appointed in 1935 concluded 'that if market
prospects and returns were improved, then the incentives for increased investment and innovative technology and production would
exist.'[7] The Commission of Government charted its fishery policy on
this principle. In 1936 it created the Newfoundland Fisheries Board[8]

and charged it with regulating most aspects of the fishery from production to distribution. In order to rationalize the marketing system, the NFB formed the Newfoundland Associated Fish Exporters Limited (NAFEL) and gave it exclusive jurisdiction over the export of salt cod.[9] In 1944 the commission finally launched a policy of financial support to fish merchants to encourage the development of fish-filleting and -refrigeration plants and the purchase of deep-sea trawlers.[10]

Such a policy ignored the problems confronting the vast majority of fishermen. Neither the commission's new plan nor its earlier plans were directed towards improving the productivity of individual fishermen. In a shrewd observation made in 1951, the Newfoundland-born and Oxford-educated political scientist H.B. Mayo wrote as follows: 'it is remarkable how little attention has been given to this fundamental problem [low productivity among individual fishermen]: official inquiries have ignored it or, having dimly perceived it, have shied away from the unpleasant implications and have concentrated instead on subsidiary issues such as credit system, or the local control of marketing.'[11]

Although fish prices were buoyed by a heightened demand for foodstuffs during the Second World War, Newfoundland had not emerged from this prosperous period with more efficient fishing methods. Saltfish merchants and the government continued to ignore the fact that the present practices among fishermen would not raise individual productivity and result in a better standard of living. Both naïvely believed that if saltfish exporters were assured adequate markets, fishermen would reap the benefits through increased investment, innovative technology, and higher prices. History had clearly shown otherwise. The fishery had been unable to provide an acceptable living for fishermen even during so-called normal years when the industry was unhampered by low prices, currency problems, or a shortage of fish. 'What is often overlooked,' Mayo argued in 1951, '... is that public relief for the fishermen, and relief disguised as public works, have always been marked recurring features of the island's finances.'[12]

II

When the 1948 Newfoundland delegation travelled to Ottawa to negotiate the final terms of union with Canada, the fishery was naturally a major priority because of its economic importance to the prospective province. More than 28,000 people, upwards of one-third of the province's labour force, found employment in the fishery, which accounted for nearly 20 per cent of the dominion's gross national product. The delegation showed little concern, however, with fishery development and the role the federal government should play in it. Instead, the focus was on the marketing of salt cod. This stemmed, in part, from the pressure exerted on the delegation by a clique from the St John's upper class involved primarily in the export of saltfish.[13] The delegation was told repeatedly that Newfoundland must retain access to European markets, despite the shortage of hard currency there, in order to prevent the impoverishment of thousands of fishermen. Since the onset of exchange difficulties in Europe after the Second World War, the Newfoundland government had arranged with Whitehall to have sterling earned from European fish sales applied against the Newfoundland sterling debt. Exporters then received payment from the Newfoundland government out of its accumulated dollar surplus.[14] Ottawa quickly realized that if it did not continue the arrangement, Newfoundland might face a severe economic slump in the wake of union. London agreed, and the Canadian government used sterling received from European purchases of fish to redeem the Newfoundland sterling debt that it inherited with union.[15] During the negotiations the Newfoundlanders argued that if their fish were shut out of Europe, markets would have to be found in the Western hemisphere at the expense of the fishing industry in Canada.[16]

The NFB and NAFEL met with less enthusiasm in Ottawa. Both were threatened by union, and Vincent C. MacDonald of the Dalhousie University Law School had prepared NAFEL for the worst. 'The whole matter of the trade in salt fish as between Newfoundland and any other Province or country,' he wrote in a legal opinion rendered at NAFEL's request, 'will come under the exclusive jurisdiction of the Parliament of Canada.'[17] Those who supported NAFEL immediately rushed to its defence. F.A.J. Laws, manager of NAFEL, complained to Governor Gordon C. Macdonald that the saltfish trade was not represented on the delegation. He claimed that NAFEL had gradually cultivated a marketing system 'considered to give the best results to our exporters and fishermen under existing world conditions.' His predictions for the industry without NAFEL were dire. Any tampering with the marketing mechanisms was tantamount to disaster for the fisheries of both Canada and Newfoundland, he warned. Raymond Gushue appeared before the delegation to support these claims. Norway, Iceland, and the Faeroe Islands, the major competitors, had exporting agencies, and all the consuming nations coordinated their buying. It made little sense, then, for Newfoundland exporters to operate individually and hope to achieve maximum returns for their products.[18] The Newfoundland Board of Trade and the Salt Codfish Association echoed these sentiments.[19]

Canadian officials disagreed. NAFEL competed with saltfish exporters in the Maritime provinces, and it had allegedly dumped saltfish in traditional Canadian markets. It was termed, 'with some justice, a Fascist monopoly', Mitchell Sharp, the director of the Economic Policy Division at the Department of Finance, pointed out. He noted, however, that NAFEL had had a successful career, in part because of a general wartime rise in fish prices, though prices had risen as much in Canada without an equivalent of NAFEL as they had in Newfoundland.[20] Fishermen in Newfoundland had received lower prices than their Canadian counterparts, but the NFB was identified with the return of high prices and strong markets and was synonymous with prosperity. If the NFB and NAFEL were dismantled at union, Canada would be seen as the culprit if, for whatever reason, the price of fish fell. That was no way to start Confederation.

Still, Canadian negotiators were worried about the political repercussions if NAFEL were allowed to continue. They feared that the Maritime provinces might demand similar boards to protect themselves. Moreover, Ottawa's bargainers did not want to create the impression that they were conceding the delegation's every demand.[21] Nevertheless, despite strong lobbying by Maritime politicians and cabinet ministers, the cabinet reluctantly agreed to keep the agencies for a transitional period of five years after it realized that the delegation might baulk at union without them. NAFEL was given control over both interprovincial and export trade involving Newfoundland saltfish. Ottawa insisted, however, on a mechanism that gave it greater control over NAFEL if it happened to act against the interests of the federal government. Canadian officials insisted that the NFB would have to be a federal agency under the authority of a federal minister because several of its powers, such as control over exporters, were not subject to any form of regulation in Newfoundland law.[22] Donald Jamieson, who covered the negotiations for one of the St John's dailies, considered the decision on NAFEL to be a Newfoundland victory. 'It is one of the biggest surprises to come out of the negotiations,' he reported.[23]

After union, sea fisheries fell under federal jurisdiction, and Newfoundland became a separate division within the Department of Fisheries. Ottawa assumed responsibility for general administration of Newfoundland's fisheries and its bait service. Many of Newfoundland's fisheries laws remained, but they were administered for Canada by the NFB until a thorough study of the effect of Canadian laws on the fishery had been completed. The federal government could, with the consent of Newfoundland during the first five years of union, repeal or alter any of the fisheries laws inherited from the new province.[24] The staff of the Newfoundland Fisheries Board was absorbed into the federal Department of Fisheries, and Gushue was appointed chief supervisor and inspector of the newly created Newfoundland Division. Gushue had become familiar with Canadian fishery policy and Canadian officials while chairman of the NFB after 1936 and while chairman of the Fishery Products Committee of the International Combined Food Board during the Second World War. Consequently, his appointment facilitated integration, as he became responsible for all federal fisheries matters in the new province. L.S. Bradbury, former secretary of the NFB, was appointed director of the Newfoundland Fisheries Branch in the federal fisheries department at Ottawa, to look after Newfoundland affairs there.[25] The Canadian Fisheries Act, though not proclaimed in Newfoundland until 1 May 1958,[26] finally brought all fisheries administration in Canada under one basic statute.

III

Ottawa wasted little time after union in announcing a five-year program to develop Canada's east-coast fisheries. On 5 May 1949, R.W. Mayhew, the minister of fisheries, announced that the time had arrived to recognize the fishery as an important national enterprise. He promised that the government would direct its efforts towards fundamental remedial action to improve the quality of the product and the catching methods, to maintain and expand the export trade, and to increase domestic consumption.[27] Unlike agriculture, he conceded, the fisheries had been given little encouragement. The program he envisaged was the first of its kind for the fishery in Canada and focused on the fishermen. 'Notwithstanding ready access to the resources, which are the world's greatest,' Mayhew said, 'the industry has been unable to provide a dependable livelihood for the people directly employed by it.' While this may have been rhetoric for the upcoming election, the expected demand for price support[28] to supplement the traditionally low incomes in the backward Newfoundland fishing industry provided much of the impetus for Ottawa's initiatives. An emphasis on saltfish destined for southern-European markets, where living standards and purchasing power were both low, held little hope for developing backward areas and improving living conditions. The industry had to be weaned from lower-grade products to ones of higher quality, such as fresh and frozen fish that could be marketed in North America.[29] Mayhew realized, though, that the saltfish industry would remain crucial to Newfoundland, and he hoped that improved fishing methods would increase individual productivity and raise incomes.[30]

Premier Joseph R. Smallwood realized, too, that the salt fishery had failed to provide a decent living for most fishermen. In fact, many fishermen had left their boats as other jobs opened up. During the Second World War, when other work and more secure incomes were available at the American and Canadian military bases, the number of fishermen declined by one-third.[31] Smallwood feared that the exodus might be massive as Confederation opened new opportunities. He promised fishermen that union would breathe new life into the fisheries. 'It is time,' he said during the May 1949 provincial election, 'for our fishermen to get their share of the good things of life, and it is our policy to bring this about without delay.'[32] This could best be achieved, he thought, by greater emphasis on the production of frozen fillets for the American and Canadian mainland using modern deep-sea draggers.[33] Consequently, the provincial government expanded the scope of the policy introduced earlier by the Commission of Government whereby capital was advanced as loans and guarantees for the development of fish-filleting and -refrigeration plants and the purchase of trawlers.[34] Though Ottawa shared Smallwood's aims, it rejected his policy of financial support for the processing companies, claiming that this might lead to over-expansion and interfere with plans to centralize the industry.

The serious difficulties encountered in the marketing of salt cod in the first years after Confederation served to reinforce the need for radical change. The prosperity brought by war disappeared as the fishing fleets of competitor nations re-emerged in a reconstructed Europe.[35] Also, despite the post-war hope for freer multilateral trade, import restrictions by some European countries and bilateral trading arrangements within the sterling bloc aggravated existing problems.

Tenders issued by Greece, for instance, stipulated that the fish sellers had to be members of the European Payment Union to revitalize intra-European trade. Governments were very reluctant to use dollar reserves for saltfish when there was urgent need for raw materials and machine tools. Monetary-exchange problems, too, made the task of selling Newfoundland fish more difficult. The devaluation of most European currencies in September 1949 made Newfoundland fish more expensive than Icelandic and Faeroese fish, and reduced Newfoundland's market share as Greece and other European nations turned to cheaper supplies. European competitors not only squeezed much of the Newfoundland fish out of Europe but also competed successfully in the Western hemisphere.[36] By 1955 Newfoundland's saltfish exports to Europe were down 75 per cent from 1947–8 levels.

Throughout this period, Newfoundland looked to Ottawa for a solution. The shortage of dollars in Europe seriously threatened the precarious existence of the Newfoundland fishermen, and only the intervention of the federal government averted a disaster. For many fishermen, Confederation had arrived just in time. Ottawa had pressed London to continue the sterling-convertibility arrangement into 1951 to clear the way for sales to Europe. Mayhew continued to help overcome the marketing difficulties abroad, and to encourage the expansion of the domestic market. In fact, the Canadian government arranged for the sale of about $4 million worth of Newfoundland fish to Europe. This was about 40 per cent of the province's 1951 production.[37] The situation was helped when Brazil agreed to purchase $1.75 million of the 1951 and 1952 production as part of a barter deal for pulp.[38] Still, the fishermen could not find a market for much of their product, and so the price for top-grade saltfish had fallen by more than 30 per cent by 1952, down to $8.80 per quintal from the already-depressed 1949 price of $13.10. Because returns throughout the period were so low, the federal government stepped in to allow the fishermen to maintain their meagre standard of living.[39] Between 1950 and 1955, to aid the slumping saltfish industry, Ottawa spent more than $4 million in direct price support and several millions more in fish purchases for United Nations relief.[40] Newfoundland's representative in the federal cabinet, Gordon Bradley, acknowledged Ottawa's assistance when he said that 'We [Newfoundland] faced disaster, and, had we been dependent entirely upon our own resources, would have been confronted with one of the most serious problems in the history of the industry.'[41] The marketing crisis continued for several years after union, and the federal government had to bail out the industry by purchasing much of the surplus between 1949 and 1954.

Ottawa became involved only because the problem was unique and because the new province was economically so far behind the rest of Canada. Yet the federal government never lost sight of the fact that the fishery had to change.[42] Mayhew had maintained throughout the crisis that government action must not prevent the conversion of production from salt to fresh frozen cod, for in this lay the long-term solution to the problem of the Newfoundland fisheries.[43] When Norman Robertson, the clerk of the Privy Council and secretary to the cabinet, visited Newfoundland in 1950, he found that both the provincial government and the fishing industry also recognized the necessity of a shift from dried salt cod to fresh and frozen fish. This transformation might take more than a decade to complete. In the meantime, Ottawa had to improve the conditions in the fishing industry for the individual fisherman and his family.[44] Throughout the marketing crisis, Ottawa expressed disappointment over the 'quality' of the argument coming from the Newfoundland saltfish industry, which was consumed with the issue of markets and paid scant attention to long-range solutions to persistent problems.[45] W.C. MacKenzie of the Markets and Economics Branch of the Department of Fisheries later remarked that Newfoundland fishermen, exporters, and the public were so concerned with fish prices that this issue tended to divert attention from the real problem of the Newfoundland fishing industry – namely, the low productivity of individual fishermen.[46] Ottawa wanted to make this the focus of fishery reforms.

IV

Persistent market difficulties underlined the necessity for major surgery, a need that both governments had recognized much earlier. On 27 January 1951 Smallwood and Mayhew announced the formation of a joint Newfoundland Fisheries Development Committee to formulate a development program for the inshore and offshore fisheries 'capable of implementation by both the Federal and Provincial Governments and those engaged in the fishing industry, and outlining the respective responsibilities of each, and their agreed shares in carrying out the programme.' The committee included representatives of fishermen, the industry, and both levels of government and was chaired by Sir Albert Walsh, Newfoundland Supreme Court justice and former chair of the delegation to negotiate the Terms of Union.[47]

Smallwood believed that the committee's recommendations should constitute a program of development for the fishery. What he did not know, however, was that Ottawa had already formulated a policy that differed markedly from his. Smallwood saw an important role for government through cash incentives and loan guarantees. But Ottawa believed that the 'development of [fishery] resources should be left to ... individuals and associations of individuals acting as private citizens,' with government performing a very limited role that would not encroach on private enterprise. Government should assume responsibility for the major part of investigative and experimental undertakings, if they contributed to an improvement in national enterprise. In other words, government should seek only to provide 'an environment in which private initiative and capital can venture and flourish through Governmental assistance.' Private enterprise, of course, should provide the capital necessary for the exploitation of the resources uncovered or expanded through federal initiatives. However, if private industry refused to become involved, 'the use of public money to exploit a resource, when such exploitation leads to social betterment, seem[ed] quite justifiable. This [was] especially so where an operation of this kind [was] necessary to overcome general inertia and the reluctance of private capital to pioneer in an area or community.' Because government was using public funds, for which there were many demands, it was 'mandatory' that government investment 'be based upon careful and objective economic analysis' because the ultimate goal was to lure private capital. Of course, if the results of government policies were not encouraging, private capital would steer away. 'Development can only be regarded as successful,' Ottawa maintained, 'if it attracts to itself investment capital from the citizens who are participating. Unwise projects carried out under the aegis of governments would only prejudice the whole fishery development scheme. Unsound works bring in their train loss of confidence, unscrupulous dealings and finally public scorn.'[48]

Ottawa's primary objective was to improve the standard of living of the people involved in the fishery. Yet it realized that 'there [was] little hope for that part of an industry [salt cod production], which use[d] methods of operation in vogue two centuries ago, to provide a satisfactory living for its dependents or, to remain in existence for very long, except by the benevolence of governments.'[49] Such benevolence Ottawa had little intention of extending. Prime Minister Louis

St Laurent's approach to the role of government in the national economy has been described elsewhere as 'minimalist,' and he was not about to make an exception for the Newfoundland fishery.[50] With such a policy, Ottawa had effectively closed the door on what Smallwood hoped to achieve through the Walsh Committee even before it had begun its investigation. Like two ships passing in the night, Ottawa and Newfoundland were on separate courses and very unlikely to meet.

On 15 April 1953, the *Report of the Newfoundland Fisheries Development Committee* was tabled in the House of Commons. The Walsh Report painted a depressing portrait of the Newfoundland fishery. The industry was characterized by extreme inefficiency, with meagre capital investment, averaging about $500 per man. Fishermen were restricted to the near-inshore waters where the season was generally short, the run of fish sporadic, and the productivity correspondingly low. The necessity of being close to the resource had drawn the fishermen to remote, isolated headlands and islands where living conditions were generally poor. In addition to being isolated, many communities lacked the amenities of civilized life. The typical family income averaged less than $1,500 annually, of which only about half was derived from fishing.[51] The Walsh Report also detected the changes sweeping the province:

The general social improvement which had been taking place in the Province for some years is resulting in the liberation of women from the hard and unsuitable work of fish-making and allowing them to devote their time to their household duties and to live in an atmosphere of human dignity as wives and mothers. It is also resulting in the liberation of children to pursue their education and receiving [*sic*] a formation preparing them properly for a career to which they should have equal opportunity with all other children. The Committee considers that in a programme of development of the fisheries, child and female labour should find no place, except in the case of young women who will be employed at suitable work in plants and senior school children who will undoubtedly continue to help in fish curing during the summer vacation.[52]

The typical family enterprise whereby the men caught the fish and the women and children dried them on the flakes was a relic of the past and, in the 1950s, peculiar to Newfoundland. The committee found a universal desire among fishermen to dispose of their fish fresh and get rid of the difficult, time-consuming, and tedious work of curing their catch.[53]

This was, in large part, a consequence of the changes evident across Newfoundland, changes that had their roots in the period of prosperity during the war.[54] 'With a suddenness that is startling,' Newfoundland minister of finance Gregory Power said in his budget speech of April 1953, 'our people in all sections of the Province seem to have awakened to a keen realization of the many ways in which Newfoundland had been lagging behind in the march of progress for most of the present century.' Power also noted that the old-time complacency and contentment of Newfoundlanders had weakened, while their 'wants have expanded enormously. A deep-seated desire for progress and improvement, sleeping through the decades, seems suddenly to have come to life.' There was a strong desire to bridge the gap with the rest of North America. Power saw the awakening in the 'sudden clamorous demand for new roads, and for improvement of old roads ... It explains the all but irresistible demand for new hospitals, hospital boats, air ambulances, and other modern health services ... [and] the swelling demand for more and better schools.'[55] Each week in the House of Assembly, members presented petitions to the government from all across the province demanding roads to end isolation, to provide better health and educational services, and, in general, to improve the standard of living.[56] There was a new consciousness among the Newfoundland people, reflected in a 'new and urgent demand for progress, [an] insatiable impatience manifest in almost every nook and corner of the Province. It is a most gratifying development,' Power concluded, 'and it must lead inevitably to great changes and improvement in our Newfoundland life.'[57]

The fishing industry had already started to show signs of change. The bank or deep-sea fishery,[58] once an integral part of the salt fishery, had practically disappeared in little more than a decade as vessels started to supply the fresh-fish industry.[59] In 1937, banking schooners had produced more than 250,000 quintals of fish for salting, but production dropped to 120,000 in 1949 and to only 5,000 quintals in 1951. The decrease in the number of vessels was equally sharp, from eighty-eight in 1949 to only two in 1951. Fresh fishing generally resulted in higher and quicker returns, and the banker crews found employment on local trawlers or in the Nova Scotia fishery.

A similar trend was discernible in the Labrador fishery, but there it was due primarily to the uncertainties of the market for the Labrador cure. Only 30 schooners or 'floaters' operated 'on the Labrador' in 1951, compared with 65 in 1950 and 144 in 1949. The decline continued into 1952.[60] Gordon Bradley thought that the greatest change in the industry was the growing reluctance of fishermen to continue in the ways of their ancestors. 'It is a definite fact,' he wrote to Hazen A. Russell of Job Brothers, a major fish company, 'that the great bulk of Bonavista fishermen have no desire whatever to salt fish nowadays. They want to sell it green [fresh]. It has taken them some time to realize that the time and labour expended by them upon the fish after it is brought to land gives them far less in the way of return than that time would afford them if they spent it in catching.'[61] His outlook was stark: 'unless we can evolve better methods of both catching and curing, the day is not far distant when the Newfoundland salt codfish industry will be a thing of the past, for the simple reason that the young men of today will not tolerate the standards of life of his [sic] forefathers. This is increasingly apparent since confederation ... opened up the growing opportunities of this vast and ever-expanding nation of ours to the youth of our province.'[62] Bradley also believed that the catching and curing of the fish had to be separated, with the latter falling to skilled and scientific management to produce a standard product of high quality.

Minister of Fisheries and Co-operatives W.J. Keough noted similar changes in early 1952. 'Many fishermen who produce light-salted or shore fish,' he said, 'have declared that they will not make [dry] fish any more. And I suppose all fishermen wish to sell their catches green from the boat.' He also noted that it was difficult for fishermen to make a decent living at light-salted or shore fish, but if the fish were cured at central shore stations, the cost of labour and investment would push the price of a quintal of fish up by two dollars. What this also meant, he said, was that 'the fishermen, who have not considered their labour as wages to be charged against the fish but rather as a service inseparable from the function of catching fish, have been subsidizing every cod's tail of light salted fish sold in export markets.'[63] Given all this, it is not surprising that the swing away from the traditional shore cure towards mass-produced fillets continued throughout most of the 1950s.[64]

The Walsh Committee reached a similar conclusion. If the fishery failed to provide an income and working conditions as attractive as those available in other occupations, fishermen would continue to leave the industry. Despite the preoccupation with fish prices in Newfoundland, it warned, an increase in the price would have only a slight effect on family income because productivity was so low. Walsh said that individual productivity had to be increased to avoid a mass exodus of fishermen and to raise their income. Moreover, fishermen had to be provided with a standard of living, including amenities and services, regarded as normal for rural areas. Walsh wrote that as far as development was concerned 'the most important feature of the programme is centralization of the industry by [the] establishment of plants capable of diversified production and economic operation. Most of the other features are auxiliary to this but necessary for success.' In order to create a productive inshore fishery, radical changes were necessary indeed.[65]

The recommendations contained in the Walsh Report were directed to the northeast coast of the island, where the industry was particularly depressed. On the ice-free south coast filleting and freezing were already developing satisfactorily, but the northern regions, ice-bound for several months each year, had not benefited from the new technology. They had continued to rely on saltfish processing, though diversification was certainly encouraged. If private enterprise failed to take the initiative, Walsh recommended, government should become involved, either to provide loans or to finance projects completely. What the Walsh recommendations implied, James Sinclair, Mayhew's successor as federal minister of fisheries, later reported to the cabinet, was the concentration of the fishing fleets around such plants, in order to ensure stability of supply. It followed that modernization involved 'withdrawal from the widely-scattered "outports" and centralization of the fishing industry at a comparatively small number of locations.'[66]

The federal government did not decide quickly on the recommendations contained in the Walsh Report, though it agreed with its analysis of the Newfoundland fishery. During the summer of 1953, in usual government fashion, St Laurent appointed an interdepartmental committee of senior officials to review the report and submit a proposal to the cabinet. Before any decision was made, however, Parliament was dissolved and an election called. Smallwood threw himself into the federal campaign. 'It is of life and death importance to all our fishermen for the Liberal Government in Ottawa to be put back in power,' he told the fishermen: 'A vote for the seven Liberal candidates in this election is a vote for your Newfoundland Government, a vote for vast and wonderful development of our fisheries, a

vote for making our fishermen prosperous.'[67] Perhaps Smallwood
hoped that a good showing by Newfoundland Liberals would make
the Prime Minister more amenable to the Walsh recommendations,
but above all he was concerned to secure the election of J.W. Pickersgill, the former secretary to the cabinet, who had agreed to run in
Bonavista-Twillingate, a strong Liberal constituency. The Liberals did
in fact win all seven seats, although Smallwood failed to convince Ottawa that his approach was the right one. Pickersgill, however, became Newfoundland's representative in the cabinet, and Smallwood
and his fishermen supporters gained an important ally in Ottawa.[68]

Before the cabinet made up its mind on Walsh's recommendations,
another group of senior bureaucrats went to Newfoundland to examine the situation at first hand. Neither this group nor the earlier
one saw any need for a radical departure from Ottawa's policy on
fishery development. Ottawa believed in an integrated, all-encom-
passing approach to fishery development that would involve both levels of government as well as private enterprise. Following a thorough
survey of potential sites, Ottawa wanted to select (as the report had
recommended) several locations for development. Various federal departments were to provide the necessary marine works, navigational
aids, and marine radio-telephone service. Power, water supply, and
other municipal services would be furnished by the provincial government. The two governments would cooperate and share costs on
vessel construction, training of personnel, and housing. In other
words, government would create the infrastructure. Once the services
were provided, private enterprise, perhaps with the help of the Industrial Development Bank, would then take over and make the projects viable.[69] Ottawa refused, however, to become involved in
undertakings in Newfoundland that it did not support elsewhere in
Canada. And so the interdepartmental committee recommended
against federal assistance to build highways and docks, as such federal encroachments would establish an undesirable precedent. In keeping with government policy, the committee warned against providing
assistance to private enterprise beyond what was available through
the normal operations of the Industrial Development Bank. There
should be no special legislation for Newfoundland to rehabilitate its
fishery, except perhaps to provide saltfish warehouses and holding
stores at winter shipping ports.[70] Moreover, the productivity of individual fishermen could be raised only with a substantial reduction in
the number of fishermen. This was a sensitive issue in Newfoundland

and one the bureaucrats warned against emphasizing publicly. The government also had to be careful that the large number of fishermen who had left their boats for higher wages on new construction sites or at other jobs in the province would not rush back to the fisheries in the expectation that the Walsh Report would create new opportunities.[71] Ottawa feared that the centralization of the industry would be seriously impeded if the province were to rehabilitate some communities without considering their long-term potentials.[72]

This approach was too slow for the provincial government. When the Walsh Committee submitted an interim report in mid-1952, Ottawa made clear to Smallwood its plans for the fishery. Above all, there would be no financial aid to private industry. This prompted an outburst from Smallwood in the House of Assembly. The fisheries, he charged, had been the greatest disappointment of union. 'Ottawa seems to have virtually no realistic understanding or appreciation of the almost incalculable importance of fisheries in the economy of Newfoundland, and the economy of Canada ... Union with Canada must always be something less than a success so long as the Government of Canada fails to do for the fisheries a fair fraction of what has been done for other primary industries and is being done.'[73] For his part, Keough believed that in the matter of saltfish production it was naïve for Ottawa to think that any of the existing fishing companies in Newfoundland would invest in the development of plants to process the product. 'Unless the Government of Canada was prepared to reach agreement in respect of capital aid for development in the salt fish industry,' he argued, 'two years would have been wasted awaiting the final report and recommendations of the Fisheries Development Committee.'[74]

Ottawa remained firm. Its goal was to improve the standard of living for fishermen, and in cooperation with the provincial government, it started a number of projects, all of them experimental and recommended by the Walsh Report, that were to overcome three basic problems faced by outport fishermen. The purpose was to increase the productivity of fishermen by separating the catching and curing processes. The projects to achieve this were undertaken at Quirpon and Seldom-Come-By. The nature of the experiment was to abandon the individual system of production in favour of a small saltfish plant in each community with centralized flakes. The plants would buy the fish green directly from the fishermen, thus giving them more time to fish.[75] The federal government hoped to achieve its second objective of more consistent quality by providing small groups of fishermen with adequate and sanitary curing facilities, a development that fore-shadowed the introduction of community stages.[76] Mayhew and St Laurent liked these projects because they promised to help fishermen to help themselves while improving the amenities available to them.[77]

Because the future development of the saltfish industry depended on the successful introduction of a low-cost dryer that would mech-anize and standardize production, an experiment along these lines was undertaken at Valleyfield–Badgers Quay. The plan was for lightly salted or semi-dried fish to be taken from the surrounding area to the experimental plant. A similar large-scale community development project, with a saltfish plant and plans for the eventual production of fresh-frozen fish and fish meal, was also approved for La Scie. By leading the way in mechanization, Ottawa hoped to demonstrate the viability of the saltfish industry. Other experiments were aimed at de-veloping better fishing craft and catching gear. In the same spirit, and with a view to promoting greater concentration of population, a sys-tematic search was undertaken for new fishing grounds. By all these means Ottawa and St John's hoped together to provide some of the amenities of life that were lacking in the isolated outports but taken for granted elsewhere in the country. The federal government believed that if the fishery could be improved through technological innova-tion, private investment would follow. Both governments accepted that the centralization of the population was the only way that ser-vices could be extended to the remote areas of the province and the curse of isolation could be overcome. It was also agreed that im-provement would mean a substantial reduction in the number of fish-ermen.[78]

In 1954 Ottawa allocated $2.3 million for the projects. The provin-cial allocation was $1.1 million.[79] The Canadian government had clearly understood the problem as presented in the Walsh Report. Yet Ottawa was timid. An indication of this was shown by its refusal to follow the recommendation in the report to stimulate the industry by an infusion of capital to private enterprise or for projects of the provincial government.[80] Ottawa's hope of stimulating investment by creating an infrastructure rather than through providing capital as-sistance to private enterprise was wishful thinking.[81] Ottawa resisted 'considerable pressure' from Smallwood to finance existing industries and become involved in various processing operations. Mayhew had told St Laurent in 1952 that such activities would lead Ottawa 'away from [its] real responsibility in that Province. We think that our responsibility is very clearly defined, and we are prepared to recognize our responsibility and take action as quickly as possible.' Mayhew did not want to establish a precedent for federal intrusion into the fishery; he realized, moreover, that if Ottawa assisted the Newfoundland fishing industry, it would be doing so 'at the expense of a neighboring [Nova Scotia] industry which was doing everything on its own.'[82] He realized too that Maritime producers would be extremely critical of the government's intervention. In sum, political considerations were put ahead of the needs of the Newfoundland fishery. The easy way out was for the federal government to fall back on capitalist ideology and persevere in the attitude that publicly sponsored enterprise was to be avoided.[83] By following this course, however, Ottawa failed to acknowledge the gravity of the problems that plagued the Newfoundland fishery. In fact, it could have silenced potential critics by making the case that the Newfoundland fishing industry was backward compared to that of the Maritimes and insisting that any special assistance given was of a temporary nature.

In the first decade of union it was the provincial government that took the initiative in providing financial assistance to the industry. Throughout that period, it gave the fishing industry more than $13 million in loans and working capital. Most of this went to the fresh-frozen business. In introducing the legislation to establish the Newfoundland Fisheries Development Authority, Smallwood advanced this justification for the action being taken: 'The only reason the Government of Newfoundland has had to lend money or guarantee loans for development is because capital, for investment in the fisheries or new industries for that matter, has not been available in Newfoundland or on the Mainland of Canada or in the United States.' The task of the new authority, the Premier explained, would be to carry out those recommendations of the Walsh Report that fell within provincial jurisdiction. According to Smallwood, Confederation had given Newfoundland entrepreneurs greater opportunity for profit in the sale of consumer items. This in turn had discouraged long-term venture-capital investment, especially in the fishery. Several of the major fishing enterprises were either shifting their operations to the fresh and frozen sectors, or getting out of the industry altogether. Bowring Brothers, one of the most powerful and largest firms in the saltfish trade, had decided by August 1950 that greater prosperity beckoned in the retail trade. One of the larger exporters engaged in the Labrador fishery, James Baird Limited, quit the fishery in 1952, and by 1957 ten companies had withdrawn from the saltfish trade. Smallwood later charged that it was the merchants, not the governments, that had lost interest in the fishery.[84]

Even with his promise of generous financial assistance, Smallwood had failed to attract private enterprise to the saltfish business, but he remained convinced that government must continue to lead if the fishing industry as a whole was to remain viable. While Ottawa hoped for a better way through experiment, Smallwood thought the way forward was to throw money at the industry so as to enable it to move quickly to producing fresh and frozen fish. 'We have refused no firm that was willing to expand and was able to meet our terms,' he told the legislature, 'and this policy we shall continue to practice.' 'We have gone further,' he continued, 'for we have approached firms and urged them to expand and offered to assist them to finance the suggested expansion, provided they were willing to meet our financial terms ... In short, by the end of the present calendar year [1951] our policy will have resulted in the filleting and freezing of a quantity of codfish that would, if salted and dried, amount to about 100,000 quintals, that would have to find markets in competition with the bulk of our codfish production.'[85] Though his policy eventually led to an overcapacity in the frozen sector,[86] its short-term effect was rapid growth and substantially improved incomes in a number of fishing settlements. Moreover, in acting as he did, Smallwood was in step with the position Ottawa itself had advocated immediately after union. This was that if private enterprise did not initiate development, then government must act to show what could be done. The Walsh Report also favoured this plan of attack.[87] Nevertheless, the federal authorities were not impressed with what Smallwood was attempting. Ottawa's reluctance stemmed in part from Newfoundland's seeming recklessness.[88] Gushue had cautioned Mayhew shortly after the Walsh Committee was formed that 'the Federal Government must avoid the head-long approach from which the Provincial Government finds it difficult to escape, and indeed, to which it is virtually committed.'[89] 'Such guarantees,' Stewart Bates, the deputy minister of fisheries, told Gushue, 'are a little like the signing of personal notes – something you do in the expectation you will never be called on to make them good. Such guarantees, moreover, are apt to be subjected to strong political pressures, to be ad hoc in their application, and to induce hasty consideration of projects.'[90]

Perhaps it was Bradley more than anyone who helped to sour Ottawa on the Walsh recommendation for public funds and steer it clear of Smallwood. Many in Ottawa were already beginning to question the Premier's development scheme.[91] Bradley had reservations about Smallwood's ability to govern effectively. 'There was not one single man in the whole outfit with any actual administrative experience, not even Joey himself,' he wrote to a friend by way of assessment of the provincial government formed in 1949. 'That in itself was a unique situation.' The only thing, Bradley concluded, that could prevent chaos with Smallwood as provincial leader was an extraordinary run of good luck.[92] When the Walsh Committee was appointed, Bradley held out little hope for it. The problem of the Newfoundland fishery, he suggested, was not one for the lawyers, merchants, civil servants, and fishermen who made up the committee. It was a problem for scientists and engineers, to be solved 'in the laboratory ... not in the committee room.' Bradley feared that the action recommended by the committee would be dictated by the provincial government and that Smallwood would simply throw money at the fishery problem, as a measure of relief, without any regard to a long-term solution.[93] 'A perusal of this interim report,' he wrote to Hazen A. Russell, one of the committee members, 'made it quite clear that it was, in fact, founded upon the policy of getting industries going by Government financing and, in this instance, at any rate, with little regard to the possibilities of success and none to the improvement of curing methods.' Bradley thought that the committee was being run by Clive Planta, Newfoundland's impulsive deputy minister of fisheries, and that its approach was in keeping with the province's general economic policy, that is to say, to plunge in, usually with generous financial aid, but without adequate knowledge or experience.[94] The schemes of economic development that were being floated in Newfoundland, he lamented, made no sense except in 'the desire of some industrialists to sneak across the Atlantic so as to provide a nest-egg for themselves if they have to fly ... in the event of a Russian advance.' Smallwood and his director general of economic development, the Latvian economist Alfred Valdmanis, were building 'castles in the air.'[95]

Ottawa's confidence in Smallwood's administrative ability was also shaken in the early years of union when the Premier landed himself in hot water on several occasions. Federal officials and politicians became sceptical about working with him, save at arm's length. It was believed in Ottawa that he had abused both the old-age-pension agreement and the unemployment-assistance program. Yet another mark against him was that, before the Newfoundland Hotel had been transferred to Canadian National Railways under the Terms of Union, he had sold to a local car dealership a parcel of land belonging to the hotel. Bradley, who gave St Laurent formal notice of Newfoundland's wish to transfer the hotel to the CNR, hastily rebuked Smallwood for what he had done. Legal questions aside, he wrote, the whole episode would 'leave the Provincial Government with a reputation for very sharp practices'; a price of even $40,000[96] was 'a poor substitute for the loss of confidence' that would result from the sale. When confidence was 'destroyed,' Bradley pronounced, cooperation became 'very difficult.'[97]

Bradley warned Smallwood that he must avoid incidents that would impair good relations between the province and Ottawa.[98] Smallwood paid him no heed. In early 1951, he announced an investigation into the price paid for the 1950 catch[99] after the federal government had announced plans to conduct a similar investigation. To make matters worse, he appointed a federal official on loan from the Dominion Bureau of Statistics to duplicate the work of the federal government. Bradley was exasperated: 'Why on earth,' he asked, 'do you embark upon projects of this kind where the Federal government is involved without first giving me any information whatever about the matter?' 'As it now stands,' he continued, 'I can only try and straighten up an awkward situation which you yourself have created ... I have told you time and again that is one of your great failings. You go ahead and on your own, make decisions and proceed to implement them without consulting others who have a stake in the matter and who can perhaps give you some sound advice.'[100] Bradley despaired when he concluded that Smallwood had not changed during his first three years in office.[101] Nor was he alone in thinking that Smallwood was unreliable. Officials such as Mitchell Sharp and R.B. Bryce recall having reservations about Smallwood's schemes for economic development, and they both claim that their views were shared by many others in the bureaucracy.[102] With such thinking in official Ottawa it is little wonder that the federal government was reluctant to follow the path, already well worn by Smallwood, of aiding private industry. Not surprisingly, Ottawa continued the established federal role of fostering a proper environment for industry. Within that environment investors would be expected to fend for themselves.

This prevailing view of Smallwood undoubtedly played a role in

Ottawa's rejection of Walsh's recommendation to establish a joint federal-provincial organization to administer a program for development. Walsh thought that a joint body might temper Smallwood's recklessness. But instead of trying to exert some measure of control, Ottawa pursued its own course, and though the two did cooperate on several experimental projects, Smallwood continued on his own. W.C. MacKenzie, who spent two years in Newfoundland as the representative of the Department of Fisheries on the Walsh Committee, saw as a grave mistake Ottawa's failure to appoint a co-ordinator to oversee Newfoundland fishery development. He feared that the provincial government, in its impatience for quick results, would ignore the recommendations for adult education and grass-roots organization to lay a foundation for fishery cooperatives, and instead opt to create such organizations from the top down. But he also realized that Ottawa was constrained by Nova Scotia, which saw the Walsh Report as a threat to its own fishing industry. In fact Nova Scotia's position was based on a misconception, as the program of modernization envisaged for Newfoundland involved contraction as well as expansion.[103] This suggests, too, that serious conflict between the interests of Nova Scotia and Newfoundland was common after union, and that Confederation did not create a unified region around the Gulf of St Lawrence.

After Ottawa introduced its program, Clive Planta told Smallwood that 'we actually gained more than we came prepared to accept as reasonable for immediate commencement, with a view to completion in 1954.' The federal government, he acknowledged, was hampered in its policy towards the Newfoundland saltfish industry by political considerations in Nova Scotia and by possible American retaliation against other Canadian fish products. Fearing countermeasures by Washington, the government had decided to purchase saltfish for overseas relief efforts rather than to initiate direct price support.[104] Certainly this was the approach of James Sinclair when he came to the fisheries portfolio in October 1952. 'If the government,' the Department of Fisheries warned, backed 'fish prices then the u.s. would have a strong case against Canadian fish entering the American market and tariff concessions would be dropped in favour of a high levy.'[105] Moreover, if support were given to Newfoundland, it would weaken the market generally and prompt protests from Nova Scotia.[106] These were not minor concerns. Planta believed that Newfoundland would gain more within the normal services and functions of the federal government than through special consideration. The latter, he noted, would depend on the willingness of the government to take a political risk, and if public debate ensued, which was quite possible, Newfoundland could not hope to win.[107]

In the end Smallwood was also conciliatory. On 1 October 1953, he stated publicly that 'the Government of Canada see clearly ... that Newfoundland's action in entering the family of Canadian Provinces can have full success for Newfoundland only if our fisheries are fully developed ... This is the real meaning of the decision that has now been reached between Ottawa and St John's.'[108]

v

In 1954, following these events, Smallwood sanctioned the absorption of NAFEL into the federal Department of Trade and Commerce. Neither St John's nor Ottawa was particularly enamoured of the saltfish marketing agency instituted by the Commission of Government. Both governments disapproved of a marketing method that left all the risks to the fishermen, though much of the antagonism towards NAFEL can be traced to the marketing crisis that wreaked havoc on the industry from 1949 to 1953. Ottawa felt that NAFEL had buried its head in the proverbial sand, and that its primary interest was to get cheap fish from the fishermen to maintain a strong competitive position in the markets.[109] Later, Stewart Bates charged that although NAFEL was a government-created monopoly and enjoyed all the advantages of a monopoly, it had refused to accept the associated responsibilities. 'It had,' he charged, 'shown no concern with development of the salt fish industry,' but had been 'satisfied with the status quo.' The deputy minister was right. NAFEL had been content to rake in the profits during the Second World War without any concern for the long-term viability of the industry. During the marketing crisis after union it called on Ottawa to bail it out and threatened to cease outfitting fishermen unless Ottawa guaranteed it a market. It had not assumed full responsibility when things went wrong in 1949–50, Bates reminded the minister; instead, it stopped buying from the fishermen and called upon the Prices Support Board to step in and take over the product.[110]

Major modifications were made to NAFEL in 1953 and again in 1954. The barrier to interprovincial trade was removed to silence the critics of the agency in Nova Scotia, though restrictions were added to regulate the purchase of saltbulk[111] for use in Nova Scotia's mechanical dryers. To do otherwise might have been to court chaos, as fishermen might have put up too much saltbulk, hoping to dispose of it on the mainland.[112] Moreover, federal officials were concerned that NAFEL had become too reliant on government to support the price to fishermen. They also wanted more direct supervision. When Ottawa assumed control, smaller firms were allowed to join NAFEL, and as a further indication of Ottawa's interest in them, fishermen were represented on the board of directors for the first time. Furthermore, merchants selling through NAFEL had to undertake at the beginning of the season to pay, subject to government approval, a minimum price to fishermen, and agree to a system of profit sharing for any increase in the general price over the minimum set.[113] The minister of trade and commerce, C.D. Howe, warned NAFEL that it must 'do everything possible to facilitate such negotiations and ... co-operate in ensuring the successful operation of any agreements ... reached.'[114]

Smallwood's perspective on the transfer of responsibility for Newfoundland's saltfish export trade to the Department of Trade and Commerce was typically expansionist.[115] He had often praised Howe, whose experience with the Canadian Wheat Board was legendary and had much impressed him. Pickersgill believed that Howe's personal interest was the 'best thing that had happened to the Newfoundland fisheries for a very long time,' and he told Smallwood that Newfoundland's interests would be best served if Howe and his officials were given a chance to make things work.[116] Howe also reminded Smallwood that since Ottawa had assumed sole responsibility in the field of export marketing, it would no longer be appropriate for the province to participate in discussions about NAFEL and fish prices. Smallwood agreed. Newfoundland's best contribution, he told Howe, might be 'to refrain from becoming involved.'[117] Thus, Smallwood gave Howe a free hand in marketing Newfoundland salt cod, and Ottawa consolidated its control over the marketing process. Within three months, Canada completed trade agreements with Italy, Spain and Greece that re-opened Newfoundland's traditional saltfish markets.[118]

VI

Protecting traditional markets, however, was not enough. The industry could survive only if it provided an acceptable standard of living. This obviously had not happened in the first years of union, and by 1955 more than 10,000 men had left the fishery. Some 17,000 remained.

It must have seemed to Ottawa that there was little hope for stability in the salt fishery: only during wartime had there been buoyant markets and relative prosperity. In the first five years of union, Ottawa had spent nearly $4 million on price support alone. This had been designed only for emergency circumstances, not as a substitute for sound production and marketing practices. Mayhew had said in 1950 that there was in price support 'an inherent danger that it may be used to subsidize inefficiency and to perpetuate rather than solve the basic problem ... [It] will not be used as a means of relieving the merchandizing branches of the industry when they find themselves with a carry over at the end of the marketing season, nor will it be used in low income areas where the low incomes are the result of causes other than a sharp decline in price.'[119] By 1955, Ottawa was doing precisely that. Price support was rarely required in mainland Canada, except for Quebec's Saguenay County, where conditions paralleled those of Newfoundland. Moreover, Newfoundland fish competed with Quebec and Nova Scotia fish, and any measure of price support for Newfoundland weakened the competitive position of mainland fish.[120]

Newfoundland quickly lost faith in Ottawa's commitment to the fishery. Political constraints and criticism from Nova Scotia, Clive Planta claimed, prevented the federal government from assuming leadership in developing the fisheries. Ottawa, he believed, felt that modernization meant concentrating on several communities and allowing the rest to die, and eventually the saltfish industry would become a shadow of the fresh-frozen industry.[121] By July 1955, Smallwood had apparently adopted a similar attitude, though he might have been playing to a national audience when he lambasted Ottawa for its failure in the Newfoundland fishery; he had a penchant for the dramatic, and he rarely missed an opportunity to berate Uncle Ottawa on the national stage for not doing enough for Newfoundland. Before the Dominion-Provincial Conference, Beland Honderich, editor-in-chief of the *Toronto Daily Star* asked him for his opinion on what Canada had done to assist Newfoundland. In a reply that perhaps gave Honderich more than he had bargained for, Smallwood delivered a scathing indictment of Canadian policy:

I am ashamed and angry to say it, but the altogether stupid, bungling, inadequate effort of Great Canada to assist the Atlantic fishing industry (which is potentially almost as valuable in dollars and cents and much more valuable in numbers of families that can be supported than the oil industry of Alberta) is a reproach to a great and progressive country. The whole policy of the Department of Fisheries of Canada, insofar as there appears to be a policy for Newfoundland, is to drive the fishermen away from fishing. The present Minister of Fisheries told one very prominent Newfoundlander that it wouldn't matter if the Newfoundland fishermen had to leave the fisheries, because they could always find work in some other part of Canada.'[122]

Smallwood had had high hopes of the Walsh Committee, and he no doubt felt that Ottawa had not done its share. Yet one must question his own commitment to the fishery, especially the salt fishery. He makes little mention of it in his memoirs. And, after all, Smallwood had initiated in 1953 a resettlement plan to remove fishermen from their isolated communities. His government's support for the industry was mainly financial aid to the producers of frozen fillets, not to the saltfish industry. When in October 1955 he appeared in St John's before the Royal Commission on Canada's Economic Prospects, chaired by Walter Gordon, Smallwood barely mentioned the fishery. On the other hand, he rambled on for quite some time about how Newfoundland's bogs could be turned into wonderful cattle-grazing areas and how federal investment could turn the province into cattle country, complete with rodeos and its own stampede. Only in the 1960s did Smallwood turn to the inshore fishermen.[123] By then it was far too late.

About 500 fishing communities depended on the salt fishery, and many of them were concentrated along the northeast coast of Newfoundland. Ottawa could not ignore them. The experimental projects for centralization and community rehabilitation were limited to a dozen communities. About 90,000 to 100,000 people in the scattered fishing villages were left to continue as before, and await the results. Many of the problems persisted in spite of the Walsh Report and increased government spending on the fishery. According to Senator Fred Rowe, more than $110 million was spent directly and another $200 million indirectly by 1971.[124] At the end of the first decade of union, incomes were still far below the national average, and no great strides had been made to provide services to the outports. A working party appointed by the federal and provincial governments to review the fishery and evaluate the changes that had occurred between 1953 and 1958 concluded that 90 per cent of the fishermen had 'hardly been touched by the development program as implemented to date and their average gross income from the cod fishery remains at from

$500 to $700 for the annual period of the fishery.' Although the number of fishermen continued to decline, the working party suggested
that the number must be further reduced. Walsh, of course, had suggested this five years before. More than 5,000 had left between 1953
and 1958, but the overall production had been maintained largely because of the shift to long-liners and company-owned trawlers. For the
majority of the fishermen who remained, there had been little increase
in productivity. Walsh's main recommendation, therefore, had gone
largely unimplemented.[125]

Nor had the community-development projects turned out as the
government had hoped. They had become much larger and more expensive than had been originally anticipated, but the community interest and cooperation needed to make the projects successful had not
materialized. Yet it was in these experiments that Ottawa had placed
its hope for a rehabilitated fishery. Quirpon, Seldom-Come-By, and
Merasheen were to demonstrate that fishermen's incomes could be
improved through increased productivity and a superior quality of
salt cod. Quality improved, but as the Newfoundland Fisheries Development Authority lamented in 1960, with few exceptions 'the fishermen have not taken advantage of [the] opportunity to increase their
earnings by extending their fishing activities at the beginning and end
of each season.' This seems to suggest that some of the persistent
problems can be attributed to the fishermen themselves.[126] Although
this may be putting the blame on the individual fishermen, it does
seem that too many of them failed to increase their annual catches.[127]
The main benefit, therefore, was freedom from the task of making or
curing saltfish.[128]

In the first decade of union the problem of Newfoundland was the
ten or twelve thousand workers who continued in the salt fishery as
their forefathers had done. They could not develop and maintain even
the most simple institutions and services. The objective of both governments continued to be the elimination of the small, remote settlements in favour of selected 'growth areas' where a modern
community might develop an acceptable standard of living. Implementation of such a policy was necessarily a gradual process, and
though the plan was carried out with some success during the 1960s
and early 1970s, the federal government sought a new strategy for the
transition period.

From at least 1955, Ottawa politicians and bureaucrats realized that
there was no easy solution to the persistence of low incomes among

Newfoundland fishermen. Consequently, they came to see the fishery in Newfoundland as a problem in social welfare as much as one in economics. J.N. Lewis of the federal Department of Fisheries noted that Ottawa's policy was 'to administer palliatives based solely on humanitarian considerations.' In 1956 James Sinclair wrote to his provincial counterpart, John T. Cheeseman, that a salt-assistance program met two of Ottawa's objectives: it was generally free of serious criticism from the Maritimes, and it put money directly into the hands of the fishermen. Sinclair agreed that the program did not address the basic problems of the salt fishery, but it would increase the incomes of individual fishermen.[129] While price support and salt rebate assistance and, later, unemployment insurance and local fishery-related construction programs contributed to the financial improvement of many fishermen and their families, they may also have put a brake upon the natural forces that might have solved, however harshly, the problem represented by the shore fishermen of Newfoundland.[130] As Lewis observed, the placebo that the government prescribed would 'prolong the transition period and stretch out the years during which these people ... [would] continue to represent a problem that ... [would] tax the resources of the province and invite crisis after crisis for [the] Department [of Fisheries].' Like the Walsh Committee much earlier, the federal department feared that each fishermen who was encouraged to remain in the inshore fishery was a potential problem for the future.[131]

Lewis could not have been more accurate if he had had a crystal ball, as the fisheries continued to be enveloped in crisis after crisis. Both levels of government usually responded to each crisis with the same ineffective policy of providing make-work projects to allow the fishermen to qualify for unemployment insurance until the fishery corrected itself.[132] This is not to suggest that changes did not occur in the fishery. The fresh-frozen sector grew rapidly – perhaps too rapidly, as capacity exceeded demand in the late 1950s. The federal plans for exploratory fishing, improved gear and boats, and mechanical drying facilities certainly paid off. On the other hand, centralization did not pay the dividends for which the planners had hoped. Despite all the criticisms of the program for removing people to the larger centres, the policy helped to bring many Newfoundlanders into the twentieth century. Yet there was little attempt to reduce and limit the number of fishermen; in fact, the opposite occurred, as the number actually increased in the decades following the release of the Walsh Report.

Because of the improvements in technology, each fisherman became more productive and, while incomes rose in the short-term for most, the growing number of fishermen placed a serious strain on a limited resource and contributed, in part, to the depletion of the cod stocks that forced the closure of much of the Newfoundland fishery in 1992 and 1993. If Walsh's recommendations had been followed, perhaps the current ecological disaster might have been avoided.

The federal government is generally blamed for not doing enough to rehabilitate the fishery.[133] But Ottawa's task after 1949 was more than rehabilitation. The fishery in Newfoundland had been largely ignored for centuries, and while Ottawa must share responsibility for what happened after 1949, especially in managing the fish stocks and for much of the overfishing by foreign ships, it cannot be blamed for the problems it inherited at union. Premier Smallwood was correct when he said in 1951 that 'what we have to overcome today is the accumulated neglect and short-sightedness of the past half-century in our fisheries.' The years of neglect prior to 1949 could not be remedied easily or quickly. Although a development strategy was devised, the federal government refused to venture outside normal government services to rehabilitate the industry. Nor was it able to administer the medicine that might have put the fishery on the road to recovery. It lacked the political will to implement the Walsh recommendations, and it was limited in its actions by political considerations in the Maritime provinces. Moreover, Smallwood expressed little interest in the fisheries until the early 1960s, when he realized the futility of his other development schemes. The structural problems cut so deep that a massive infusion of funds was required rather than the timid approach finally adopted by the federal government. If Ottawa had followed the Walsh Report and accepted the views expressed by its own Department of Fisheries and by St John's, the fishery would have been concentrated in several areas around the province, a change that would have meant relocating people and taking many fishermen out of the industry. There is no evidence that Ottawa sought alternate strategies to reform the fishery. Massive unemployment would inevitably have resulted if a large number of fishermen had been forced out of the industry to create an élite body of fishermen operating modern and efficient boats to supply the needs of mechanized saltfish and fresh-fish processors. Other opportunities for working did not exist in Newfoundland. In other words, the federal government was hampered by humanitarian and social concerns. The number of fishermen had to be drastically reduced if the fishery was to be improved, and this would create the additional problem of massive unemployment.[134] Ottawa also came to realize that fishing in Newfoundland was not just a means of livelihood. It was also a way of life that could not be changed overnight.[135] In the end, the federal policy amounted to little more than a subsidy to increase the incomes of fishermen. This was a far cry from what was needed.

The Canadian approach to the fishery demonstrates clearly that while Newfoundland made major gains in social welfare as the incomes of fishermen improved after Confederation, the new province received little assistance in developing its economy. Ottawa avoided bold economic action in Newfoundland. And even if the federal government had possessed the political will to divert vast quantities of public money into the fishery, it is quite conceivable that the outcome in Newfoundland might not have been very much different and that the frozen-fish trade would still have largely supplanted the traditional saltfish industry. The fate of the inshore salt fishery, carried out as it was *at the time of union*, was already sealed and, *ipso facto*, it would have declined in the social reformation of the 1950s. Perhaps the best Ottawa could do was to treat the symptoms and ignore the cause of the ailment. In practice, that is precisely what it did.

Conclusion

This day marks 'the fulfilment of a vision of great men who planned the nation of Canada more than eighty years ago,' F. Gordon Bradley reminded the crowd gathered on Parliament Hill in Ottawa on 1 April 1949 to mark the union of Newfoundland and Canada. In 1864, the Fathers of Confederation had a plan for the union of all British North America and, 'in fancy we can see them now, bending over this scene in silent and profound approval.' Newfoundland had finally surrendered all claims to independence and dominion status and, at long last, had become a province of Canada. Confederation was now complete.

Union with Newfoundland was an important event in the national development of Canada. The grand design of 1864 was finally complete. The map of Canada had looked pretty odd for years without Newfoundland, and union removed for all time the peculiarities of the nation's eastern boundaries. Canada's cartographers could finally extend the Canadian boundary eastward to include Labrador and the island of Newfoundland, making Canada truly a dominion from sea to sea. More important, though, Confederation was an expression of a new mood felt throughout Canada. After playing an important role in the Second World War, Canada had emerged from the conflict confident and ambitious for both the prospects at home and its role on the world stage. The pre-1939 policy of avoiding international commitments was largely a relic of the past, and a national survey showed that 78 per cent of Canadians accepted the new internationalism and favoured a greater role for the country in foreign affairs. Domestically, Canadians expected a good life and welcomed the coming of the welfare state. Union with Newfoundland must be seen as an expression of this new-found confidence and ambition. It is perhaps no coincidence that, in the same year that Newfoundland entered Confederation, the St Laurent government established the Supreme Court of Canada as the final court of appeal for Canadians and Canadian statesmen played an important role in the creation of the North Atlantic Treaty Organization.

Confederation also brought greater security to Canada. It removed the threat that the United States would secure territory on the east coast as it had earlier done with the acquisition of Alaska on the west coast. Ottawa need not worry any more that an independent Newfoundland would drive a hard bargain over matters of civil aviation or defence, matters very important to Canada in the dangerous world of the period. After 31 March 1949, the federal government had a free hand in those areas. Gone, too, was the fear that Newfoundland might strike a deal that would earn its fish a special place in the American market at the expense of frozen fish from the Maritime provinces. Canadian exporters could breathe easier knowing that their Newfoundland markets were secure and should expand with union. Ottawa also rejoiced in the fact that the vast iron-ore deposits in Labrador were now assured for Canadian use.

The confidence and optimism that abounded in Canada facilitated Newfoundland's integration into the federal system. Many in Canada saw union as a benevolent and paternalistic act; Confederation with Newfoundland demonstrated Canada's willingness to play an important role in the world and its desire to help a less fortunate cousin. In admitting Newfoundland Canada was acting from a source of strength. All of Canada welcomed union (although the Maritime provinces, long the poor cousins of Confederation, did not wish to see the newest province benefiting more from the arrangement than they were).

The process of integration was made considerably easier because of the traditions common to both Newfoundland and Canada. Their association within the British Commonwealth and their triumphs and losses on the battlefields of Europe in two world wars accelerated the process of integration. Moreover, they shared language, religion, and history, and, more recently, their banking system, currency, and educational system. The federal system also assisted integration. The former dominion of Newfoundland retained sovereignty over a number of jurisdictions, including education, local and municipal institutions, and other local matters. In joining Canada, Newfoundland ensured the security of its traditions, culture, and distinctive characteristics within the federal system. Integration thus became mostly a bureaucratic and administrative affair. There were few radical changes to have a negative impact on the people's daily routine.

Canada was not greatly troubled by the cost of union. Of course, Newfoundlanders were eligible immediately for most federal social-welfare programs. In fact, officials had worked assiduously since late December 1948 to have those programs ready for Newfoundlanders in the first month of union. Hence, in April 1949, Newfoundlanders received their family-allowance cheques on the same day that Canadians in all the other provinces received theirs. Workers in the new province qualified for unemployment assistance and insurance on the same terms as those elsewhere in the dominion. Such government munificence had never before been seen in Newfoundland, and the Canadian social programs clearly had a salutary effect. Reports from the outports during 1949 praised family allowances for helping mothers – many with money in their purses for the first time – to buy clothing and shoes for their children. In fiscal 1951, for instance, family allowances alone injected more than $10 million into the provincial economy, and millions more poured in from Ottawa each year. In a province where cash income was appallingly low, federal money made a noticeable improvement in the standard of living and the people's purchasing power. The elimination of the Newfoundland tariff also helped to improve the standard of living. After union, prices on many items dropped by as much as 30 to 40 per cent, and competition with Canadian products forced many wholesalers and distributors to lower prices even further.

While this drop in prices benefited consumers, the manufacturing enterprises suffered in the early months of union. Yet the federal and provincial governments refused to institute a comprehensive assistance program for the manufacturing sector after union. Ottawa provided limited help on an individual basis to help the process of integration and offered a 15 per cent premium in 1949 on government tenders to allow firms to adjust to the new conditions. The premium was removed three years later. C.D. Howe, the minister of trade and commerce, decided then that it was time Newfoundland manufacturers competed on an equal footing with others throughout the dominion. In retrospect, Ottawa's limited assistance proved sufficient, as most of the secondary-manufacturing firms survived to take advantage of the increased purchasing power made possible with federal money, and continued to produce for local consumption much as they had prior to union; now, however, they did so more cheaply, because most underwent a period of retrenchment to streamline operations and become more efficient to meet Canadian competition. By 1952, Ottawa treated the manufacturing firms in Newfoundland the same as it treated industries in the rest of Canada. Several Newfoundland firms even lost their pre-union tax privileges, after the Supreme Court of Canada ruled that, in areas of federal jurisdiction such as income tax, the Canadian government had the power to repeal Newfoundland laws made prior to 1949.

The Newfoundland government was quick to use the benefits that Confederation provided, another indication of the rapid integration of the province into Canada. When the province encountered serious problems with unemployment in the first year of union, Premier Joseph R. Smallwood devised a make-work project to transfer the unemployed from the provincial public relief rolls to Ottawa's unemployment-insurance program, by using scarce provincial funds to put the unemployed to work on road repair just long enough for them to qualify for unemployment insurance. Over the next forty years, this became a favourite income-support strategy for both the provincial and the federal governments. When unemployment became a serious problem, as it too often did, Ottawa hastily created short-term employment. This approach did little to build a strong economy and provide permanent jobs, but it gave the people a source of income. Yet, in this respect, Newfoundland was treated no differently than any of the other have-not provinces, where the federal government routinely used unemployment insurance and federal make-work projects as an important means of income support. It was clearly in the area of social welfare that Newfoundland benefited most from union.

Ottawa's paternalism was also evident in the fishery. Both the federal and the provincial governments realized that, to allow fishermen to share in the standard of living that all Canadians had come to expect, the fishery had to be weaned from the precarious and unpredictable saltfish markets of Europe to produce frozen fish for North America. At the same time, fishermen themselves were demanding improved living conditions and an end to their isolation. Governments realized that the number of fishermen had to be reduced and the remainder furnished with efficient and modern equipment, operating from centralized communities that would allow them to increase their productivity, raise their incomes, and improve their standard of living. But other means of employment had to be found for displaced fishermen and this proved to be the sand in the gears of change, as such pursuits simply did not exist in Newfoundland. Ottawa realized that it could not solve one problem without creating an equally serious one. As a result, an efficient, prosperous fishery failed to emerge, and after 1949 the Newfoundland fishery went from crisis to crisis. From 1954 onwards, Ottawa came to view the fishery as a social problem. As such, it tried to improve the lives of fishermen through various mechanisms such as a salt rebate, make-work projects, and unemployment insurance. The federal and provincial governments and industry did not seek alternatives until the mid-1960s and simply allowed those who wanted to fish to do so, practice that made most fishermen dependent for much of their livelihood on the federal government. Still, this was remarkably similar to the federal approach to underemployment in other depressed regions of the country.

Fears of a political backlash from the Maritime provinces acted as a restraint on Canadian policy makers and limited Ottawa's initiative in Newfoundland. The federal government insisted that Newfoundland be treated like all other provinces, even though it was quite different and lagged far behind the others in most respects. Thus, Newfoundland learned early on that Ottawa was afraid to implement policies that other provinces might consider discriminatory. This was Ottawa's pat (but honest) answer to many problems raised during the negotiations in 1948. After union, when Newfoundland needed bold steps to reform its fishery, for instance, Ottawa was clearly timid and refused to invest the necessary capital for fear of political repercussions from the Maritimes. There was serious competition between Newfoundland and the Maritime provinces after 1949 and little evidence of a coherent 'Atlantic provinces.' This was obviously a case where regional resentment and jealousy served as a brake on the level of federal involvement in developing Newfoundland's natural resources.

It is true that during the final negotiations for union in 1948, Ottawa made several concessions to Newfoundland. The question remains, however, whether a better case could have been made for 'special status' in 1949. Was the opportunity lost to transform Newfoundland's economy because the delegation to Ottawa failed to have the province's uniqueness better recognized? Although the federal government increased the transitional grant, provided an unemployment-assistance program, and permitted the manufacture and sale of oleomargarine, the supporters of a return to responsible government thought more could have been achieved, especially in economic matters. They argued, correctly, that their country was unique and that it required special measures to bring its standard of living, its level of services, and its economy up to par even with those in the depressed Maritimes. Newfoundland could have achieved much more from Ottawa, they insisted, if it had also pursued negotiations with the United States as an independent nation, or had it had better negotiators in 1948. In hindsight, perhaps, the Newfoundlanders who negotiated the terms of union might have been too preoccupied with transitional grants and tapping into Ottawa's existing programs to help provide their people with a better standard of living. Both the delegation and Ottawa ought to have been more concerned with building a secure foundation for the province's precarious economy. They all realized, nonetheless, that Newfoundland faced an uncertain future if it chose to stand alone. It clearly had either to throw in its lot with Canada, or forge a special link with the United States, or stay with Britain. If Newfoundland had demanded too much in 1948, there might well have been no union in 1949, and the dominion would have fared worse on its own than it had with Canada. The delegation fully realized in 1948 that provincial status ensured that there would be no repeat of the embarrassing bankruptcy of the 1930s.

Newfoundland's decision to throw away the status of a self-governing dominion for that of a province demonstrates clearly the difficulties facing small nations in a world surrounded by big powers. Despite Canada's new confidence after the war, it too realized that it was often at the mercy of the Americans, as was demonstrated when it renegotiated the 1941 Leased Bases Agreement. Before consenting to modify the agreement, Washington exacted its pound of flesh from Canada in the form of a long-term lease to Goose Bay. Ottawa could say publicly by 1952 that Canadian law governing U.S. troops at other military establishments throughout the dominion also applied to those in Newfoundland, but the Americans continued to enjoy the same privileges they had before union, and throughout the 1950s the Canadian government continued to worry about the increasing American military build-up in Newfoundland. The episode clearly demonstrates that in a world where a nation the size of Canada often failed to hold its own, there was likely little hope for an independent Newfoundland. The necessity of economic and political integration into a larger entity was clear, and the best choice seemed to be Canada, which offered the best insurance against the problems of the past. Being Canadian promised a brighter and more secure future than being independent.

This conclusion is borne out by post-Confederation politics to 1957. When they realized that Confederation was inevitable, those who had demanded a return to self-government and fought against union quickly dropped their struggle for independence and threw their support behind the union. Although these people were unhappy with some of the Terms of Union, they realized that Newfoundland could not survive as an independent nation. In their first electoral campaigns, they promised to negotiate better terms with Ottawa rather than to undo the union. That they chose to do so within the Progressive Conservative party was, without doubt, a clear sign of their acceptance of union and demonstrates the rapid integration of Newfoundland into Canada. While it remains true that it was administratively and financially easier for the supporters of responsible government to forge an alliance with the Conservatives than to create a nationalist political party, there is no indication whatsoever that the Newfoundland wing harboured separatist sentiments. They guaranteed their ineffectiveness, however, by choosing the Tories, who were out of power in Ottawa until 1957. On the other hand, the Confederate Association, led by Smallwood and Bradley, who also teamed up with the Canadians, created the Newfoundland Liberal party and held power for the next twenty years. One more word is necessary here: Newfoundlanders who were not entirely happy with the Terms of Union followed the path of dissent well trodden by their Maritime neighbours within the traditional political parties.

By 1957, Newfoundland had clearly become a province like the others, subject to the Terms of Union. Administratively, union had long been complete and the process of union had bound Newfoundland firmly to Canada. In the years after 1957, however, Ottawa and Newfoundland had many quarrels, including disputes over finances and undersea resources. The latter opened up issues not even considered in 1948–9. Still, after a decade, there were few Newfoundlanders who did not share in the benefits of union with Canada and fewer still who believed that union had been a wrong move. Most were happy with union, and never once did the province seriously consider leaving Confederation. In this sense, then, Canada had succeeded in integrating Newfoundland into the federation. On the other hand, Prime Minister Louis St Laurent's promise to Newfoundland on 1 April 1949 of 'full and equal' partnership in Canada had not been realized by the end of the first decade of union. In the fifteen years prior to Confederation, Newfoundland was little more than a British dependency. Instead of finding economic prosperity within Canada, Newfoundland found instead a new and wealthier benefactor in Ottawa. During most of his time as premier, Joseph R. Smallwood affectionately referred to the federal government as 'Uncle Ottawa.' For the first forty years, it proved a very benevolent uncle, and consequently all Newfoundlanders now share a better standard of living. Unfortunately, union with Canada has not helped Newfoundland to bridge the gap between itself and the other provinces, in large part, because of the Terms of Union and the decisions made during the process of integration. In 1949 Newfoundland ranked lowest among the provinces on all indices used to measure economic wealth, and several decades later it retains that dubious position.

Notes

Introduction

1 The constitutional status of Newfoundland from 1934 to 1949 is the subject of considerable debate. See Gilmore, 'Law, Constitutional Convention, and the Union of Newfoundland and Canada,' and his *Newfoundland and Dominion Status*. Ottawa and St John's fought several legal battles over the ownership of the offshore oil resources off Newfoundland in the 1980s. Gilmore has written widely on this subject and claims that, in the strict rule of law, Newfoundland was a dominion.
2 In the first poll of the referendum, Commission of Government won 14.32 per cent, Responsible Government 44.5 per cent, and Confederation 41.13 per cent. In the second, Confederation polled 52.34 per cent and Responsible Government 47.66 per cent.
3 See Buckner, Waite, and Baker, 'CHR Dialogue: The Maritimes and Confederation.'

CHAPTER 1 The stage is set: from dominion to province

1 Bridle, ed., *Documents*, 1690–2
2 Ibid., 1662
3 St John's *Evening Telegram*, 4 Apr. 1949
4 Bridle, ed., *Documents*, 1692
5 Ibid., 156–8, 169–71
6 Canada, House of Commons, *Debates*, 8 Sept. 1939, 35. King's role in the union with Newfoundland is frequently overshadowed by that of Louis St Laurent. Although St Laurent had succeeded King as prime minister before the final negotiations with Newfoundland, King had presided over the gov-

ernment that laid the foundation for union. To achieve his objective, King adopted a simple strategy: he never gave the Newfoundlanders reason to suspect that Canada was overzealous or aggressive in its approach, but at every opportunity he tried to improve relations with the dominion. One thing is clear: if King had not wanted union in 1946–7, Newfoundland would not have become a Canadian province. By the time St Laurent took the helm, events had proceeded too far to turn back. See Blake, 'William Lyon MacKenzie King's Attitude towards Newfoundland's Entry into Confederation.'

7　National Archives of Canada (NAC), W.L.M. King Papers, Diaries, 18 Aug. 1940, and Conn and Fairchild, *The Western Hemisphere*, 55–6

8　For Newfoundland's role in the negotiations, see Neary, *Newfoundland in the North Atlantic World*, 135–53.

9　MacKenzie, *Inside the Atlantic Triangle*, 60–1. On Pearson's reaction, see English, *Shadow of Heaven*, 240–1, 246–7.

10　NAC, King Papers, J4, vol. 401, file 77, 'Memorandum' from Skelton to King, 22 Aug. 1940. American bases in Newfoundland turned out to be a thorn in the Canadian side after union, see ch. 5 below.

11　See Hayman, 'Origins and Function of the Canadian High Commission in Newfoundland'; and Stacey, *Canada and the Age of Conflict*, 2: 418.

12　Cited in MacKenzie, *Inside the Atlantic Triangle*, 64; See also Neary, *Newfoundland in the North Atlantic World*, 158–62.

13　By the end of 1946 seven nations had established legations in Ottawa, but Canada had been unable to reciprocate. St John's was the only capital where Canada had established a diplomatic post that did not have similar representation in Ottawa. Spencer, *Canada in World Affairs*, 412–14

14　MacKenzie, *Inside the Atlantic Triangle*, 65

15　See Granatstein, *A Man of Influence:*, 203.

16　Bridle, ed., *Documents*, 156–8, 169–71

17　Ibid., 73–4. Earlier in the session the Department of External Affairs had prepared a memorandum for King on a question raised in Parliament regarding the transfer of Labrador to Canada. The memo was detailed and 'hinted at the possibility of Canada considering the incorporation of Newfoundland into Confederation.' Ibid., 67

18　NAC, King Papers, J4, vol. 308, file 3270, 'Memorandum' prepared by N.A. Robertson for King, 18 Aug. 1943

19　NAC, King Diaries, 20 Apr. 1941 and 5 Dec. 1941

20　Bridle, ed., *Documents*, 97–102. For a full discussion of MacKay's memo, see MacKenzie, *Inside the Atlantic Triangle*, 149–51.

21　Bridle, ed., *Documents*, 130–4, 157, 169–71. On 24 July 1948, a few days after the second referendum, Keenleyside recorded in his diary that 'our policies of sympathetic interest and restraint rather than pressure have been justified by what has now occurred.' See Keenleyside, *Memoirs*, 199–216.

22 MacKenzie, *Inside the Atlantic Triangle*, 150–1. On the post-war reconstruction plan, see Neary, *Newfoundland in the North Atlantic World*, 220–6.

23 Bridle, ed., *Documents*, 133–5, 161–3, 167, 191–2, and *passim*

24 Quoted in MacKenzie, *Inside the Atlantic Triangle*, 150

25 Bridle, ed., *Documents*, 151–2, 158–9, 162–3, 173, 174–8

26 Ibid., 176–8

27 NAC, King Diaries, 27 Sept. 1945

28 Ibid., 27 Sept. and 18 Oct. 1945

29 Bridle, ed., *Documents*, 180–2

30 Ibid., 180; and MacKenzie, *Inside the Atlantic Triangle*, 163. Neary argues that it was Britain's initiative that made union possible: 'When it came to Confederation, the United Kingdom led, Canada followed, and Newfoundland consented ... Canada was more influenced than influencing.' Neary, *Newfoundland in the North Atlantic World*, 230–5, 354. For a discussion of the differences between Neary and MacKenzie, see Hiller, 'Twentieth Century Newfoundland Politics,' 180–91.

31 For a full discussion of the Commission of Government, see Noel, *Politics in Newfoundland*; and Neary, *Newfoundland in the North Atlantic World, passim*.

32 Great Britain, House of Commons, *Debates*, 11 Dec. 1945, 210–11

33 For a discussion of Smallwood's life see Gwyn, *Smallwood*; Neary, *Newfoundland in the North Atlantic World*, 281–4; and Horwood, *Joey*. For Burchell's views on Smallwood see Bridle, ed., *Documents*, 231–3, 241–2, 296.

34 MacKenzie, *Inside the Atlantic Triangle*, 171–3

35 See Burns, *The Acceptable Mean*.

36 Bridle, ed., *Documents*, 464–5, 470–80

37 See ibid., 517–39.

38 NAC, King Diaries, 24 June 1947

39 Cited in David MacKenzie, 'Canada and the Entrance of Newfoundland into Confederation,' 278

40 See Bothwell and Kilbourn, *C.D. Howe*, 272; Canada, House of Commons, *Debates*, 24 June 1946, 2753–4; and Smallwood, *I Chose Canada*, 571.

41 Thomson, *Louis St. Laurent*, 208–9, 234; NAC, King Diaries, 25 Aug. 1947; and NAC, Brooke Claxton Papers, vol. 114, file 3, 1947–8. On 9 Oct. 1948, the *Evening Telegram* reported that Duplessis had written to Prime Minister King objecting to union. 'It [union] is not justified, either from the economical or constitutional points of view or, for that matter, from that of national unity.'

42 For a discussion of the 1947 negotiations, see Bridle, ed., *Documents*, 535–697, *passim*.

43 Canada, Department of External Affairs, *Report and Documents*, esp. 57–70

44 Bridle, ed., *Documents*, 807–12, 823–5

45 Ibid., 840–1

46 Webb, 'The Responsible Government League and the Confederation Campaigns of 1948'

47 *The Independent*, 29 Apr. 1948. The rival publication, *The Confederate*, countered with equally effective ads. In one issue, it featured two babies with the caption, 'Are Our Daddies and Mommies Going to Remember Us on the 22nd?'

48 See Jamieson, *No Place for Fools*, 87–92, 124–5. Although Jamieson tells us that he cried when responsible government was defeated, he was not averse to making money from the Canadians. Within days of the second referendum, he had established a consulting firm to help Canadians get established in Newfoundland.

49 Cashin, Horwood, and Harris, 'Newfoundland and Confederation, 1948–9,' 240

50 Interview with Michael Harrington, 20 Mar. 1990

51 Interview with Grace Sparkes, 23 Mar. 1990

52 Morgan, 'Newfoundland, Our Tenth Province,' and Newell, 'Newfoundland, Canada'

53 NAC, King Diaries, 23–30 July 1948, *passim*

54 NAC, King Papers, vol. 246, file 2352, MacKay to Pearson, 29 July 1948

55 Bridle, ed., *Documents*, 1326

56 Ibid., 979–91

57 Centre for Newfoundland Studies, Memorial University Archives (MUN), Higgins Papers, file 3.01.018, 'Correspondence F.M. O'Leary, 1944–48,' O'Leary to Collins, 13 Aug. 1949

58 Provincial Archives of Newfoundland and Labrador (PANL), Governor's Office, Miscellaneous Despatches and Local Correspondence, file 1/48, 'National Convention – Confederation,' Crosbie to Governor Macdonald, 3 Aug. 1948

59 The Supreme Court of Newfoundland rejected the RGL's appeal for an injunction against the government to prevent it from proceeding with union. The court termed the appeal as 'vexatious and frivolous,' but the RGL then appealed to the Judicial Committee of the Privy Council. See *Evening Telegram*, 12 Feb. 1949; Neary, *Newfoundland in the North Atlantic World*, 337–9; and Gilmore, 'Law, Constitutional Convention and the Union of Newfoundland and Canada.'

60 St John's *Daily News*, 2 Aug. 1948

61 *Evening Telegram*, 4 Oct. 1948

62 Bridle, ed., *Documents*, 1352

63 NAC, King Diaries, 27 July 1947, and NAC, R.A. MacKay Papers, vol. 3, ICCNR – General Correspondence and Memoranda, Jan.–Aug. 1948, 'Memos of Mac-Kay's Visit to Newfoundland'

64 Bridle, ed., *Documents*, 1010–11. The Newfoundland governor had earlier invited Charles E. Hunt and R. Gordon Winter, both leading St John's businessmen who had been associated with the Responsible Government League, to be members of the delegation; they declined.

65 The only personal account of the negotiations from a Newfoundlander is Channing, *Effects of Transition to Confederation*. Channing was secretary to the delegation.

66 MUN, Joseph R. Smallwood (JRS) Collection, file 4.01.005, 'Newfoundland Delegation, Minutes of Meetings,' 28 Aug. 1948

67 Bridle, ed., *Documents*, 1046–7

68 MUN, JRS Collection, file 4.01.005, 'Minutes of Meeting,' 13 Sept. 1948

69 Ibid., 'Minutes of Meeting,' 13–14 Sept. 1948

70 PANL, Sir Albert Walsh Papers, file 5, 'Memorandum Submitted by Newfoundland Delegation to Ottawa,' Oct. 1948

71 See Neary, *Newfoundland in the North Atlantic World*, 220–6 for the commission's reconstruction plan.

72 NAC, Privy Council Office (PCO), Cabinet Conclusions, 10 and 25 Sept. 1948

73 *Daily News*, 30 Oct. 1948, and Bridle, ed., *Documents*, 1813

74 Interview with Mitchell Sharp, 12 Feb. 1990; and with Alan Hockin, 23 Feb. 1990

75 Bridle, ed., *Documents*, 1002

76 NAC, PCO, vol. 128, file N–18 Newfoundland, Aug.–Sept. 1948, MacKay to St Laurent, 30 Sept. 1948

77 C.D. Howe, minister of trade and commerce, D.C. Abbott, minister of finance, J.J. McCann, minister of national revenue, M.F. Gregg, minister of veterans affairs, R.W. Mayhew, minister of fisheries, and L.B. Pearson, secretary of state for external affairs, were the other members of the cabinet negotiating committee.

78 Bridle, ed., *Documents*, 1231 and 1371–2

79 Ibid., 1149–51

80 Ibid., 1070

81 Ibid., 1107

82 Public Record Office, London (PRO), DO 114, vol. 103, no. 339: 200, telegram from high commissioner, 16 Oct. 1948

83 Bridle, ed., *Documents*, 1149–51. In June 1947, Clark referred to Newfoundland as a 'little Ireland' full of 'disgruntled people.' Cited in Neary, *Newfoundland in the North Atlantic World*, 358

84 Interview with Mitchell Sharp, 12 Feb. 1990

85 See Bryce, *Maturing in Hard Times*, for a history of the finance department. J.G. Channing, secretary to the Newfoundland delegation, recalls that 'there were occasions when the Newfoundland delegation appeared to be on the verge of achieving a desired objective only to run into a stumbling block as a result of some Finance representative expressing a contrary or admonitory view. Finance was probably the leading proponent of the principle that all provinces must receive equal treatment, and its officials obviously kept in mind at all times the ominous warning sounded by Mr. King in his letter of 29 July 1947 to the Governor of Newfoundland ... that the financial arrangements proposed in 1947 constituted just about the limit of what Canada was prepared to offer.' Channing, *Effects of Transition to Confederation*, 46

86 Bridle, ed., *Documents*, 1149

87 Ibid., 1162–3

88 NAC, PCO, Cabinet Conclusions, 3 Nov. 1948

89 NAC, PCO, vol. 130, file N–18, vol. 3, Pearson to St Laurent, 5 Nov. 1948

90 Bridle, ed., *Documents*, 1174–8

91 NAC, PCO, Cabinet Conclusions, 9 and 15 Nov. 1948. The transitional grant for years nine through twelve remained unchanged from the 1947 proposal. As well, a royal commission was promised within eight years to review the financial position of Newfoundland. The dispute between Ottawa and Newfoundland over Term 29 – the review of Newfoundland's financial positions – that occurred in 1959 is not covered in this study. For an account, see Gwyn, *Smallwood*, 181–98.

92 Bridle, ed., *Documents*, 1189–91

93 Skelton thought a precedent might have existed because of the 1937 Bank of Canada *Report on the Financial Position of the Prairie Provinces*, which noted that Saskatchewan had a lower level of taxation than the other provinces. Officials from the federal and provincial governments agreed that Saskatchewan should impose a sales tax. See ibid., 1191.

94 Ibid., 1191–2, 1208–9

95 Ibid., 1194–6, 1202–6

96 NAC, PCO, Cabinet Conclusions, 15 Nov. 1948

97 Bridle, ed., *Documents*, 1214

98 Ibid., 1210, 1219, 1225–6

99 NAC, PCO, vol. 130, file N–18, vol. 3, Channing to acting secretary, cabinet committee on Newfoundland, 1 Dec. 1948. The Newfoundland income-tax act required payment in arrears; that is, taxpayers paid their 1947 taxes in 1948.

100 This is covered in detail in ch. 5.

101 Bridle, ed., *Documents*, 1200, 1204–5, 1207, 1209, 1214–15

102 Ibid., 1252. Newfoundland was given the option of entering the existing Tax

Rental Agreement between Ottawa and the provinces, due to expire in 1952, or continuing on the basis of that agreement until 1957. The latter proposal was offered to provide stability during the transitional period. See Burns, *Acceptable Mean*, 88–90.

103 Bridle, ed., *Documents*, 1299–1301

104 PANL, Government of Newfoundland, Governor's Office, file 1/48, 'National Convention – Governor's Office,' Chesley A. Crosbie to Governor Macdonald, 9 Feb. 1949

105 *Newfoundland Journal of Commerce*, Feb. 1949

106 Bridle, ed., *Documents*, 1360–2

107 See Canada, House of Commons, *Debates*, 14–15 Feb. 1949, and Queen's University Archives, Grant Dexter Collection, box 14, folder 76, 'The Newfoundland Debate,' 17 Feb. 1949. During the debate on 8 February, Drew criticized the fact that if Newfoundland entered into the Tax Rental Agreement it would remain unchanged until 1957. He pointed out that other provinces had secured adjustments to financial arrangements with Ottawa if another province worked out a better deal. Drew was obviously trying to establish himself as a defender of provincial rights.

108 See Bridle, ed., *Documents*, 1606–7; and Smallwood, *I Chose Canada*, 199–200, 336, 380. In fact, the commission was something of an embarrassment for most of the delegation. Bradley disliked the commission immensely, and Smallwood, whose views are better known through his own writings, chastised it for ignoring Newfoundland's economic development. Moreover, the Newfoundland Industrial Development Board, created by the Commission of Government in 1942 to encourage economic development and expansion, was allowed to die by the provincial government in the first year of union. Also, the delegation wanted to minimize the role played by the commission in approving the Terms of Union.

109 Bridle, ed., *Documents*, 1739

110 Ibid., 1786–7

111 Ibid., 1750, 1784, 1774, 1797–8

112 See Canada, External Affairs, *Report and Documents*, especially Terms of Union, 13–32.

113 NAC, MacKay Papers, vol. 3, file ICCNR Apr. 1948 – May 1949, C.H. Bland to MacKay, 7 Jan. 1949

114 NAC, PCO, Cabinet Conclusions, 13 Jan. 1949

115 Interview with Burnham Gill, St John's, Newfoundland, 27 Mar. 1990

116 Bridle, ed., *Documents*, 1066–7

117 Ibid., 1571, 1135, 1066–7

118 Ibid., 1160

119 NAC, Louis St Laurent Papers, vol. 59, file L–25–10, F. Gordon Bradley to St Laurent, 4 Mar. 1949

120 Jamieson, *No Place for Fools*, 147; and interview with Mitchell Sharp, 12 Feb. 1949

121 Pickersgill, *My Years with Louis St Laurent*, 84; Grand Falls *Advertiser*, 5 Feb. 1949; and *Evening Telegram*, 9 Mar.1949

122 See Bridle, ed., *Documents*, 1570–1603.

123 NAC, St Laurent Papers, vol. 59, 'Memorandum for Mr. Harris and Mr. Bradley,' 25 Mar. 1949. Marked 'approved by the Prime Minister.'

124 Ibid., file L–25–5, secretary of state for external affairs to high commissioner for Canada in Newfoundland, 25 Mar. 1949. Marked 'approved by PM.'

125 Pickersgill, *My Years with Louis St. Laurent*, 84–5

126 NAC, St Laurent Papers, vol. 66, file P–30–10, St Laurent to Sir Albert Walsh, 8 Mar. 1949

127 Ibid, vol. 59, file L–25–10, St Laurent to Albert Walsh, 8 Mar. 1949, and file L–25–5, St Laurent to Burchell, 25 Mar. 1949

CHAPTER 2 Back to politics: political organization in post-Confederation Newfoundland, 1948–1951

1 St John's *Evening Telegram*, 29 Apr. 1949

2 Party organization has often been regarded as the key to victory in other Canadian elections. See Cuff, 'The Conservative Party Machine'; and Stevens, 'Laurier, Aylesworth, and the Decline of the Liberal Party.'

3 Noel, *Politics in Newfoundland*, 274–7

4 See Gwyn, *Smallwood*; Horwood, *Joey*; and Smallwood, *I Chose Canada*.

5 Centre for Newfoundland Studies, Memorial University of Newfoundland Archives (MUN), Joseph R. Smallwood (JRS) Collection, file 7.01.002, David Lewis to J.R. Smallwood, 31 July 1948; National Archives of Canada (NAC), M.J. Coldwell Papers, vol. 46, file Smallwood, M.J. Coldwell to Smallwood, 12 July 1948; NAC, Cooperative Commonwealth Federation (CCF) Papers, vol. 16, file 1948, Convention Correspondence, Smallwood to Lewis, 3 Aug. 1948, and vol. 25, file Nfld General Correspondence, 1947–53, Coldwell to Edward Russell, 5 May 1951. See Lewis, *The Good Fight*, 333.

6 NAC, CCF Papers, vol. 4, file National Council and Executive Minutes, 1949–50, 'Meetings of CCF National Council,' 22 Aug. 1948, 19 Sept. 1948, and vol. 25 file Nfld General Correspondence, 1947–53, Lewis to Margaret Lazarus, 2 Dec. 1948

7 Ibid., vol. 364, file CCF Council and Executive Minutes, 1948–50, 'Meeting of National Council,' 29–30 Jan. 1949

8 Ibid., vol. 25, file Nfld General Correspondence, 1947–53, Lewis to Donald

MacDonald, 12 Apr. 1949. Desmond Morton writes in *The New Democrats*, that as late as 1969 the NDP was still searching 'unavailingly to find some new indigenous roots' in Newfoundland.

9 Explanations for the failure of the CCF and the limited success of third parties in the Maritimes are scarce. In *The Anatomy of a Party*, Walter Young perpetuates the stereotypical view that the Maritimes, a very conservative society, did not support the CCF because it conflicted with the region's 'rigid traditionalism' in politics. More recently, scholars have questioned the regional stereotypes, though much work remains to be completed on the CCF in the Atlantic region. See also Forbes, *Challenging the Regional Stereotype*; and Young, 'Teaching and Research in Maritime Politics.'

10 Gillespie, *A Class Act*, 95–6

11 Horwood, *Joey*, 73–6, 106–9; and Gillespie, *A Class Act*, 93–8

12 See Gillespie, *A Class Act*, 93.

13 Horwood, *Joey*, 144–5; and Gwyn, *Smallwood*, 129. See also Smallwood, *I Chose Canada*. Here Smallwood states on a number of occasions that he is a socialist. See particularly 72, 78–9, 109–10.

14 NAC, CCF Papers, vol. 25, file Nfld General Correspondence, 1947–53, Eamon Park to M.J. Coldwell, 18 May 1949

15 MUN, JRS Collection, file 4.03.002, Smallwood to Kevin Barry, 18 Apr. 1949. J.W. Pickersgill claims that Coldwell told him the same story. Although the CCF leader does not mention the particulars of his meeting with Mrs Russell in a May 1951 letter to Edward Russell (after the latter resigned from the Smallwood cabinet), Coldwell alluded to her meeting him at the airport: 'I also recollect Mrs. Russell's kindness in meeting me at the Airport in May 1949.' See NAC, CCF Papers, vol. 25, file Nfld, General Correspondence, 1947–53, Coldwell to Edward Russell, 5 May 1951.

16 Ibid., vol. 25, file Nfld, General Correspondence, 1949–53, David Jackman to David Lewis, 12 Apr. 1949

17 Ibid., Betty Massey to Fred Massey, 16 June 1949, and Park to Coldwell, 18 May 1949

18 Ibid., Lorne Ingle to A.M. Nicholson, 22 Oct. 1953

19 NAC, Progressive Conservative Party of Canada (PC) Papers, vol. 177, file N–N–1, Collins to Bell, 26 Oct. 1948, and Bell to Collins, 6 Nov. 1948

20 Ibid., Nowlan to Bell, 3 Aug. 1948; Bell to Nowlan, 13 Aug. 1948; Bell to Nowlan, 28 Aug. 1948; and Bell to A.L. Payne, 11 Aug. 1948

21 Toronto *Globe and Mail*, 30 Sept. and 1 Oct. 1948

22 The George Drew Papers (NAC) are closed.

23 NAC, PC Papers, vol. 177, file N–N–1, J.C. MacKeen to Bell, 17 Feb. 1949

24 Ibid., and MUN, John G. Higgins Collection, file 3.01.014, 'List of Memberships and Supporters'; NAC, PC Papers, vol. 177, file N–N–1, 'Nfld PC Association,

Agenda St John's,' 25 Feb. 1949; and Provincial Archives of Newfoundland and Labrador (PANL), Peter Cashin Papers, box 1, file 'Cashin's Radio Speeches, 1949'

25 NAC, PC Papers, vol. 177, file N–N–1, Bell to MacKeen, 8 Mar. 1949, and 'Report of Committee,' 27 Feb. 1949

26 Interview with Richard A. Bell, Ottawa, 27 Aug. 1987; see Jamieson, *No Place for Fools.*

27 NAC, PC Papers, vol. 178, file N–N–1A, Bell to MacKeen, 8 Mar. 1949

28 *Evening Telegram,* 4 Apr. 1949

29 Ibid., 9–11 Apr. 1949

30 St John's *Daily News,* 9–11 Apr. 1949

31 Ibid., 28 Apr. 1949

32 *Evening Telegram,* 12 and 28 Apr. 1949

33 Perlin argues that Smallwood had a profound understanding of the political culture of Newfoundland while his opponents did not. 'They were patronizing towards the outports ... addressed local elites from the authority of their status, and often as creditors to debtors,' but Smallwood 'accorded them the prestige of formal recognition [and] perceiv[ed] their instrumental role in opinion formation at the community level.' Nonetheless, Perlin argues that 'probably the decisive factor was the profound influence of the Canadian social security system, the benefits of which began to be felt in the province well in advance of the first general election.' See Perlin, 'Political Support in a Transitional Society,' 11–14.

34 *Evening Telegram,* 6 Jan. 1949; and NAC, CCF Papers, vol. 25, file Nfld General Correspondence, 1947–53, Leo Cousins to CCF, 13 Mar. 1949

35 See Gwyn, *Smallwood,* 100; Cashin, Horwood, and Harris, 'Newfoundland and Confederation,' 250–1; and MacKenzie, *Inside the Atlantic Triangle,* 203–4. Gregory Power, assistant campaign director in the Confederate Association, claims that Ray Petten's attempt to raise funds in Ottawa was unsuccessful until Power contacted Prime Minister King and told him that if the Confederates did not receive immediate financial assistance the struggle for union would have to be abandoned. Interview with G.J. Power, St John's, 23 July 1986. Bradley and Smallwood also wrote directly to C.D. Howe requesting additional funds: 'We need money desperately. Taking into account what we will raise locally, we must have at least another $20,000 ... We need it quickly.' NAC, C.D. Howe Papers, vol. 58, file 26 (1), Bradley and Smallwood to Howe, 21 June 1948

36 Rowe, *The Smallwood Era* 4–7

37 See Hiller, 'Career of F. Gordon Bradley.'

38 *Evening Telegram,* 7 Apr. 1948

39 Ibid., 7 Aug. 1948; and Pickersgill and Forster, eds, *The Mackenzie King Record*, 4: 360

40 MacKenzie, *Inside the Atlantic Triangle*, 174–5

41 NAC, Brooke Claxton Papers, vol. 114, file 2, J.S. Macdonald to the secretary of state for external affairs, 19 Mar. 1948; and NAC, R.A. MacKay Papers, vol. 6, files, 'Semi-official and Personal Correspondence,' and 'J.B. McEvoy, Personal Correspondence, 1948–49'

42 Bridle, ed., *Documents*, 1574

43 Smallwood, *I Chose Canada*, 322–3

44 NAC, Louis St Laurent Papers, vol. 59, file L–25–10, St Laurent to Walsh, 8 Mar. 1949

45 Ibid., vol. 223, file E–3–37–2, 'Memorandum for Prime Minister,' from J.W. Pickersgill, 9 Dec. 1948

46 *Evening Telegram*, 6 Jan. 1949, and NAC, CCF Papers, vol. 25, file Nfld General Correspondence, 1947–53, Cousins to CCF, 13 Mar. 1949

47 MUN, JRS Collection, file 3.10.024, Smallwood to Bradley, 4 Apr. 1949

48 Ibid., file 4.03.001, 'Liberal Party, Founding Convention, 194'; and Whitaker, *The Government Party*, 395

49 MUN, JRS Collection, file 4.01.006, 'Misc. Corresp.,' 1948–9

50 *Evening Telegram*, 25 Apr. 1949

51 Ibid., 28 Apr. 1949. Burnham Gill, editor of the Corner Brook *Western Star*, was on the train with the delegates. He recalls that both money and liquor flowed liberally. He estimates that one person had a pouch containing $50,000 to be distributed as needed. Interview, 27 Mar. 1990

52 *Evening Telegram*, 28 Apr. 1949; and *Daily News*, 29 Apr. 1949

53 MUN, JRS Collection, file 4.03.001, Smallwood to Angus L. Macdonald, John B. McNair, J. Walter Jones, 12 Apr. 1949; file 3.10.024, Smallwood to Bradley, 4 Apr. 1949, and *Daily News*, 26 and 28 Apr. 1949. See Horwood, *Joey, passim*.

54 For Cook's career, see Neary, *Newfoundland in the North Atlantic World, passim;* and Smallwood, ed., *The Encyclopedia of Newfoundland and Labrador*, 1: 515.

55 *Evening Telegram*, 2 May 1949

56 *Daily News*, 28 and 29 Apr. and 2 May 1949; Smallwood, *I Chose Canada*, 505–6. See also Horwood, *Joey*, 148–51.

57 Although most political parties had a recognized leader of the federal wing from each province, Bradley's election as federal leader seems an anomaly in Canadian politics.

58 See Pickersgill, *My Years with Louis St Laurent*, 91–2.

59 NAC, St Laurent Papers, vol. 75, file S–20–10, Bradley to St Laurent, 28 Apr. 1949

60 *Evening Telegram*, 20, 21, and 22 May 1949

61 NAC, PC Papers, vol. 177, file N–N–1, Furlong to Bell, 7 Apr. 1949
62 *Evening Telegram*, 20 Apr. 1949
63 Ibid., 26 Apr. 1949; and *Daily News*, 7 May 1949. The correspondent for the *Daily News* reported from Carbonear that the Conservative party launched its campaign in that town on 16 May, just eleven days before the balloting. *Daily News*, 25 May 1949
64 *Evening Telegram*, 28 Apr. 1949; and Browne, *Eighty-four Years a Newfoundlander*, 339. Throughout the campaign, the Tories continued to emphasize that the constitutional issues of 1948 were settled. 'The old issues are dead, we are now a part of Canada, and must now seek the best way to live as a province,' Mews said in Bell Island. See *Daily News*, 5 May 1949.
65 See Noel, *Politics in Newfoundland*, 279–80; and Neary, 'Party Politics in Newfoundland,' 207–8.
66 MUN, Higgins Collection, file 3.02.001, 'Drew's Speech on Newfoundland,' 7 Feb. 1949, delivered to Newfoundland households during May 1949
67 MUN, JRS Collection, 7.02.002, 'Speeches, 1949,' no date, but the speech was given just a few days before the provincial election.
68 *Evening Telegram*, 3, 13, and 14 May 1949; and NAC, PC Papers, vol. 177, file N–N–1, J.S. Currie to Bell, 20 May 1949
69 See Browne, *Eighty-four Years a Newfoundlander*, 380–1.
70 *Evening Telegram*, 14 and 20 Apr. 1949
71 PANL, Cashin Papers, box 1, 'Cashin's Radio Speeches, 1949'
72 NAC, PC Papers, vol. 177, file N–N–1, Mews to Bell, 30 Apr. 1949
73 *Evening Telegram*, 10 May 1949
74 Ibid., 12 May 1949
75 Ibid., 12 and 14 May 1949
76 Ibid., 5 May 1949
77 Correspondence with George Rowsell, Fortune, Newfoundland
78 *Evening Telegram*, 23 May 1949
79 *Daily News*, 21 Apr. 1949
80 William J. Keough, leader of the cooperative organizations on Newfoundland's west coast, was minister of cooperatives; Samuel J. Hefferton, vice-president of the Anglican Church College and president of the Newfoundland Teachers' Association was minister of education; Charles H. Ballam, past-president of the Federation of Labour, was minister of labour; Dr H.L. Pottle, minister of welfare, and H.W. Quinton, minister of health, had both been members of the Commission of Government; Michael J. Sinnott, chief magistrate at Placentia, became minister of public works; Gordon A. Winter, minister of finance, was the only merchant in the cabinet; Leslie Curtis, who became minister of justice, had been a law partner of Sir Richard Squires, former Lib-

eral prime minister; and former Confederate Philip F. Forsey was minister of home affairs. NAC, St Laurent Papers, vol. 59, file L–25–10, St Laurent to Walsh, 8 Mar. 1949

81 NAC, Howe Papers, vol. 59, file 6, 'Documents Submitted by Newfoundland, Canadian Government Office, St John's to Secretary of State for External Affairs, 4 April, 1949'

82 *Evening Telegram*, 25 Feb. 1949

83 MUN, JRS Collection, file 4.01.003, Smallwood to C.H. Ballam, 18 Dec. 1948; and *Evening Telegram*, 25 Feb., 14 Mar., 23 Mar., 29 Mar., 19 Apr. 1949

84 *Evening Telegram*, 22 Apr. 1949

85 Ibid., 19 Apr. 1949

86 Ibid., 9 May 1949

87 Ibid.

88 Ibid., 13, 14, and 21 May 1949 (reports from *Evening Telegram* correspondents)

89 Ibid., 25 May 1949

90 MUN, JRS Collection, file 4.00.001, John R. Courage to Smallwood, nd, but obviously during the campaign

91 Ibid., file 7.02.002, 'Speeches 1949'

92 See Horwood, *Joey*, 150.

93 *Daily News*, 29 Apr. 1949

94 *Evening Telegram*, 16 and 21 May 1949; and Gillespie, *A Class Act*, 93

95 MUN, JRS Collection, file 7.02.002, 'Speeches 1949.' Smallwood also told his audience: 'It's all for nothing. We don't have to pay for it, because the Government of Canada really gets it from the three very rich provinces of Ontario, Quebec, and British Columbia.'

96 MUN, Higgins Collection, file 3.01.307, 'Speeches'

97 MUN, JRS Collection, file 7.02.002, 'Speeches 1949'

98 NAC, St Laurent Papers, vol. 66, file P–30–10, vol. 1, Smallwood to St Laurent, 10 May 1949, and St Laurent to Smallwood, 20 May 1949

99 Ibid., vol. 75, file S–20–10, Bradley to St Laurent, 28 Apr. 1949

100 Ibid., vol. 66, file P–30–10, vol. 1, Walsh to St Laurent, 20 Apr. 1949; and *Evening Telegram*, 3 May 1949

101 *Evening Telegram*, 25 Apr., 27 Apr. and 2 May 1949

102 Ibid., 30 May 1949

103 Bridle, ed., *Documents*, 1590. The memo was written after Harris's visit to St John's, 13–15 Mar. 1949.

104 In the second referendum, responsible government polled more than 60 per cent of the vote in the two St John's ridings.

105 Independent Peter Cashin won in the district of Ferryland.

106 See Noel, *Politics in Newfoundland*, 279–80; Neary, 'Party Politics in New-foundland,' 207–8; and Matthews, 'Perspective on Recent Newfoundland Politics.'
107 Correspondence with George Rowsell, Fortune, Newfoundland
108 *Evening Telegram*, 30 May 1949; see Neary, 'Party Politics in Newfoundland,' 206–9
109 *Daily News*, 30 May 1949
110 Noel, *Politics in Newfoundland*, 283
111 *Evening Telegram*, 21 May, 25 and 26 June 1949; and Browne, *Eighty-seven Years a Newfoundlander*, 339–81
112 NAC, PC Papers, vol. 178, file N–N–1, Butt to W.H. Kidd, 19 Aug. 1950
113 Ibid., Butt to Kidd, 13 Dec. 1949
114 Ibid., vol. 178, file N–S–1, Gordon Higgins to W.H. Kidd, 1 Aug. 1952
115 NAC, Claxton Papers, vol. 17, Claxton to St Laurent, 21 July 1949
116 MUN, JRS Collection, file 4.03.003, Eric Cook to H.E. Kidd, 25 Mar. 1949
117 NAC, Liberal Papers, vol. 679, file 'Liberal Association of Newfoundland,' Kidd to Garland, 7 Dec. 1953; Garland replied 10 Dec. 1953.
118 Interview with Gregory Power, 23 July 1986
119 Interview with Chesley W. Carter, St John's, 26 June 1988. Smallwood and Petten corresponded regularly about the Newfoundland MPs in Ottawa. See MUN, JRS Collection, especially files 4.04.018 and 4.04.001.

CHAPTER 3 Sharing the wealth: Canadian social programs come to New-foundland

1 Newfoundland, *Budget Speech* of Honourable H.W. Quinton, minister of finance, 30 Nov. 1949
2 Horwood, *Joey*, 137
3 National Archives of Canada (NAC), Department of National Health and Welfare, vol. 38, file 35–2–0 pt 2, 'Minutes, Interdepartmental Committee on Newfoundland,' 19 Aug. 1949
4 Ibid., vol. 38, file 35–2–0, pt 1, Davidson to Pearson, 11 May 1948; Pearson to Davidson, 7 May 1948; and Escott Reid to Davidson, 30 May 1946
5 Ibid., 'Memorandum,' Curry to Martin, 11 Aug. 1948. For a brief history of family allowances in Canada, see Vadakin, *Family Allowances*, esp. 47–72.
6 NAC, National Health and Welfare, vol. 38, file 35–2–0, pt 3, 'Memorandum,' Curry to Martin, 11 Aug. 1948
7 Ibid., vol. 38, file 35–2–0, pt 3, Curry to Davidson, 30 Aug. 1948
8 Ibid., Curry to Martin, 11 Aug. 1948
9 Provincial Archives of Newfoundland and Labrador (PANL), Commission of

Government, s6–1–5A, no. 11, Paul Bridle to Quinton, 11 Oct. 1948, and Quinton to Bridle, 12 Oct. 1948

10 NAC, R.A. MacKay Papers, vol. 3, file ICCNR Apr. 1948 – May 1949, Curry to J.E. Howes, 14 Oct. 1948

11 NAC, National Health and Welfare, vol. 38, file 35–2–0, pt 3, Davidson to Martin, 15 Oct. 1948

12 Ibid.

13 Ibid.

14 PANL, Sir Albert Walsh Papers, file 5, 'Memorandum Submitted by Newfoundland Delegation to Ottawa,' Oct. 1948; and NAC, National Health and Welfare, vol. 2358, file 260–1–1 (Nfld), 'Memorandum' from Curry to all regional directors, 12 Jan. 1949

15 Ibid., Davidson to Martin, 15 Oct. 1948

16 Ibid., vol. 38, file 35–2–0, pts. 1 and 2, Pett to Dr G.D.W. Cameron, 24 Aug. 1948

17 Most regional centres had banks and, if parents wished to save their family allowance, they made deposits through the post office. See Canada, Department of National Health and Welfare, *Annual Report*, 1950.

18 NAC, National Health and Welfare, vol. 38, file 35–2–0, pt 3, Davidson to Martin, 15 Oct. 1948

19 NAC, MacKay Papers, vol. 3, file ICCNR Apr. 1948 – May 1949, Curry to Howes, 14 Oct. 1948

20 Bridle, ed., *Documents*, 1773–5

21 NAC, National Health and Welfare, vol. 38, file 35–2–0, pt 3, Davidson to Reid, 30 Nov. 1948. On 16 Dec. 1948, Pearson wrote to St Laurent: 'You will recall that the Minister of National Health and Welfare has already been given authority in respect of family allowances only.' See Bridle, ed., *Documents*, 1782–3.

22 NAC, National Health and Welfare, vol. 38, file 35–2–0 pt 3, Davidson to Reid, 30 Nov. 1948; and Acc. 82–83/52, box 2, file 260–1–1 (Nfld), Bridle to Pearson, 17 Dec. 1948

23 St John's *Daily News*, 18 Dec. 1948; and NAC, Louis St Laurent Papers, vol. 61, file N–19–2, Burchell to St Laurent, 29 Jan. 1949

24 See Carl Abbott, 'Family Allowances and Old Age Security,' in Smallwood, ed., *The Book of Newfoundland*, 253–5.

25 *Daily News*, 22 Dec. 1948

26 St John's *Evening Telegram*, 23 Dec. 1948

27 Grand Falls *Advertiser*, 29 Jan. 1949

28 NAC, National Health and Welfare, vol. 38, file 35–2–0, pt 3, 'Memorandum,' Curry to Martin, 11 Aug. 1948

29 NAC, MacKay Papers, vol. 3, file, ICCNR Sept. 1948–May 1949, J.T. Marshall to Howes, 27 Nov. 1948; Marshall to Howes, 20 Sept. 1948; and H.G. Page to C.H. Tobin, 22 Jan. 1949; and NAC, National Health and Welfare, vol. 38, file 35–2–0, pt 3, Davidson to Martin, 15 Oct. 1948

30 Rice, a native Newfoundlander, had resigned his position as district treasury officer for the Unemployment Insurance Commission in London to become district treasury officer of family allowances for Newfoundland. After a brief training period at the Toronto office and an orientation at Ottawa, Rice assumed control of preparing the Newfoundland cheques in Halifax.

31 NAC, National Health and Welfare, vol. 2359, file 260–1–11, pt 1, T.F. Phillips, chief treasury officer, to Rice, 28 June 1949

32 Ibid., Curry to Hoganson, 4 Apr. 1949

33 Port Union *Fishermen's Advocate*, 16 May 1949. Similar reports came from other communities: the *Daily News*, Lewisporte Notes, reported that 'Many homes were brighter a short while ago, when the first family allowances was received ... to all it is very acceptable and gratefully received,' 14 May 1949. See also the *Newfoundland Journal of Commerce* 16, no. 4 (Sept. 1949).

34 *Evening Telegram*, 14 May 1949

35 NAC, National Health and Welfare, vol. 2361, file 264–1–17, pt 1, Parsons to Curry, 14 May 1949; and interview with Carl Abbott, 28 Mar. 1990

36 In her biography of George Nowlan, Margaret Conrad suggests that federal social programs such as family allowances and unemployment insurance introduced during the 1940s paid big dividends for provincial parties, since most people did not distinguish between the federal and provincial wings of federal parties. Conrad, *George Nowlan*, 76–7

37 Canada, National Health and Welfare, *Annual Report*, 1955. For a discussion of changes in Newfoundland society since union see Noel, *Politics in Newfoundland* 262–78.

38 *Daily News*, 2 May 1949. See Rowe, *Education and Culture in Newfoundland;* Andrews, *Post-Confederation Developments in Newfoundland Education;* and Frederick Kirby, 'Education since 1949 and a Forecast,' in Smallwood, ed., *The Book of Newfoundland*, 179–83.

39 NAC, Brooke Claxton Papers, vol. 117, Claxton to St Laurent, 21 July 1949

40 NAC, Department of Labour, vol. 836, file 1–31, vol. 1, Mitchell to Pelletier, 16 Oct. 1948

41 For the introduction of Canadian unemployment insurance in 1940, see Struthers, *No Fault of Their Own*.

42 NAC, Department of Labour, vol. 836, file 1–31, vol. 1, 'Memorandum prepared for the Commission' by Laberge, 21 Oct. 1948; and file 1–2–2–25, pt 1, 'Memorandum' prepared by R.G. Barclay, 4 Oct. 1948

43 Ibid., 'Memorandum,' McCord to MacNamara, 8 Nov. 1948

44 Ibid., 'Memorandum prepared for the Commission' by Laberge, 21 Oct. 1948; file 1–2–2–25, pt 1, 'Memorandum' prepared by R.G. Barclay, 4 Oct. 1948; file 1–31, pt 1, 'Memorandum,' McCord to MacNamara, 8 Nov. 1948; Acc. 83–84/351, box 13, file 10300–J–40, pt 1, 'Minutes, Subcommittee on the Organization of Administrative Services,' 23 Oct. 1948; and NAC, MacKay Papers, vol. 3, file ICCNR, Sept. 1948–May 1949, Bisson to Howes, 18 Oct. 1948

45 NAC, Department of Labour, vol. 836, file 1–31, pt 1, 'Memorandum,' McCord to MacNamara, 8 Nov. 1948

46 See N.S. Batten, 'Unemployment Insurance in Newfoundland,' in Smallwood, ed., *The Book of Newfoundland*, 255–8.

47 NAC, Department of Labour, vol. 836, file 1–31, pt 2, Bisson to Humphrey Mitchell, 24 Jan. 1949

48 NAC, Unemployment Insurance Commission, vol. 25, file 1–2–2–25, pt 1, 'Memorandum' prepared by Barclay for the Commission, 15 Jan. 1949; and Bisson to regional supervisor, 17 Jan. 1949

49 *Advertiser*, 26 Feb. 1949

50 NAC, Unemployment Insurance Commission, vol. 25, file 1–2–2–25, pt 2, R.H. Sims to Laberge, 31 Mar. 1949. S.B. O'Brien, staff trainer with the Maritime Region, was in charge of the training at Corner Brook.

51 Ibid., vol. 25, file 1–2–2–25, pt 1, Coy to Hartley, 28 Feb. 1949

52 Ibid., file 1–2–2–25, pt 2, Curry to Barclay, 2 Mar. 1949

53 Ibid.

54 NAC, Department of Finance, vol. 3912, file 5765–2, pt 2, 'Memorandum, Unemployment Assistance Payments in Newfoundland,' 1 Mar. 1949

55 NAC, Unemployment Insurance Commission, vol. 25, file 1–2–2–25, pt 2, Barclay to Curry, 14 Mar. 1949; Curry to Barclay, 19 Mar. 1949; and Curry to Barclay, 30 Mar. 1949. A. Burden and J.G. O'Grady were appointed as managers of the Grand Falls and St John's offices respectively.

56 Canada, Department of Labour, *Labour Gazette* 46, no. 4 (Apr. 1949), 395

57 NAC, Unemployment Insurance Commission, vol. 25, file 1–2–2–25, pt 2, Curry to Barclay, 6 Apr. 1949; Curry to Grant, 8 Apr. 1949; and Hartley to McLaren, 17 Apr. 1949

58 Newfoundland, *Budget Speech*, 1949

59 NAC, Unemployment Insurance Commission, vol. 25, file 1–2–2–25, pt 2, Curry to Barclay, 6 Apr. 1949; Curry to Horace Grant, 8 Apr. 1949; and Hartley to S.H. McLaren, 17 Apr. 1949. See Centre for Newfoundland Studies, Memorial University of Newfoundland Archives (MUN), Joseph R. Smallwood (JRS) Collection, file 3.18.004.

60 NAC, Privy Council Office (PCO), vol. 199, file U–11–J, 'Unemployment – New-

foundland,' Mitchell to D.C. Abbott and Norman A. Robertson, 21 Mar. 1950; *Evening Telegram*, 3 May 1949; and *Daily News*, 11 May 1949

61 NAC, St Laurent Papers, vol. 29, file R–21, 'Employment Conditions in Newfoundland,' report prepared by the Department of Labour, 1 Nov. 1949

62 Smallwood, *I Chose Canada*, 338

63 PANL, Department of Natural Resources, file 611–29, vol. 1, C.H. Ballam to O'Grady; 'Memorandum' from Ballam to all Newfoundland cabinet ministers, 1 Nov. 1949; and NAC, PCO, vol. 199, file U–11–J, 'Unemployment – Newfoundland,' Mitchell to Abbott and Robertson, 21 Mar. 1950

64 Ibid.

65 *Evening Telegram*, 15 Mar. 1950. Premier Smallwood was quoted as saying, 'From the Standpoint of the amount of work done and the money received by those on relief, the program was startlingly successful ... [but the program] was too rich for our blood.'

66 Canada, Unemployment Insurance Commission, *Annual Reports*, 1949–55

67 MUN, JRS Collection, file 3.18.004, Pottle to Gregg, 25 Mar. 1955

68 NAC, National Health and Welfare, vol. 38, file 35–2–0, pt 3, Davidson to Martin, 15 Oct. 1948

69 Ibid., vol. 145, file 208–6–0, J.W. MacFarlane to R.E. Curran, 9 Oct. 1948

70 See Bryden, *Old Age Pensions*.

71 Ibid.

72 Bridle, ed., *Documents*, 1235–7; and NAC, PCO, Cabinet Conclusions, 8 Dec. 1948

73 Canada, House of Commons, *Debates*, 10 Feb. 1949, 449–51

74 NAC, PCO, Cabinet Conclusions, 11 Feb. 1949

75 NAC, PCO, vol. 130, file N–18 1949 (Jan.–Mar.); and Bridle, ed., *Documents*, 1792

76 Canada, House of Commons, *Debates*, 17 Feb. 1949, 636–7

77 Neary, *Newfoundland in the North Atlantic World*, 275

78 See Channing, *Effects of Transition to Confederation*, 53–4. Channing was a career civil servant in the Newfoundland public service beginning with the Commission of Government in 1934 and retiring as deputy minister of the Office of the Premier in 1978. His book is a brief overview of the changes he witnessed in the Newfoundland public service throughout this time. In fact, the title is somewhat misleading, as he does not deal in any great detail with the effect of union on public administration in Newfoundland.

79 MUN, JRS Collection, file 3.29.001, Pottle to Davidson, 21 Apr. 1949; and Smallwood to Pottle, 26 Apr. 1949

80 Ibid.

81 NAC, National Health and Welfare, vol. 131, file 208–5–0, pt 2, Swettenham to

Davidson, 26 Apr. 1949; Davidson to Swettenham, 26 Apr. 1949; and NAC, PCO, Cabinet Conclusions, 4 May 1949

82 NAC, National Health and Welfare, vol. 131, file 208–5–0, pt 2, Swettenham to MacFarlane, 25 Apr. 1949; and *Evening Telegram*, 29 Apr. 1949 and 22 May 1949

83 NAC, National Health and Welfare, vol. 131, file 208–5–0, pt.2, Swettenham to MacFarlane, 28 Apr. 1949; Swettenham to MacFarlane, 2 May 1949; and Swettenham to MacFarlane, 5 May 1949

84 Ibid. This is an interesting point and one worthy of further study. Andrews, *Post-Confederation Developments in Newfoundland Education*, 24–5

85 NAC, National Health and Welfare, vol. 131, file 208–5–0, pt 2, Swettenham to MacFarlane, 11 May 1949

86 There was such a large number of new applicants because the qualifying age was lowered from seventy-five to seventy years of age.

87 NAC, National Health and Welfare, vol. 131, file 208–5–0, pt 2, MacFarlane to Swettenham, 19 May 1949

88 Ibid., Swettenham to MacFarlane, 24 May 1949. See *Evening Telegram*, 27 Apr. and 4 May 1949.

89 PANL, Department of Finance (Newfoundland), file 204.01. 'Broadcasting, 1949–53,' broadcast given by F.W. Rowe, 20 Oct. 1949

90 NAC, National Health and Welfare, vol. 131, file 208–5–0, pt 2, 'Memorandum' from MacFarlane to Davidson, 18 Jan. 1950; and 'Memorandum' from Mac-Farlane to Davidson, 13 June 1949

91 Ibid., MacFarlane to Roberts, 30 Jan. 1950

92 Ibid., MacFarlane to V.D. McElary, 10 June 1950

93 Ibid., Pottle to Davidson, 17 Feb. 1950; and McElary to MacFarlane, 1 June 1950 (Included in the McElary letter is a memo on the matter from the Newfoundland Old Age Pension Board.)

94 Ibid., Davidson to Pottle, 27 June 1950

95 Ibid., Davidson to Pottle, 14 Dec. 1950

CHAPTER 4 Going it alone: the federal government and secondary manufacturing in Newfoundland, 1948–1953

1 Provincial Archives of Newfoundland and Labrador (PANL), Records of the National Convention, box 1, file 10, 'Memorandum Concerning Secondary Manufacturing Industries in Newfoundland,' Prepared by the Associated Newfoundland Industries (ANI) Limited for Presentation to the Newfoundland Delegation, Sept. 1948; and National Archives of Canada (NAC), Depart-

ment of National Health and Welfare, Acc. 82–3/52, box 2, file 260–1–1 (Nfld), 'Newfoundland Reference Bulletin No. 3, Background Data, re Population, Government, Resources, and Industries, etc.,' Sept. 1948

2 Statistics on individual enterprises could not be located for the period of this study. This number comes from *The Newfoundland Market* (Montreal 1949), 10–12.

3 In 1946, Canadian manufacturing industries (with the exception of pulp and paper and fish curing) had a gross production value of $458 per capita. The manufacturing industries of Newfoundland had a gross production of $102 per person compared with Nova Scotia's $233 and New Brunswick's $251. See Donald, Ross and Co., *Industrial Survey*, 100–20.

4 See Yannopoulos, 'Development of the Newfoundland Economy since Confederation.'

5 PANL, National Convention, box 1, file 10, Angel to Walsh, 6 Aug. 1948

6 Ibid., 'Memorandum Concerning Secondary Manufacturing Industries in Newfoundland,' prepared by the ANI for presentation to the Newfoundland Delegation, Sept. 1948

7 Centre for Newfoundland Studies, Memorial University of Newfoundland Archives (MUN), Joseph R. Smallwood (JRS) Collection, file 4.01.005, 'Newfoundland Delegation, Minutes of Meetings,' 10 Sept. 1948

8 PANL, National Convention, box 1, file 10, 'Memorandum Concerning Secondary Manufacturing Industries in Newfoundland,' prepared by the ANI for presentation to the Newfoundland Delegation, Sept. 1948

9 PANL, Sir Albert Walsh Papers, box 2, file 9, H.T. Renouf to Walsh, 13 Aug. 1948, and 'Memorandum by the Newfoundland Board of Trade to the Newfoundland Delegation,' 16 Sept. 1948

10 Ibid., box 1, file 5, 'Memorandum Submitted by Newfoundland Delegation to Ottawa,' Oct. 1948

11 Bridle, ed., *Documents*, 1184, 1218, 1221, 1225, 1708–9; and NAC, C.D. Howe Papers, vol. 57, file 26, W.F. Bull to Howe, 23 Nov. 1948

12 NAC, Howe Papers, vol. 59, file 26, 'Survey of the Implications of Confederation for Secondary Industries in Newfoundland and Comments on Potential Industrial Development,' 23 Nov. 1948

13 Ibid.

14 Ibid., 'Memorandum on the Probable Effects of Confederation on the Secondary Manufacturing Industries of Newfoundland, A Supplementary Submission on Behalf of ANI,' 24 Nov. 1948

15 NAC, Privy Council Office (PCO), vol. 130, file N–18–1, 'Newfoundland, 1948–9,' Howe to St Laurent, 27 Nov. 1948

16 Bothwell and Kilbourn, *C.D. Howe*, 189, 206–7, and 237

17 NAC, PCO, vol. 130, file N–18–1, 'Newfoundland, 1948–9,' 'Memorandum, re Newfoundland's Secondary Industries,' 8 Dec. 1948; and Howe to St Laurent, 27 Nov. 1948

18 Channing, *Effects of Transition to Confederation*, 41

19 Canada, Department of External Affairs, *Report and Documents*, 39–40

20 Bridle, ed., *Documents*, 1184, 1218, 1221, 1225, 1708–9; and NAC, Howe Papers, vol. 57, file 26, Bull to Howe, 23 Nov. 1948

21 PANL, Walsh Papers, box 2, file 1, 'Memorandum re Local Manufacturing Industries in Newfoundland,' nd

22 NAC, PCO, vol. 130, file N–18–1, 'Nfld Industries, 1948–49,' 'Memorandum re Newfoundland's Secondary Industries,' 8 Dec. 1948

23 PANL, Governor's Office, file 1/48, 'National Convention – Confederation, Governor's Office,' Crosbie to governor of Newfoundland, 9 Feb. 1949

24 MUN, JRS Collection, file 4.01.005, 'Newfoundland Delegation, Minutes of Meetings,' 10 Sept. 1948

25 NAC, Howe Papers, vol. 59, file 26, folder 7, Campbell Smith to Bull, 27 Jan. 1949

26 Ibid., file 26, folder 8, Bull to Howe, 23 Nov. 1948

27 Ibid., Howe to Bull, 14 Feb. 1949

28 Ibid., vol. 59, file 26, folder 7, Bull to T.M. Beaupre, executive assistant to Howe, 1 Feb. 1949, and vol. 59, file 26, folder 8, 'Survey of Implications of Confederation for Secondary Industries in Newfoundland and Comments on Potential Industrial Development,' 23 Nov. 1948

29 *Newfoundland Journal of Commerce* 15, no. 3 (Mar. 1949)

30 Ibid. During Howe's visit, Bowring Brothers, one of the oldest business firms in Newfoundland, issued an open letter to the minister in which they called for an adjustment period to allow local firms to find their feet in a new environment: 'Mr. Howe, this is a small Island and we must necessarily be at a disadvantage when we first enter the Canadian scene. We will be like a new boy during his first term at school and we do not want to be knocked around any more than is necessary. It won't take long to learn … but first we must pass through this difficult period of transition and you are one of the people who can help us.' St John's *Evening Telegram*, 5 Feb. 1949

31 NAC, Howe Papers, vol. 59, file 5, Angel to Howe, 16 Feb. 1949

32 See Cuff and Granatstein, *American Dollars – Canadian Prosperity*, 44–63.

33 *Newfoundland Journal of Commerce* 16, no. 5 (May 1949), 16, no. 7 (July 1949), and 19, no. 10 (Oct. 1952)

34 *Financial Post*, 4 June 1949 and 3 June 1950

35 I do not discuss freight rates here. The issue was a contentious one after union, and Newfoundland joined with the other Atlantic provinces to argue

its case for lower rates in Ottawa. See Forbes, *Challenging the Regional Stereotype*, 114–47, and Newfoundland, *Report of the Royal Commission on Transportation*.

36 NAC, Howe Papers, vol. 59, file 26, folder 7, A.D.P. Heeney to Howe, 18 Jan. 1949

37 Bridle, ed., *Documents*, 1730–2; and NAC, PCO, Cabinet Conclusions, 13 Jan. 1949

38 Bridle, ed., *Documents*, 1730–2

39 NAC, R.A. MacKay Papers, vol. 4, file ICCNR–Secondary Industries, 1949–51, 'Minutes of Interdepartmental Sub-Committee on Newfoundland Secondary Industries and Purchasing,' 7 Mar. 1949

40 Ibid., 9 May 1949

41 At a later meeting, R.M. Bullock from the Department of Reconstruction and Supply made a similar claim. NAC, PCO, vol. 130, file N–18–1, 'Nfld Industries, 1948–9,' 'Minutes of Interdepartmental Sub-Committee on Newfoundland Secondary Industries and Purchasing,' 3 Aug. 1949

42 Newfoundland, *Report of the Royal Commission on the Cost of Living in Newfoundland*, 85–8

43 NAC, PCO, vol. 130, file N–18–1, 'Nfld Industries, 1948–9,' Smith to D.M. McDonald, secretary, Interdepartmental Sub-Committee, Secondary Industries and Purchasing, 30 June 1949

44 Ibid.

45 Canadian products were available in Newfoundland long before union, but the removal of the tariff on 1 Apr. 1949 made them much cheaper. In fact, more than 50 per cent of all imports came from Canada. The average import duty on those goods was 25 per cent. See PANL, National Convention, box 1, file 12, Renouf to Channing, 17 Sept. 1948, and 'Memorandum by the Newfoundland Board of Trade to the Newfoundland Delegation,' 16 Sept. 1948.

46 NAC, PCO, vol. 130, file N–18–1, 'Nfld Industries, 1948–9,' Smith to McDonald, 21 Apr. 1949

47 Ibid., 'Minutes of Meeting, Interdepartmental Sub-Committee on Newfoundland Secondary Industries and Purchasing,' 3 Aug. 1949

48 NAC, Department of Finance, vol. 778, file 201–13–3, McDonald to Mitchell Sharp, 8 Aug. 1949, and NAC, PCO, Cabinet Conclusions, 17 Aug. 1949

49 NAC, PCO, vol. 130, file N–18–1, 'Newfoundland Industries, 1948–49,' 'Memorandum for Prime Minister' by N.A. Robertson, 22 Aug. 1949

50 NAC, Department of Trade and Commerce, vol. 947, file 7–657, pt 8, Mallory to Bull, 15 Nov. 1949

51 NAC, MacKay Papers, vol. 4, file ICCNR – Secondary Industry, 1949–51, Angel to McDonald, 11 Mar. 1950; MUN, JRS Collection, file 3.08.045, Renouf to Smallwood, 10 Mar. 1951; and NAC, PCO, Cabinet Conclusions, 25 Mar. 1950

52 NAC, PCO, vol. 172, file N–18–1, 'Newfoundland Industries 1949–51,' White to McDonald, 15 Mar. 1950

53 Ibid., 'Minutes of Interdepartmental Sub-Committee on Newfoundland Secondary Industries and Purchasing,' 17 Mar. 1949

54 NAC, MacKay Papers, vol. 4, file 4, ICCNR – Secondary Industry, 1949–51,' 'Memorandum' prepared by Bull for the cabinet, 22 Mar. 1950

55 MUN, JRS Collection, file 3.08.045, 'Request for Continuation of the Fifteen Percent Preference to Newfoundland Secondary Industries Tendering on Federal Contracts,' submitted by ANI, 2 Mar. 1951

56 NAC, Howe Papers, vol. 4, file ICCNR – Secondary Industries, 1949–51, 'Minutes of Interdepartmental Sub-Committee on Newfoundland Secondary Industries and Purchasing,' 12 Mar. 1951, 'Memorandum Prepared by W.F. Bull on the Continuation of Assistance to Newfoundland Secondary Industries for the Cabinet,' 16 Mar. 1951; and NAC, PCO, Cabinet Conclusions, 21 Mar. 1951

57 NAC, Department of Finance, vol. 778, file 201–13–3, Smallwood to St Laurent, 14 Feb. 1952

58 NAC, PCO, vol. 228, file P–100–1–N, Howe to St Laurent, 28 Feb. 1952, and St Laurent to Smallwood, 15 Mar. 1952

59 Interview with J.B. Angel, 4 Aug. 1949; and NAC, MacKay Papers, vol. 4, file ICCNR – Secondary Industry, 1949–51, 'Minutes of Interdepartmental Sub-Committee on Newfoundland Secondary Industries and Purchasing,' 7 Mar. 1949

60 MUN, JRS Collection, file 3.10.028, Smallwood to Howe, 5 Oct. 1949, and Howe to Smallwood, 13 Oct. 1949

61 NAC, PCO, vol. 172, file N–18–1, 'Newfoundland Industries, 1950–51,' 'Minutes of Meeting of Interdepartmental Sub-Committee on Newfoundland Secondary Industries and Purchasing,' 17 Mar. 1950

62 MUN, JRS Collection, file 3.07.041, Angel to Smallwood, 4 May 1951; Smallwood to Howe, 4 May 1951; and Howe to Smallwood, 8 May 1951. In a subsequent letter to Smallwood, Howe reminded him of the special assistance Angel had received: 'The Island's nail firms, I am sure you will agree, have received assistance of an exceptional character during this [transitional] period. However, this type of assistance could only be a temporary expedient, since trade must flow freely throughout the Dominion.' Howe to Smallwood, 19 June 1951

63 Ibid., file 3.07.041, H.G. Hilton, president of Stelco, to Smallwood, 23 July 1951

64 Newfoundland, *Report of the Royal Commission on the Cost of Living in Newfoundland*, 85

65 Interview with Angel, 4 Aug. 1988

66 Smallwood, *I Chose Canada*, 346

67 NAC, Department of Trade and Commerce, vol. 947, file 7–657, pt 8, 'Supple-

ment to the Bull Report on Implications of Confederation for Secondary Industries in Newfoundland and Comments on Potential Industrial Development,' 15 Nov. 1949

68 See Newfoundland, *Budget Speech*, 30 Nov. 1949 and 26 Apr. 1950.

69 MUN, JRS Collection, file 3.08.031, Angel to Smallwood, 19 Nov. 1949; file 3.08.045, Eric White to Smallwood, 8 Dec. 1950; and file 7.02.004, New Year's Broadcast 1951

70 Ibid., file 3.08.097, A.L. Graudins to R. Rieker, 21 Dec. 1951

71 The Colonial Cordage Company expanded its operation after Confederation and began to market its products in the Maritime provinces. The same was true of United Nail and Foundry. See Perlin, *Story of Newfoundland*, 203–5.

72 MUN, JRS Collection, file 3.08.032, Gordon Pushie to L. MacIsaac, 25 Apr. 1953

73 *Newfoundland Journal of Commerce* 18, no. 1 (Jan. 1951), and *Evening Telegram*, 28 June 1950. Donald Jamieson was appointed director.

74 *Newfoundland Journal of Commerce* 17, no. 1 (Jan. 1950), and 17, no. 4 (Apr. 1950)

75 Ibid., 18, no. 1 (Jan. 1951)

76 *Financial Post*, 3 June 1950

77 *Newfoundland Journal of Commerce* 22, no. 8 (Aug. 1955), 7. The *Journal* reported that a representative from the packaged meat industry claimed that 'Confederation made us sharper operators. We've modernized our plant, [and] learned cheaper ways of producing.'

78 Ibid., 18, no. 1 (Jan. 1951); and *Evening Telegram*, 28 June 1950

79 See, Canada, *Report of the Royal Commission on Newfoundland Finances* 90.

80 *Newfoundland Journal of Commerce* 22, no. 8 (Aug. 1955), 8

81 Yannopoulos, 'Development of the Newfoundland Economy since Confederation,' 247

82 See *Submission of Newfoundland Branch of the Canadian Manufacturers' Association to the Royal Commission on Canada's Economic Prospects*, 9–12. The *Submission* gives a list of the old established secondary industries in Newfoundland, and it is not significantly different from a 1949 inventory of industries. Newfoundland manufacturers joined the Canadian Manufacturers Association on 1 Dec. 1953.

83 The percentages are calculated from Atlantic Provinces Economic Council, *Atlantic Provinces Statistical Review*, 1970.

84 See Neary, 'The Supreme Court of Canada'; and Reader, *Bowater*.

85 Grand Falls *Advertiser*, 26 Nov. 1949, and *Financial Post*, 3 June 1950

86 There were three other companies in addition to Bowater that enjoyed certain tax privileges from the Newfoundland government: the United Towns Electric Company, Dominion Iron and Nova Scotia Steel Companies, and

Bell Island Transportation Company. I concentrate on Bowater, as that company lobbied hardest for the continuation of its privileges after union.

87 PANL, Walsh Papers, box 1, file 5, 'Memorandum Submitted by Newfoundland Delegation to Ottawa,' Oct. 1948, 6

88 Bridle, ed., *Documents*, 1214–15; and NAC, Department of External Affairs, Acc. 83–84/351, box 11, file 10300–40, pt 2, 'Notes for Conversation with Sir Alexander Clutterbuck on Newfoundland Negotiations,' prepared by R.A. MacKay, 17 Nov. 1948

89 Bridle, ed., *Documents*, 1214–15

90 Ibid., 1159, 1214–15

91 Public Records Office (PRO), London, Dominion Office Records (DO) 35, 3470, Bowater to Noel-Baker, 7 Dec. 1948

92 NAC, PCO, vol. 173, file N–18–9, Lewin to St Laurent, 24 Nov. 1948; and NAC, St Laurent Papers, vol. 61, file N–19–2, Bowater to St Laurent, 22 Dec. 1948

93 Ibid., vol. 61, file N–19–2, Bowater to St Laurent, 22 Dec. 1948; St Laurent to Bowater, 23 Dec. 1948; and NAC, Department of Finance, vol. 701, file 201–13–3–1, Bowater to St Laurent, 23 Dec. 1948

94 PRO, DO 35/3470, R.L. James to H.N. Tait, 30 Nov. 1948

95 Ibid., Bowater to Noel-Baker, 7 Dec. 1948, Memo attached; and C.G.L. Syers to Gordon-Walker, 23 Dec. 1948

96 PRO, DO 114/103, (No. 450), Syers to Clutterbuck, 1 Jan. 1949

97 Ibid., 114/103: 272–3, telegram from acting high commissioner in Canada, 8 Sept. 1949

98 Ibid., (No. 451), telegram to Commonwealth Relations Office (CRO) from high commissioner in Canada, 18 Jan. 1949

99 NAC, PCO, vol. 173, file N–18–9, Clutterbuck to St Laurent, 17 Jan. 1949. Clutterbuck sent Abbott a copy of this letter, and he also spoke to Pearson about it. See NAC, Department of Finance, vol. 701, file 201–13–3–1, Pearson to St Laurent, 18 Jan. 1949, and Clutterbuck to Abbott, 17 Jan. 1949

100 NAC, PCO, vol. 173, file N–18–9, St Laurent to Clutterbuck, 24 Jan. 1949

101 NAC, External Affairs, Acc. 83–4/351, box 14, file 10519–40, Clutterbuck to Pearson, 1 Feb. 1949

102 NAC, PCO, vol. 173, file N–18–9, Pickersgill to Pearson, 8 Feb. 1949

103 PRO, DO 35/3470, CRO memorandum, 22 Mar. 1949

104 NAC, External Affairs, Acc. 83–84/351, box 14, file 10519–40, pt 1, Clutterbuck to Abbott, 8 Apr. 1949

105 NAC, Department of Finance, vol. 701, file 201–13–3–1, Abbott to C.G. Heward, 8 Apr. 1949

106 PRO, DO 35/3470: 33, 'Memorandum' by J.S. Gandee, CRO, 22 Sept. 1949; PANL, Department of Justice, box 389, file 55(1), G.W.R. Morley to L.R. Cur-

tis, 5 Oct. 1949; and NAC, Department of Finance, vol. 701, file 201–13–3–1,
Heward, Holden, Hutchison, Cliff, Meredith and Ballantyne (law firm representing Bowater), to Abbott, 17 Nov. 1949

107 NAC, Department of Finance, vol. 4765, file 5600–03(47)–3/308, pt 1, Varcoe
to Abbott, 15 Oct. 1949

108 Ibid., vol. 701, file 201–13–3–1, D.H.W. Henry to Mitchell Sharp, 29 Nov.
1949. For a thorough treatment of the court case, see Neary, 'Supreme Court
of Canada.'

109 PANL, Department of Justice (Nfld), box 389, file 55(2), 'Factum of the Attorney General of Newfoundland in the Supreme Court of Canada'; and Toronto
Globe and Mail, 28 Feb. 1950

110 Halifax Chronicle-Herald, 10 June 1950

111 NAC, PCO, The Canadian Abridgement, vol. 7 (Toronto 1967), 61–2

112 NAC, PCO, vol. 173, file N–18–9, 'Written Judgement of the Chief Justice,' 24–7

113 Ibid., 'Written Judgement of Justice R. Taschereau,' 8; see Dupré, 'Fiscal Policy in Newfoundland, 124–6.

114 NAC, PCO, vol. 173, file N–18–9, Bowater to St Laurent, 29 Sept. 1950

115 Ibid., Currie to St Laurent, 3 Apr., 1951; and NAC, St Laurent Papers, vol. 163,
file 1–20–5–B, Pickersgill to Currie, 5 Oct. 1951

CHAPTER 5 Canada establishes sovereignty in Newfoundland, 1948–1952

1 Bridle, ed., Documents, 1847–8

2 Canada, House of Commons, Debates, 16 Nov. 1949. The British government
was particularly incensed that Canada refused to consider aviation agreements as conferring proprietary rights. It had granted traffic rights at Gander
to eleven national airlines in exchange for concessions elsewhere that benefited British airlines. Pearson, too, realized the importance of Gander and
planned to use it to full Canadian advantage. Although Ottawa extended
the rights held by airlines using Gander to 1 July 1949, the Canadian government eventually negotiated new bilateral aviation agreements that won major
benefits for Canadian airlines. Gander was the Canadian ace in civil aviation.

3 See Bridle, ed., Documents, 1839–54.

4 See Stacey, Canada and the Age of Conflict, 360–1. By the end of the war, the
United States had a strong presence in the Canadian North, though Arnold
Heeney, clerk of the Privy Council, recalls that Ottawa was unaware of the
extent and nature of American intrusions into Canada. Stacey adds that
King was willing to share facilities with the Americans but not give them
leases to Canadian territory. On this subject see Heeney, The Things That Are
Caesar's, 71–2; and Granatstein, Canada's War, 321–5.

5 On this point see Bercuson, 'SAC vs Sovereignty,' 214–22. Bercuson suggests that Canadian control over U.S. forces was more *de jure* than *de facto*. See also Barry, ed., *Documents* 1137–8.

6 National Archives of Canada (NAC), Brooke Claxton Papers, vol. 116, file 5, Pearson to Wrong, 6 Jan. 1949

7 For a discussion of the Visiting Forces Acts, see Stacey, *Arms, Men and Governments*, 210–12.

8 See Cardoulis, *A Friendly Invasion.*

9 NAC, Louis St Laurent Papers, vol. 235, Pearson to St Laurent, 9 Feb. 1949

10 Canadian Institute of Public Opinion, Gallup Poll of Canada, 10 Mar. 1948

11 NAC, Claxton Papers, vol. 116, file 5, Pearson to Wrong, 6 Jan. 1949. Pearson had written in a 1946 issue of *Foreign Affairs* that Canadians would cooperate with the United States in matters of defence, but that the Americans would have to respect Canadian sovereignty. See Jockel, *No Boundaries Upstairs*, 2.

12 Bridle, ed., *Documents*, 1898–9

13 See Pearson, *Mike*, 211–20; and English, *Shadow of Heaven*, 257–66.

14 NAC, Claxton Papers, vol. 116, file 5, Pearson to Wrong, 6 Jan. 1949

15 NAC, Department of External Affairs, Acc 89–90/029, box 27, file 17 D(s), file pocket, 'Text of Joint Statement Issued in Ottawa and Washington,' 12 Feb. 1947; 'Text of Supplementary Statement by Prime Minister of Canada made in House of Commons on Defence Cooperation with the United States,' 12 Feb. 1947; and NAC, Claxton Papers, vol. 116, file 5, Claxton to Pearson, 28 Oct. 1948

16 Ibid.

17 NAC, External Affairs, Acc. 83–84/351, box 13, file 10477–A–40, pt 2, Heeney to Wrong, 12 Feb. 1951

18 National Archives, Washington (NAW), State Department, 811.24543/8–3048 and 843.7962/11–1048, Snow to Harrington, 30 Aug. and 10 Nov. 1948

19 Ibid., 843.7962/11–1048, Snow to Hickerson, 10 Nov. 1948; and NAC, Claxton Papers, vol. 116, file 5, 'Memorandum on U.S. Bases in Newfoundland' prepared in Privy Council Office, 12 Nov. 1948

20 Bridle, ed., *Documents*, 1896; and NAW, State Department, 843.7962/12–2848, Snow to Hickerson, 28 Dec. 1948

21 Canada, House of Commons, *Debates*, 10 Feb. 1949, 433

22 NAC, Privy Council Office (PCO), Cabinet Conclusions, 3 Nov. 1948; NAC, Claxton Papers, vol. 116, file 5, Claxton to Pearson, 28 Oct 1948, and 'Memorandum on U.S. Bases' prepared in Privy Council Office, 12 Nov. 1948. See Newfoundland, *Report of the Royal Commission for the Preparation of the Case of the Government of Newfoundland*, 589–610.

23 See Bercuson, 'SAC vs Sovereignty,' 209; and Dziuban, *Military Relations between the United States and Canada*, 162–89.

24 NAC, Claxton Papers, vol. 116, file 5, 'Memorandum on U.S. bases in New-foundland' prepared by Escott Reid for Claxton, 30 Oct. 1948

25 Ibid.

26 *Foreign Relations of the United States (FRUS), 1951*, 2: 877–8

27 NAC, Claxton Papers, vol. 116, file 5, 'Memorandum on U.S. Bases in New-foundland' prepared by Escott Reid for Claxton, 30 Oct. 1948; and Bridle, 'ed., *Documents*, 1914, 1922

28 NAC, St. Laurent Papers, vol. 235, Pearson to St Laurent, 9 Feb. 1949

29 Bridle, ed., *Documents*, 1909. See MacKenzie, *Canada and International Civil Aviation*.

30 NAC, Claxton Papers, vol. 116, file 5, Pearson to Wrong, 6 Jan. 1949. In 1952 there were 3,800 Canadian civilians employed at the bases. Moreover, during the renegotiations of the Bases Agreement, the Americans were pressed to purchase more of their supplies in Canada, particularly in Newfoundland. See Barry, ed., *Documents*, 1143.

31 NAC, Claxton Papers, vol. 116, file 5, Wrong to Claxton, 13 Nov. 1948; and Claxton to Wrong, 16 Nov. 1948

32 NAC, External Affairs, Acc 85–90/027, box 27, file 17 D(s), file pocket, Wrong to Robert A. Lovett, 19 Nov. 1948

33 See Bridle, ed., *Documents*, 1903–6.

34 NAC, Claxton Papers, vol. 116, file 5, Wrong to secretary of state for external affairs, 19 Nov. 1948. Pearson had hoped to reduce the tenure of the agreement from ninety-nine to twenty-five years, but he told Wrong that they would have to be very careful about bringing this issue before the Americans. Ibid., Pearson to Wrong, 6 Jan. 1949

35 Bridle, ed., *Documents*, 1905–6

36 NAC, Claxton Papers, vol. 116, file 5, Pearson to Wrong, 6 Jan. 1949

37 Ibid., Pearson to Wrong, 6 Jan. 1949; and Wrong to Pearson, 12 Jan. 1949

38 Ibid., Wrong to Pearson, 12 Jan. 1949; and Bridle, ed., *Documents*, 1911–13. In *No Boundaries Upstairs*, 9, Jockel suggests that after 1945 the United States had designs on other bases in Newfoundland. James Eayrs makes a similar claim. See his *In Defence of Canada*, 323, 344–5, 353–5.

39 NAC, Claxton Papers, vol. 116, file 5, Wrong to Pearson, 12 Jan. 1949

40 NAC, External Affairs, Acc. 83–84/351, box 13, file 10477–A–40, pt 1, Wrong to Pearson, 28 Jan. 1949

41 Ibid., Pearson to Wrong, 18 Jan. 1949

42 Ibid.

43 NAC, St Laurent Papers, vol. 235, 'Memorandum prepared for the Prime Minister,' 9 Feb. 1949

44 At a news conference on 27 Jan. 1949 when Truman announced that the

Canadian prime minister would be visiting Washington, a reporter asked him the PM's name. Truman said he was trying to avoid using the Canadian's name because he did not know how to pronounce it. *Public Papers of the Presidents of the United States … Truman.* 4: 118

45 NAC, External Affairs, Acc. 83–84/351, box 13, file 10477–A–40, pt 1, Pearson to St Laurent, 24 Jan. 1949

46 Bridle, ed., *Documents*, 1917

47 NAC, External Affairs, Acc. 89–90/029, box 27, file 17 D(s), pt 1, Wrong to Pearson, 12 Jan. 1949

48 Ibid., Acc. 83–84/351, box 13, file 10477–A–40, pt 1, 'Memorandum' prepared while St Laurent was in Washington, 12 Feb. 1949; NAC, Claxton Papers, vol. 116, file 5, Wrong to Pearson, 12 Jan. 1949; and *FRUS, 1949*, 2: 394–6, 400

49 NAC, External Affairs, Acc. 89–90/029, box 27, file 17 D(s), file pocket, 'Oral Message' presented to U.S. embassy in Ottawa, 19 Mar. 1949

50 NAC, St Laurent Papers, vol. 235, Pearson to St Laurent, 24 Feb. 1949

51 NAC, Claxton Papers, vol. 116, file – Newfoundland Defence (1), Heeney to Claxton, 17 May 1949

52 NAC, External Affairs, Acc. 89–90/029, box 27, file 17 D(s), file pocket, R.E.C. to acting U.S. secretary of state, 2 June 1949. See Canada, *Treaty Series*, 1952, no. 14, for 'Exchange of Notes between Canada and the United States Constituting an Understanding Relating to Civil Aviation at the Leased Bases in Newfoundland, effective 4 June 1949.'

53 NAC, External Affairs, Acc. 89–90/029, box 27 file 17 D(s), pt 1, A.G.L. McNaughton to Heeney, 28 June 1949

54 NAC, Claxton Papers, vol. 117, Claxton to St Laurent, 21 July 1949

55 Ibid., vol. 116, file 4, 'Memorandum' of Claxton's visit to Newfoundland, 27 July 1949. Earlier in July, an American military police officer had shot and wounded a Newfoundlander near Harmon Air Force Base in a dispute. St John's *Evening Telegram*, 13 July 1949. See Blair Fraser, 'Where the Yanks Rule a Part of Canada,' *Maclean's*, 15 Nov. 1949; and MacLeod, *Peace of the Continent*, 22–4.

56 NAC, Claxton Papers, vol. 116, file 4, 'Memorandum' of Claxton's visit to Newfoundland, 27 July 1949

57 *Evening Telegram*, 12 Nov. 1949. For Smallwood's attitude towards the Leased Bases Agreement, see Neary, *Newfoundland in the North Atlantic World*, 149.

58 NAC, Claxton Papers, vol. 116, file 4, 'Memorandum of Claxton's visit to Newfoundland,' 27 July 1949

59 Ibid. See MacLeod, *Peace of the Continent*, 11–12. The Commission of Government had agreed with lower wages for Newfoundlanders because it prevented them from deserting traditional occupations.

60 NAW, Office of Secretary of State, file co9–4–3, Symington to Johnson, 5 Aug. 1949; Bercuson, 'SAC vs Sovereignty,' 208–9; and Eayrs, *In Defence of Canada*, 336ff, 351–4

61 *FRUS, 1946.* 5: 58–61, and Bercuson, 'SAC vs Sovereignty,' 208–9. On the strategic importance of Goose Bay to the Americans also see Eayrs, *In Defence of Canada*, 352–6; and Smith, *Diplomacy of Fear*, 165–7.

62 NAC, External Affairs, Acc. 89–90/029, box 27, file 17 D(s) pt 1, MacKay to under-secretary of state for external affairs, 14 July 1949

63 See *FRUS, 1951*, 2: 888–92.

64 Quoted in Neary, *Newfoundland in the North Atlantic World*, 334

65 NAC, External Affairs, Acc. 89–90/029, box 27, file 17 D(s), pt 2, 'Memorandum' prepared by McNaughton on his conversation with Hickerson, 31 Aug. 1949. Claxton received this memorandum in early September, and Heeney discussed the McNaughton-Hickerson conversation in a letter to Claxton dated 15 Sept. 1949.

66 Ibid., McNaughton to Claxton, 12 Sept. 1949

67 Ibid., C.C. Eberts to MacKay, 14 Sept. 1949, and Heeney to Claxton, 15 Sept. 1949. On the relationship between Hickerson and Canadian officials in Washington see Bothwell and Kirton, 'A Sweet Little Country,' 1078–1102.

68 NAC, External Affairs, Acc. 89–90/029, box 27, file 17 D(s), pt 2, McNaughton to Eberts, 8 Nov. 1949; and NAC, Claxton Papers, vol. 116, file 5, Acheson to Pearson, 9 Nov. 1949. See also *FRUS, 1949*, 2: 402, 410–11.

69 NAC, External Affairs, Acc. 89–90/029, box 27, file 17 D(s), pt 2, McNaughton to Eberts, 8 Nov. 1949; and Claxton Papers, vol. 116, file 5, Acheson to Pearson, 9 Nov. 1949, and McNaughton to Heeney, 16 Oct. 1949

70 NAC, External Affairs, Acc. 89–90/029, box 27, file 17 D(s), pt 2, Heeney to Wrong, 25 Oct. 1949. The message was dispatched after Heeney's discussion with Pearson.

71 *Maclean's*, 15 Nov. 1949; and NAC, Claxton Papers, vol. 116, file 5, Heeney to Wrong, 21 Oct. 1949. See Neary, *Newfoundland in the North Atlantic World*, 335–6.

72 NAC, Claxton Papers, vol. 116, file 5, Heeney to Canadian permanent delegate to the U.N., 21 Oct. 1949

73 Ibid., Wrong to Heeney, 27 Oct. 1949

74 NAW, State Department, Permanent Joint Board on Defence, box 22, Nfld Bases (Oct.–Dec. 1949), unsigned message from U.S. Embassy in Ottawa to Acheson, 26 Oct. 1949

75 President Truman was not involved in the negotiations, and he had not been informed of the progress of the negotiations after St Laurent's visit to Washington in February 1949. See *FRUS, 1950*, 584. Nevertheless, in a memoran-

dum he composed on 27 Oct. 1949, Acheson claims that Truman 'had emphatically assured him that in the interests of maintaining good relations with Canada, he would go into the matter of the Newfoundland bases any time the Secretary felt it was necessary to do so.' See *FRUS, 1949*, 2: 402, 410–11.

76 NAC, Claxton Papers, vol. 116, file 5, Wrong to Heeney, 27 Oct. 1949; and Wrong to Pearson, 26 Oct. 1949

77 NAC, External Affairs, Acc. 89–90/029, box 27, file 17 D(s), pt 2, Heeney to Wrong, 25 Oct. 1949; and NAC, Claxton Papers, vol. 116, file 5, Pearson to Claxton, 8 Dec. 1949

78 Ibid., Wrong to Heeney, 26 Oct. 1949; and McNaughton to Eberts, 8 Nov. 1949

79 Ibid., vol. 116, file – Newfoundland Defence (1), 'Memorandum prepared by Post Office Department for Canadian Section, PJBD,' 10 Dec. 1949

80 Ibid., 'Memorandum' prepared for Pearson by MacKay, 22 Dec. 1949

81 Ibid., file 4, 'Memorandum prepared by Canadian Section, PJBD, for 28–31 Mar. 1950 meeting,' 14 Mar. 1950

82 Ibid.; and NAC, Lester B. Pearson Papers, vol. 5, Heeney to Pearson, 13 Jan. 1950

83 NAC, PCO, Cabinet Conclusions, 31 Mar. 1949

84 NAC, Department of National Defence, Directorate of History (DHist) file 112.3M2 (565), 'Memo to Cabinet Defence Committee,' 20 Apr. 1950. See Bercuson, 'SAC vs Sovereignty,' 210–11.

85 NAC, Claxton Papers, vol. 116, file Nfld – file 4, McNaughton to Claxton, 1 Apr. 1950

86 For the exchange of notes between Canada and the United States regarding the lease of Goose Bay, see *United States Treaties*, 5295–9. See also Swettenham, *NcNaughton*, 3: 193–5; and NAC, PCO, Cabinet Conclusions, 31 Mar. 1949.

87 NAC, National Defence, DHist, 'Extracts from unpublished memoirs of General Guy Henry held in the U.S. Military History Institute, Carlisle, Penna'

88 See Bercuson, 'SAC vs Sovereignty,' 212.

89 NAC, PCO, Cabinet Conclusions, 25 Oct. 1950

90 Canada, House of Commons, *Debates*, 9 June 1950, 3421–2

91 Barry, ed., *Documents*, 1113–18

92 NAC, Claxton Papers, vol. 116, file 4, 'Memorandum on Explanation of the PJBD Recommendation of Mar. 30 on the U.S. Bases in Newfoundland,' 5 Apr., 1950; and McNaughton to Claxton, 30 Mar. 1950

93 NAC, External Affairs, Acc. 83–84/351, box 13, file 10477–A–40, pt 1, 'Memorandum on Legislation to Protect Security Interests of United States Forces in Canada,' 14 Apr. 1950; and NAC, Claxton Papers, vol. 116, file 4, 'Memorandum on Explanation of the PJBD Recommendation of Mar. 30 of the U.S. Bases in Newfoundland,' 5 Apr. 1950, and McNaughton to Claxton, 30 Mar. 1950

94 NAC, External Affairs, Acc. 83–84/351, box 13, file 10477–A–40, pt 2, Heeney to Wrong, 12 Feb. 1951; and NAC, St Laurent Papers, vol. 223, file L–3–37–3, Heeney to Pearson, 24 Apr. 1951
95 Ibid., vol. 223, file L–3–37–3, 'Memorandum prepared for file' by J.W. Pickersgill, 23 Apr. 1951
96 MacKay, ed., *Canadian Foreign Policy, 1945–1954*, 250–2
97 On this point see Barry, ed., *Documents*, 1113–93; *FRUS, 1951*, 2: 877–81; and Bercuson, 'SAC vs Sovereignty.'
98 *FRUS, 1951*, 2: 886
99 Pearson, 'Canadian Foreign Policy.' See Eayrs, *In Defence of Canada*, 354–5, for Pearson's reaction to the American request for the use of Goose Bay in 1946.

CHAPTER 6 The problem of Newfoundland: Ottawa and the fisheries, 1948–1957

1 Statistics for the fisheries are not easy to find. Here, I have relied on Canada, Department of Fisheries, *Annual Reports;* Canada, Department of Fisheries, *Trade News* 1, no. 10 (Apr. 1949); Newfoundland, *Historical Statistics of Newfoundland;* and Atlantic Provinces Economic Council, *Atlantic Provinces Statistical Review.*
2 Great Britain, *Report of the Newfoundland Royal Commission*
3 Centre for Newfoundland Studies, Memorial University of Newfoundland Archives (MUN), Queen Elizabeth II Library, Dunn, 'Fisheries Re-organization in Newfoundland,' radio address, 21 Jan. 1944
4 See Newfoundland Fisheries Board, *Report of the Fisheries Post-War Planning Committee.*
5 Hiller and Harrington, eds, 'Report of the Fisheries Committee of the National Convention'
6 See Innis, *The Cod Fisheries*, esp. 418–43.
7 See Newfoundland, *Report of the Commission of Enquiry Investigating the Seafisheries of Newfoundland and Labrador.*
8 See Alexander, *The Decay of Trade*, and Neary, *Newfoundland in the North Atlantic World.*
9 See Alexander, *The Decay of Trade.* For fishery policy under the Commission of Government, see Neary, *Newfoundland in the North Atlantic World;* and Sinclair, *State Intervention and the Newfoundland Fisheries*, 22–35.
10 For an alternate view see Alexander, *The Decay of Trade*, 16. He argued that low productivity of fishermen 'was a response to inadequate markets and few employment opportunities. If market development had been more satisfactory, there would have been an expansion of productive investment from private rather than public sources, generating higher labour and capital productivity and higher incomes, without any real or disguised reduction in the

size of the fishing labour force.' When the export value of fish nearly tripled between 1939 and 1948, there was no appreciable increase in capital in the producing sector.

11 Mayo, 'Economic Problems of the Newfoundland Fisheries,' 488–90
12 See ibid., 482–93.
13 See Provincial Archives of Newfoundland and Labrador (PANL), Sir Albert Walsh Papers, box 2, 'Submissions by various organizations and institutions to the Newfoundland Delegation, July–Sept. 1948.'
14 Bridle, ed., *Documents*, 1106–10
15 National Archives of Canada (NAC), Department of Fisheries and Oceans, vol. 1739, file 794–7–4 [1], Alexander Clutterbuck to Dr W.C. Clark, 30 Nov. 1948
16 PANL, Walsh Papers, box 1, file 5, 'Memorandum Submitted by Newfoundland Delegation to Ottawa,' Oct. 1948, 5–6. By 1948, most of the Canadian saltfish was marketed in the Caribbean and South America.
17 PANL, National Convention, box 2, file 20, F.A.J. Laws to Gordon C. Macdonald, governor of Newfoundland, 2 Aug. 1948, and 'Memorandum on Salt Fish Marketing for Consideration of Newfoundland Delegation to Ottawa' submitted by NAFEL, 21 Sept. 1948
18 Ibid., box 2, file 20, 'Notes Prepared by the Newfoundland Fisheries Board [Raymond Gushue] for Consideration in Discussions of Fishery Matters between Canada and Newfoundland, Memorandum No. 1,' 1 Sept. 1948
19 Ibid., Newfoundland Board of Trade to Walsh, 13 Aug. and 17 Sept. 1948. See PANL, Walsh Papers, esp. boxes 3 and 4
20 NAC, Fisheries and Oceans, vol. 1132, file 721–54–4 [8], 'Memorandum to the Cabinet on Points Likely to be raised by Newfoundland Delegation,' 25 Sept. 1948; and Bridle, ed., *Documents*, 1066–71
21 NAC, Fisheries and Oceans, vol. 1132, file 721–54–4 [8], 'Memorandum to the Cabinet on Points Likely to be raised by Newfoundland Delegation,' 25 Sept. 1948
22 Bridle, ed., *Documents*, 1171–2, 1195
23 St John's *Daily News*, 1 Dec. 1948
24 Canada, Department of External Affairs, *Report and Documents*, 18–19. Eleven fisheries items were included in 'Statements on Questions Raised by the Newfoundland Delegation,' including reference to market representatives of NAFEL and the Newfoundland Bait Service. See 36–8.
25 PANL, Department of Natural Resources, file 830, vol. 2, Bates to Gushue, 2 Apr. 1949. See also, NAC, Fisheries and Oceans, vol. 63, file 710–202–3, pt 1, 'Minutes of Meeting of the Newfoundland Fisheries Board,' 11 Apr. 1949; St John's *Evening Telegram*, 2 June 1949; and Canada, External Affairs, *Report and Documents*.

26 Canada, Department of Fisheries, *Trade News* 10, no. 11 (May 1958). The Fisheries Act was a comprehensive document that outlined the powers of the minister and fishery officers and matters relating to the conservation and protection of various species of fish, authority for fisheries regulations, pollution and obstruction of streams, and the licensing of vessels and fishermen.

27 NAC, Privy Council Office (PCO), vol. 125, file D–14, 'Dept of Fisheries, 1949.' 'Memorandum to Cabinet on Fisheries Development,' by R.W. Mayhew, 12 Oct. 1949; and NAC, Fisheries and Oceans, vol. 541, file 711–25–36 [2], 'Statement to the House of Commons,' by R.W. Mayhew, 6 Dec. 1949

28 The Price Support Board was established in July 1947 under the direction of the minister of fisheries. It was part of Ottawa's plan to promote orderly adjustment in the fishery from wartime to peacetime conditions and to ensure an adequate return from the fishery compared with other occupations. The board was authorized to purchase fish or to pay fishermen the difference between a price set by the board and that which the industry paid them. See Dominion Bureau of Statistics, *Canada Year Book, 1950*, 493–4.

29 PANL, Newfoundland Department of Fisheries, file 11/4, vol. 2, and NAC, Fisheries and Oceans, vol. 541, 711–25–36 (1), 'Background Notes to Minister of Fisheries' Statement on Developmental Programme,' 6 May 1949, and 'Memorandum as to a Programme for the Development of the Fisheries,' May 1949

30 NAC, Fisheries and Oceans, vol. 125, file D–14, 'Memorandum to Cabinet on Fisheries Development,' by R.W. Mayhew, 12 Oct. 1949; and vol. 541, file 711–25–36 [2], 'Statement to House of Commons on Government Programme for Fisheries Development,' by R.W. Mayhew, 6 Dec. 1949

31 See Sinclair, *State Intervention and the Newfoundland Fisheries.* The number of fishermen declined from 25,220 in 1939 to 17,645 in 1942 and rose again to 28,000 by 1948. The boom on the bases had ended by 1942.

32 MUN, Joseph R. Smallwood (JRS) Collection, file 3.06.042

33 PANL, Newfoundland Department of Fisheries, file 96/1, 'Federal Government Assistance to the Fishing Industry in Various Provinces,' memorandum unsigned and undated; and MUN, JRS Collection, file 3.12.046, Smallwood to H.G. Dunstan, manager, Bank of Nova Scotia, 26 July 1951

34 In *Newfoundland in the North Atlantic World*, Neary suggests that the mould for the development of the fishery was cast in the early 1940s. See 357.

35 PANL, Newfoundland Board of Trade, box 51, file 4, 'Review of the Newfoundland Fisheries for 1949,' prepared by the Newfoundland Fisheries Board, 15 Dec. 1949

36 PANL, Governor's Office, file 140/39, Gushue to Bates, 25 June 1949

37 NAC, Fisheries and Oceans, vol. 1740, file 794–7–4 [5], 'Statement in House of

Commons,' by Mayhew, 17 May 1951, and D.C. Abbott to Clutterbuck, 4 May 1951. Also, NAC, PCO, vol. 195, file T–50–9, vol. 1, 'Cabinet Memorandum Prepared by Mayhew on Price Support Policy for Fisheries – 1951 Production Season,' 14 May 1951

38 NAC, Fisheries and Oceans, vol. 1740, file 794–7–4 [7], secretary of the Interdepartmental Fisheries Trade Committee to J.N. Lewis, chief, Market Branch, Department of Fisheries, 4 Jan. 1952; MUN, JRS Collection, file 3.12.073, Smallwood to Phil Grouchy, 23 June 1951, and to Bowater Newfoundland Ltd, 23 June 1951; Smallwood to Howe, 16 July 1951; and NAC, Louis St Laurent Papers, vol. 225, file F–11, 'Summary on Canadian Fisheries Markets,' nd

39 NAC, PCO, vol. 177, file P–100–C, vol. 1, Provincial Governments – Newfoundland, 'Record of Cabinet Decisions,' 26 Sept 1951; and Canada, Department of Fisheries, Annual Report, 1951–2, 45

40 See Canada, Fisheries Price Support Board, Annual Reports, 1949–55. For a fuller discussion of the problems with the marketing of salt cod after 1949, see Blake, 'The Making of a Province.'

41 MUN, Bradley Collection, 'Radio Broadcasts, 1949–53,' 27 Oct. 1951

42 NAC, Fisheries and Oceans, vol. 1740, file 794–7–4 [2], 'Minute for File: Re: Newfoundland Salt Fish Situation,' prepared by Stewart Bates, 22 Apr. 1950; and NAC, PCO, vol. 195, file T–50–9, vol. 1, Bates to Robertson, 26 Apr. 1950. Also included was a statement dealing with the saltfish situation in Newfoundland, and Canada's desire to initiate a long-term strategy for the industry.

43 NAC, PCO, vol. 1654, file 20–191, pt 1, Cabinet Conclusions, 18 Apr. 1950; and NAC, Fisheries and Oceans, vol. 1740, file 794–7–4 [2], 'Minute for file,' 22 Apr. 1950

44 NAC, PCO, vol. 195, T–50–9, vol. 1, Bates to Robertson, 20 Mar. 1950; and NAC, Fisheries and Oceans, vol. 1740, file 794–7–4 [2], Robertson to Mayhew, 3 Apr. 1950

45 Evening Telegram, 6 May 1950; and NAC, PCO, vol. 195, file T–50–9, vol. 1, James to Robertson, 29 May 1950

46 NAC, J.W. Pickersgill Papers, box 2, Newfoundland Series, file N1–29, 'Fish Marketing Part 1, Memorandum on Newfoundland Fisheries,' by W.C. MacKenzie, 14 July 1953

47 NAC, Fisheries and Oceans, vol. 1748, file 784–17–1 [1], 'Joint Announcement by Premier Smallwood and Mayhew, Re: Fisheries Development in Newfoundland,' 27 Jan. 1951; and PANL, Newfoundland Department of Fisheries, file 27/1, 'Fishery Conference,' F. Scott, deputy minister of cooperatives, to Keough, 10 July 1950

48 PANL, Newfoundland Department of Fisheries, file 27/1, 'Fishery Conference.'

'A Development Program for the Fisheries of the Atlantic Coast Provinces', memorandum attached to letter from Bates to Scott, 7 June 1950

49 Ibid.

50 See Bothwell, Drummond, and English, *Canada since 1945*, 165. For a different view, see Forbes, 'Consolidating Disparity.'

51 NAC, Pickersgill Papers, box 2, Newfoundland Series, file N1–28, 'Memorandum of Inter-Departmental Committee, Re Walsh Report of Newfoundland Development,' 9 May 1953

52 Newfoundland, *Report of the Newfoundland Fisheries Development Committee*, 102. This was commonly referred to as the Walsh Report.

53 PANL, Newfoundland Department of Fisheries, file 8/45/9. 'Proposals by C. Planta and C.M. Lane for Alternate Market Set-up to NAFEL,' Nov. 1952. See Innis, *The Cod Fisheries*, and the Walsh Report, 13.

54 On this point, see Noel, *Politics in Newfoundland*, 262–4.

55 Newfoundland, *Budget Speech*, presented by Gregory Power, 29 Apr. 1953. In 1951, the growing independence of fishermen was discernible but Raymond Gushue described it as a 'we won't fish unless ... attitude.' He blamed the change on the 'vote-catching propaganda of the past several years,' particularly on Smallwood whom he regarded as a propagandist by nature. Unfortunately, Gushue failed to see the new attitude as a product of changing social conditions and a growing awareness among fishermen of their condition in Newfoundland. See Fisheries and Oceans, vol. 1748, file 794–17–1 [1], Gushue to Mayhew, 14 May 1951

56 See *Evening Telegram*, 10 Aug., 1949, 15 Oct. 1949, 28 Feb. 1950, 1 May 1951. The *Evening Telegram* reported on 10 Aug. 1949 that '[d]aily in the House of Assembly the electorate in Newfoundland are voicing their demands for roads.' That day alone, one member presented five petitions from five separate communities.

57 Newfoundland, *Budget Speech*, 29 Apr. 1953; and NAC, Fisheries and Oceans, vol. 1748, file 794–17–1 [1], Gushue to Mayhew, 14 May 1951. See Smallwood, *I Chose Canada*, 370–2.

58 The bank fishery was prosecuted in large vessels or schooners. Each carried a number of dories, small flat-bottomed boats, which fished near the schooner. See Raoul Andersen, 'Usufruct and Contradiction.'

59 The fresh-frozen industry in Newfoundland received its impetus from the demand for food during the Second World War. See Smallwood, ed., *Encyclopedia of Newfoundland and Labrador*, 2: 159–60; and MacKay, ed., *Newfoundland*, 92–6.

60 Gushue, 'Newfoundland Fisheries in 1951,' *Newfoundland Journal of Commerce* 19 (1): 55; and Canada, Department of Fisheries, *Annual Report*, 1950–1 and 1951–2

61 MUN, Bradley Collection, file: 'Hazen Russell Correspondence, 1949–52,' Bradley to Russell, 14 Sept. 1951

62 Ibid., file: 'Radio Broadcasts 1949–53,' 'Radio Broadcast,' 27 Oct. 1951

63 NAC, Fisheries and Oceans, vol. 1749, file 794–17–1, [3], 'Speech made by Keough over Radio Station CJON,' 12 Jan. 1952. Keough also said that '[T]his would seem to shed some light on why salt fish export merchants have never built up central splitting, salting and curing stations to make light-salted or shore fish.'

64 MUN, J.W. Pickersgill, *Report from Parliament Hill*, 23 Jan. 1954

65 Walsh Report, various references

66 NAC, Pickersgill Papers, box 2, Newfoundland Series, file N1–28, 'Fisheries Development, Memorandum of Inter-Departmental Committee, Re Walsh Report of Newfoundland Development,' 9 May 1953

67 MUN, JRS Collection, file 7.02.006, 'Radio Broadcast' by Smallwood, 16 July 1953. On the relationship between Pickersgill and Smallwood, see Smallwood, *I Chose Canada*, Gwyn, *Smallwood*, and Pickersgill, *My Years with Louis St. Laurent*.

68 Pickersgill claims that he was largely responsible for changes in the Unemployment Insurance Act that allowed fishermen to receive benefits in 1957. See Pickersgill, *My Years with Louis St. Laurent*, 227–9.

69 NAC, Pickersgill Papers, box 2, Newfoundland Series, file N1–28, 'Fisheries Development, Memorandum of Inter-Departmental Committee, Re Walsh Report of Newfoundland Development,' 9 May 1953

70 NAC, Fisheries and Oceans, vol. 1749, file 794–17–1 [6], 'Memorandum to Cabinet by Robert H. Winter, Re: Report of the Newfoundland Fisheries Development Committee,' 15 May 1953

71 Ibid., vol. 1750, file 794–17–1 [7], 'Memorandum to Cabinet, Re: Newfoundland Fisheries Development,' 8 Sept. 1953. This was the report of the party of senior officials.

72 MUN, JRS Collection, file 3.12.040, Smallwood to A.H. Monroe, President, Fishery Products Limited, 25 Mar. 1953

73 Ibid., file 7.02.005, 'Speech file, 1952'

74 PANL, House of Assembly, file 11/4/5, 'Notes on Discussion between Sinclair, Keough and Bates, Memorandum to Executive Council, Subject: Submission of Memorandum Received from Fisheries Development Committee,' 17 Dec. 1952

75 NAC, Fisheries and Oceans, vol. 1750, file 794–17–1 [8], 'Memorandum on Newfoundland Fisheries Development Programme,' nd, but obviously late Dec. 1953

76 NAC, PCO, vol. 237, file T–50–11–N, Mayhew to St Laurent, 29 May 1952

77 NAC, PCO, Cabinet Conclusions, 8 May 1952
78 NAC, PCO, vol. 237, file T–50–11–N, 'Memorandum to Cabinet Re: Newfound-land Fisheries Development,' prepared by Mayhew, 7 May 1952; MUN, Bradley Collection, file: 'Newfoundland Fisheries Development Committee, Consider-ation of Proposals of Newfoundland Fisheries Development Committee,' 22 Apr. 1952; and NAC, Fisheries and Oceans, vol. 1750, file 794–17–1 [8], 'Mem-orandum on Newfoundland Fisheries Development Programme'
79 Ibid.
80 See Walsh Report, 116–21.
81 PANL, Newfoundland Department of Fisheries, file 11/4/5, 'Notes on Discus-sion between Sinclair, Keough and Bates, Memorandum to Executive Council, Subject: Submission of Memorandum Received from Fisheries Development Committee,' 17 Dec. 1952
82 NAC, PCO, vol. 237, file T–50–11–N, Mayhew to St Laurent, 29 May 1952
83 NAC, Pickersgill Papers, box 2, Newfoundland Series, file N1–28, 'Fisheries Development, Memorandum of Inter-Departmental Committee, Re Walsh Report of Newfoundland Development,' 9 May 1953
84 Alexander, *Decay of Trade*, 139–40; and Smallwood, *The Time Has Come to Tell*, 72–3. See Vince Walsh, 'Stagnant Capital and Mobile People,' in Rex Clark, ed., *Contrary Winds*, 21–3.
85 Newfoundland, *Budget Speech*, 9 May 1951
86 See Canada, Department of Fisheries, *Annual Report*, 1956–60.
87 MUN, JRS Collection, file 3.12.023, 'Fisheries Development Authority Legisla-tion,' a speech by Smallwood, 1953. In the 1954 *Budget Speech*, Gregory J. Power, minister of finance, said that during 1953, the plants to which the government had loaned $7 million employed 3,000 workers and paid $6.25 million in wages.
88 For Smallwood's industrial development policy see Gwyn, *Smallwood*, Hor-wood, *Joey*, and Bassler, 'Develop or Perish,' 93–119.
89 NAC, Fisheries and Oceans, vol. 1748, file 794–17–1 [17], Gushue to Mayhew, 5 May 1951
90 Ibid., file 794–17–1 [1], Bates to Gushue, 3 July 1951
91 On the relationship between Smallwood and Bradley see Hiller, 'Career of F. Gordon Bradley.'
92 MUN, Bradley Collection, 'G. Sellars, Correspondence 1952–53,' Bradley to Sellars, 3 Apr. 1952. After all, Bradley said, 'Smallwood himself was a man of no experience. He had been a doctrinaire socialist with a hobby for public-ity and a desire to get into public life.' Bradley to Sellars, 11 Feb. 1952
93 MUN, JRS Collection, file 3.10.024, Bradley to Smallwood, 7 Oct. 1949
94 MUN, Bradley Collection, 'Hazen Russell (Job Brothers & Company Ltd.)

Correspondence,' Bradley to Russell, 8 May 1952. W.C. MacKenzie who served for a time as Ottawa's representative on the committee denies that Planta had such control. Interview with MacKenzie, Feb. 1990

95 MUN, Bradley Collection, 'G. Sellars, Correspondence 1952–53,' Bradley to Sellars, 11 Feb. 1952. On the career of Valdmanis, see Gwyn, *Smallwood*, 140–69, and Horwood, *Joey*, 170 ff.

96 Bradley later said that the property was valued at $200,000 within a few months.

97 MUN, JRS Collection, file 3.10.024, Bradley to Smallwood, 7 Oct. 1949

98 Ibid., Bradley to Smallwood, 29 Mar. 1950

99 Because Ottawa had control over support payments for a sudden drop in prices, there was little Smallwood could do to correct the situation without the aid of the federal government. His rationale for the inquiry may be found in a letter to Bradley in early 1951: 'Our fishermen generally are in a poor mood. They feel, or had begun to feel, that the Liberal Party and Governments had abandoned them to the tender mercies of the merchants. Our appointment of Clive Planta as Deputy Minister of Fisheries, the joint appointment of the new Fisheries Development Committee, the fisheries price investigation by the Federal Government and the fish prices and fish profits investigation by the Provincial Government, together with this drive initiated by us to organize the fishermen – all these should go far to show the fishermen that they have not become the "forgotten men" of liberalism.' Ibid., Smallwood to Bradley, 24 Feb. 1951

100 Ibid., Bradley to Smallwood, 20 Feb. 1951

101 MUN, Bradley Collection, 'G. Sellars, Correspondence 1952–3,' Bradley to Sellars, 13 Mar. 1952

102 Interviews with R.B Bryce, 14 Feb. 1990, and Mitchell Sharp, 12 Feb. 1990

103 NAC, Pickersgill Papers, box 2, Newfoundland Series, file N1–29, G.R. Clark, assistant deputy minister of fisheries, to Theresa Maloney, executive assistant to Pickersgill, 15 July 1953. MacKenzie's memorandum was also included.

104 Ibid., file N1–29, Bates to Pickersgill, 7 Oct. 1953

105 Ibid., file N1–28, Charlie Granger to Pickersgill, 16 Sept. 1953, and Ian S. McArthur to C.M. Lane, general secretary, Newfoundland Federation of Fishermen, 21 Oct. 1953. See NAC, PCO, Cabinet Conclusions, 12 June 1953. St Laurent wrote to President Dwight Eisenhower expressing his disappointment about threats of American countervailing duties on Canadian groundfish and oats. For a discussion of U.S. demands for higher tariffs against Canadian fish, see Dewar, *Industry in Trouble*, esp. 43–76.

106 NAC, Pickersgill Papers, box 2, Newfoundland Series, file N1–28, Charlie

Granger to Pickersgill, 16 Sept. 1953; Ian S. McArthur to C.M. Lane, 21 Oct. 1953

107 MUN, JRS Collection, file 3.12.011, Planta to Smallwood, 28 and 29 Sept. 1953

108 Ibid., 'Smallwood Press Release,' 1 Oct. 1953

109 NAC, Fisheries and Oceans, vol. 1740, file 794–7–4 [7], McArthur to Bates, 27 Feb. 1952

110 Ibid., vol. 1133, file 721–54–16 [1], 'Memorandum, Re: NAFEL,' prepared by Bates, 26 Mar. 1953

111 Salt bulk is heavily salted fish that has not been dried. During the 1940s several Nova Scotia firms had installed mechanical dryers, but as fishermen started to sell their catch fresh, the source of supply for the dryers was cut off. Then, Nova Scotia looked to Newfoundland for its supplies of salted fish.

112 NAC, Fisheries and Oceans, vol. 1133, file 721–54–16 [1], James Sinclair to Percy M. Crosbie, chairman of NAFEL, 27 Mar. 1953

113 PANL, Newfoundland Department of Fisheries, file 8/45/7, 'Discussions in Ottawa, 5 Mar. 1954, to Decide Alternative System of Marketing Salt Codfish, News Release, Department of Fisheries,' 22 Mar. 1954

114 NAC, Fisheries and Oceans, vol. 1133, file 721–54–16 [3], Howe to Crosbie, 11 May 1954

115 J.W. Pickersgill maintains that Ottawa did this to placate Smallwood, who, Pickersgill says, could not agree with James Sinclair on anything. Interview with J.W. Pickersgill, 11 Feb. 1989

116 NAC, Pickersgill Papers, box 7, Newfoundland Series, file N1–161–1, Pickersgill to Smallwood, 3 Apr. 1954

117 MUN, JRS Collection, file 3.10.028, Howe to Smallwood, 7 Apr. 1954, and Smallwood to Howe, 20 Apr. 1954

118 Alexander claims that the Department of Trade and Commerce was interested in helping NAFEL, but it was inexperienced in the overseas saltfish trade. See Alexander, *Decay of Trade*, 132.

119 NAC, PCO, vol. 195, file T–50–9, vol. 1 (Trade, Commerce, Industry), 'Draft Statement for the Minister of Fisheries,' June 1950

120 NAC, PCO, Cabinet Conclusions, 12 May 1955

121 MUN, JRS, Collection, file 3.12.002, Planta to Smallwood, 21 Apr. and 3 July 1954

122 Ibid., file 3.06.016, Smallwood to Beland Honderich, editor-in-chief, *Toronto Daily Star*, 5 July 1955

123 Canada, *Hearings of the Royal Commission on Canada's Economic Prospects*, 18 Oct. 1955 at St John's, 50–60, and Alexander, *Decay of Trade*, 159–60

124 Rowe, *The Smallwood Era*, 42

125 NAC, Fisheries and Oceans, vol. 1750, file 794–17–1 [11], 'Report of the

Working Party on Newfoundland Fisheries Development,' 7 Jan. 1958

126 A similar work ethic was discernible in the forest industry. When H.M.S. Levin, the manager of the Bowater pulp-and-paper mill in Corner Brook, appeared before the Gordon Commission he complained that the average man came to work for not more than fifty days at a time. As soon as he had earned enough money to keep him going for a while he left, only to return when it ran out. Canada, *Hearings of the Royal Commission on Canada's Economic Prospects*, St John's, 18 Oct. 1955

127 Shortly before his premature death, David Alexander had turned to the subject of illiteracy among the Newfoundland workforce and the relationship between educational levels and economic development. Though his conclusion was tentative, he wrote that 'it is difficult to see how the country could rise to meet its opportunities and challenges when its educated population was so small ... It is difficult to believe that this deficiency did not impose heavy costs upon the country in limiting its capacity to adapt, innovate, and face the external world with pride and self-confidence.' David Alexander, 'Literacy and Economic Development in Nineteenth Century Newfoundland,' in Alexander, *Atlantic Canada and Confederation*, 136–7. Even today, Newfoundland would benefit from a program of adult education.

128 Newfoundland, Newfoundland Fisheries Development Authority, *Annual Report*

129 Maritime History Group Archives, Memorial University of Newfoundland, John T. Cheeseman Collection, 31–D–4–33, Sinclair to Cheeseman, 15 Mar. 1956

130 NAC, Department of Trade and Commerce, vol. 1962, file 20–191–4, pt 1, 'Memorandum on Newfoundland and the Salted Fish Industry' by J.N. Lewis, 26 June 1958

131 Ibid.

132 See Toronto *Globe and Mail*, 9 Nov. 1990. The federal fisheries minister, Bernard Valcourt, announced a $10-million aid package for fishermen. The money was designed for community-development projects that would allow fishermen to qualify for unemployment-insurance benefits.

133 See Alexander, *Decay of Trade*, 1–19, 158–65.

134 It is worth pointing out that between 1951 and 1961 the number of loggers in Newfoundland decreased by nearly 40 per cent, but individual productivity increased by more than 30 per cent. Between 1954 and 1963 the number of inshore fishermen increased by 25 per cent but their share of landed fish dropped from 78 to 75 per cent. See McAllister, ed., *Newfoundland and Labrador*, 99–101, 123–5.

135 See Pross and McCorquodale, *Economic Resurgence and the Constitutional Agenda*, 20–1.

Illustration Sources and Credits

St John's *Daily News*: first page of the souvenir edition, 31 March 1949.

National Archives of Canada: St Laurent and Walsh sign the Terms of Union, PA 186927; Smallwood meets with reporters, PA 189779; Colin Gibson presents Sir Albert Walsh with certificate, PA 189780; typical Newfoundland fishing village, PA 186925; the Newfoundland fishery involved more, PA 186930; women were often responsible, PA 186933. *Parliament/Senate Collection*: crowd gathered on Parliament Hill, Acc. 1979-185, PA 187349; St Laurent welcomes Newfoundland, Acc. 1979-185, PA 187350. *National Film Board of Canada*: workers wrapping fillets, Acc. 1971-271, PA 142652; Gertrude Everard, Phoebe Moore, and Doris Moore, Acc. 1971-271, PA 128003. *Canada Public Works*: following union there was a small boom, Acc. 1985-104, volume 5292, PA 187346.

Provincial Archives of Newfoundland and Labrador: St Laurent and Smallwood on the campaign trail, NA 2596; Canadian National coastal boat ss *Burgeo*, B6-29.

Centre for Newfoundland Studies Archives, Memorial University of Newfoundland: Progressive Conservative campaign poster, OMF-33B; fishermen preparing codfish, Coll-075, Neg. no. 504.517; construction of a modern fish-processing plant, Coll-075, Neg. no. 504.672; Smallwood and Pickersgill campaigning, Coll-075, Neg. no. 504–243.

Bibliography

I ARCHIVAL COLLECTIONS

A *Centre for Newfoundland Studies, Memorial University of Newfoundland Archives, St John's*

Bradley, F. Gordon
Dunn, P.D.H.
Hattenhauer, Rolf G.
Hefferton, Samuel J.
Higgins, John Gilbert
Job, Robert Brown
Newell, Isaac
Responsible Government League
Rowe, Frederick W.
Smallwood, Joseph R.
Sparks, Walter Stanley

B *Maritime History Group Archives, Memorial University of Newfoundland, St John's*

Cheeseman, John T.
Newfoundland Association of Fish Exporters Limited

C *National Archives, Washington*

Department of State. General Records. Record Group 59

D *National Archives of Canada, Ottawa*

1 Government Records
Department of External Affairs
Department of Finance
Department of Fisheries and Oceans
Department of Labour
Department of National Defence
Department of National Health and Welfare
Department of Trade and Commerce
Historical Section, DHist, Department of National Defence
Privy Council Office
Public Service Commission
Unemployment Insurance Commission

2 Manuscript Collections
Bell, Richard A.
Browne, William J.
Carter, Chesley W.
Chevrier, Lionel
Claxton, Brooke
Coldwell, M.J.
Co-operative Commonwealth Federation (CCF)
Diefenbaker, John
Eggleston, Wilfrid
Evans, George H.
Granger, Charles R.
Grosart, Allister
Howe, C.D.
Kidd, H.E.
King, W.L.M.
Lewis, David
Liberal Party of Canada
McDonald, John H.
MacKay, Robert A.
McNaughton, A.G.L.
Martin, Paul
Noseworthy, J.W.
Pearson, Lester B.
Pickersgill, J.W.

Progressive Conservative Party of Canada
St Laurent, Louis
Winters, Robert

E *Provincial Archives of Newfoundland and Labrador, St John's*

1 Government of Newfoundland Record Groups
Colonial Secretary
Commission of Government
Department of Career Development and Advanced Studies
Department of Economic Development
Department of Education
Department of Finance
Department of Fisheries
Department of Fisheries and Co-operatives
Department of Justice
Department of Marine and Fisheries
Department of Natural Resources
Department of Public Health
Department of Public Welfare
Department of Public Works
Executive Council
Fisheries Loan Board
Governor's Office
House of Assembly
National Convention
Newfoundland Fisheries Board
Voters' List / Electoral Office

2 Manuscript Collections
Baine Johnson and Co., Ltd
Cashin, Peter J.
Chalker, James R.
Curtis, Leslie R.
Dyer, George
Ellis, Eric
F.G. House and Co., Ltd
Frecker, G. Alain
Manning, Raymond
Newfoundland Association of Public Employees

Newfoundland Board of Trade
Newfoundland Federation of Fishermen
Newfoundland Federation of Labour
Newfoundland Ranger Force Association
Newfoundland Savings Bank
Walsh, Albert J.

F *Public Records Office, London, United Kingdom*

Dominions Office, DO 35, 41

G *Queen's University Archives, Kingston, Ontario*

Deutsch, John
Dexter, Grant

II BOOKS AND PUBLIC DOCUMENTS

Alexander, David. *Atlantic Canada and Confederation: Essays in Canadian Political Economy.* Compiled by Eric Sager et al. Toronto 1983
– *The Decay of Trade: An Economic History of the Newfoundland Saltfish Trade, 1935–1965.* St John's 1977
Andersen, Raoul, ed. *North Atlantic Maritime Cultures: Anthropological Essays on Changing Adaptations.* The Hague 1979
Andrews, Ralph. *Post-Confederation Developments in Newfoundland Education, 1949–75.* St John's 1985
Atlantic Provinces Economic Council. *Atlantic Provinces Statistical Review.* Halifax 1970
Barry, Donald, ed. *Documents on Canadian External Relations.* Vol. 18. 1952. Ottawa, 1990
Bothwell, Robert, Ian Drummond, and John English. *Canada since 1945: Power, Politics, and Provincialism.* Toronto 1989
Bothwell, Robert, and William Kilbourn. *C.D. Howe. A Biography.* Toronto 1979
Bridle, Paul, ed. *Documents on the Relations between Canada and Newfoundland.* Vol. 2. 1940–49. Confederation. Ottawa 1984
Browne, W.J. *Eighty-four Years a Newfoundlander. Memoirs of William J. Browne.* Vol. 1. 1897–1949. St John's 1981
– *Eighty-seven Years a Newfoundlander. Memoirs of William J. Browne.* Vol. 2. 1946–1965. St John's 1981

Brox, Ottar. *Newfoundland Fishermen in the Age of Industry. Sociology of Economic Dualism.* St John's 1972

Bryce, R.B. *Maturing in Hard Times: Canada's Department of Finance through the Great Depression.* Kingston and Montreal 1986

Bryden, Kenneth. *Old Age Pensions and Policy-Making in Canada.* Montreal and Kingston 1974

Brym, Robert J., ed. *Regionalism in Canada.* Toronto 1986

Burns, R.M. *The Acceptable Mean: The Tax Rental Agreements, 1941–1962.* Toronto 1980

Bursey, Brian. *A Half Century of Progress? A History of Economic Growth and Development in Newfoundland during the Modern Period, 1930–1980.* St John's 1980

Canada. Department of External Affairs. *Report and Documents Relating to the Negotiations for the Union of Newfoundland with Canada.* Ottawa 1949

– Department of Fisheries. *Annual Reports.* Ottawa 1948–57

– Department of Fisheries. *Trade News.*

– Department of Labour. *Annual Reports.* Ottawa 1949–55

– Department of National Health and Welfare. *Annual Reports.* Ottawa 1950–5

– Department of Trade and Commerce. *Annual Reports.* Ottawa 1949–53

– Fisheries Price Support Board. *Annual Reports.* Ottawa 1948–53

– *Hearings of the Royal Commission on Canada's Economic Prospects.* Ottawa

– House of Commons. *Debates.*

– *Proposed Arrangements for the Entry of Newfoundland into Confederation.* Ottawa 1948

– *Report of Royal Commission on Newfoundland Finances.* Ottawa 1958

– *Treaty Series.* 1952, no. 14. Ottawa 1953

Cardoulis, John N. *A Friendly Invasion: The American Military in Newfoundland, 1940–1990.* St John's 1990

Chadwick, St John. *Newfoundland: Island into Province.* London 1967

Channing, J.G. *The Effects of Transition to Confederation on Public Administration in Newfoundland.* Toronto 1982

Clark, Rex, ed. *Contrary Winds: Essays on Newfoundland Society in Crisis.* St John's 1986

Conn, Stetson, and Byron Fairchild. *The Western Hemisphere: The Framework of Hemisphere Defense.* Washington 1960

Conrad, Margaret. *George Nowlan. Maritime Conservative in National Politics.* Toronto 1986

Copes, Parzival. *St John's and Newfoundland – An Economic Survey.* St John's, 1961

– *The Resettlement of Fishing Communities in Newfoundland.* Ottawa 1972

Coward, Laurence E., ed. *Pensions in Canada. A Compendium of Fact and Opinion.* Don Mills, Ont. 1964

Creighton, Donald G. *The Road to Confederation. The Emergence of Canada, 1863–1867.* Toronto 1964

Cuff, R.D., and J.L. Granatstein. *Ties that Bind. Canadian-American Relations in Wartime: From the Great War to the Cold War.* Toronto 1975

– *American Dollars – Canadian Prosperity: Canadian-American Economic Relations, 1945–50.* Toronto 1978

Dewar, Margaret E. *Industry in Trouble: The Federal Government and the New England Fisheries.* Philadelphia 1983

Dominion Bureau of Statistics. *Canada Year Book.* Ottawa 1950–7

Donald, Ross, and Co. *Industrial Survey of the Resources of Newfoundland.* Montreal 1950

Dyck, Rand. *Provincial Politics in Canada.* Scarborough 1986

Dziuban, Stanley W. *Military Relations between the United States and Canada, 1935–45.* Washington 1959

Eayrs, James. *In Defence of Canada: Peacemaking and Deterrence.* Toronto 1972

Eggleston, Wilfrid. *Newfoundland. The Road to Confederation.* Ottawa 1974

English, John. *Shadow of Heaven. The Life of Lester Pearson.* Vol. 1, *1897–1948.* Toronto 1989

Forbes, E.R. *Challenging the Regional Stereotype: Essays on the 20th Century Maritimes.* Fredericton 1989

Foreign Relations of the United States, 1946, 1949, 1950, 1951. Washington 1969, 1975, 1977, 1979

Fraser, Blair. *The Search for Identity. Canada, 1945–1967.* Toronto 1967

Fullerton, Douglas H. *Graham Towers and His Times.* Toronto 1986

Gillespie, Bill. *A Class Act: An Illustrated History of the Labour Movement in Newfoundland and Labrador.* St John's 1986

Gilmore, William C. *Newfoundland and Dominion Status.* Toronto 1988

Goulding, Jay. *The Last Outport. Newfoundland in Crisis.* Toronto 1982

Government of Newfoundland and Labrador. *Historical Statistics of Newfoundland and Labrador.* Vol. 1. St John's 1970

Granatstein, J.L. *Canada's War: The Politics of the Mackenzie King Government, 1939–45.* Toronto 1975

– *A Man of Influence: Norman A. Robertson and Canadian Statecraft, 1926–68.* Toronto 1981

– *The Ottawa Men: The Civil Service Mandarins, 1935–1957.* Toronto 1982

Grant, Ruth Fulton. *The Canadian Atlantic Fishery.* Toronto 1934

Great Britain. *Report of the Newfoundland Royal Commission.* London, 1933

Guest, Dennis. *The Emergence of Social Security in Canada.* Vancouver 1982

Gwyn, Richard. *Smallwood: The Unlikely Revolutionary.* Toronto 1972

Hawes and Company (London Ltd.). *Annual Review of the Salt Codfish Trade.* London 1930– and 1948–9

Heeney, Arnold. *The Things That Are Caesar's: Memoirs of a Canadian Public Servant.* Toronto 1972

Hiller, James, and Peter Neary, eds. *Newfoundland in the Nineteenth and Twentieth Centuries: Essays in Interpretation.* Toronto 1980

Hollohan, Francis, and Melvin Baker, eds. *A Clear Head in Tempestuous Times. Albert B. Perlin: The Wayfarer. Observations on the National Convention and the Confederation Issue, 1946–1949.* St John's 1986

Horwood, Harold. *Joey: The Life and Political Times of Joey Smallwood.* Toronto 1989

Innis, Harold A. *The Cod Fisheries: The History of an International Economy.* Toronto 1954

Inverson, Noel, and Ralph Matthews. *Communities in Decline: An Examination of Household Resettlement in Newfoundland.* St John's 1968

Jamieson, Don. *No Place For Fools: The Political Memoirs of Don Jamieson.* St John's 1989

Jockel, Joseph T. *No Boundaries Upstairs: Canada, the United States, and the Origins of North American Air Defence, 1945–1958.* Vancouver 1987

Keenleyside, Hugh L. *Memoirs of Hugh L. Keenleyside. On the Bridge of Time.* Toronto 1982

Leacy, F.H., ed. *Historical Statistics of Canada.* 2nd ed. Toronto 1965

Lewis, David. *The Good Fight: Political Memoirs, 1900–1958.* Toronto 1981

McAllister, R.I., ed. *Newfoundland and Labrador: The First Fifteen Years of Confederation.* St John's 1964

McEvoy, John B. *Confederation Papers and Correspondence.* Compiled by Centre for Newfoundland Studies, Memorial University 1974

MacKay, R.A., ed. *Canadian Foreign Policy 1945–1954: Selected Speeches and Documents.* Toronto 1970

– *Newfoundland: Economic, Diplomatic and Strategic Studies.* Toronto 1946

MacKenzie, David. *Canada and International Civil Aviation, 1932–1948.* Toronto 1989

– *Inside the Atlantic Triangle: Canada and the Entrance of Newfoundland into Confederation, 1939–49.* Toronto 1986

MacLeod, Malcolm. *Peace of the Continent: The Impact of the Second World War and American Bases in Newfoundland.* St John's 1986

Martin, Paul. *A Very Public Life.* Vol. 2. *So Many Worlds.* Toronto 1985

Mathias, Philip. *Forced Growth. Five Studies of Government Involvement in the Development of Canada.* Toronto 1971

Matthews, Ralph. *'There's No Better Place Than Here.' Social Change in Three Newfoundland Communities.* Toronto 1978

Morton, Desmond. *A Military History of Canada.* Edmonton 1985

– *The New Democrats, 1961–1986: The Politics of Change.* Toronto 1986

Neary, Peter. *Newfoundland in the North Atlantic World, 1929–1949.* Kingston and Montreal 1988

– *The Political Economy of Newfoundland, 1929-1972.* Toronto, 1973

Newfoundland. *Building on Our Strength: Report of the Royal Commission on Employment and Unemployment.* St John's 1986

– Department of Education. *Annual Reports.* St John's 1944–57

– Fisheries Development Authority. *Annual Report.* St John's 1960

– *Historical Statistics of Newfoundland.* St John's 1970

– Minister of Finance. *Budget Speeches.* St John's 1949–55

– *Report of the Commission of Enquiry Investigating the Seafisheries of Newfoundland and Labrador.* St John's 1937

– *Report of the Newfoundland Fisheries Development Committee.* St John's 1953

– *Report of the Royal Commission for the Preparation of the Case of the Government of Newfoundland for the Revision of the Financial Terms of Union.* St John's 1957

– *Report of the Royal Commission on the Cost of Living in Newfoundland.* St John's 1950

– *Report of the Royal Commission on Transportation.* St John's 1966

– *Submission by the Government of the Province of Newfoundland to the Royal Commission on Canada's Economic Prospects.* St John's 1955

– *Submission of Newfoundland Branch of the Canadian Manufacturer's Association to the Royal Commission on Canada's Economic Prospects.* St John's 1956

Newfoundland Fisheries Board. *Report of the Fisheries Post-War Planning Committee.* St John's 1944

Noel, S.J.R. *Politics in Newfoundland.* Toronto 1971

Parker, John. *Newfoundland, 10th Province of Canada.* London 1950

Pearson, Lester B. *Mike: The Memoirs of the Right Honourable Lester B. Pearson. Volume I. 1897–1948.* Toronto 1972

– *Mike: The Memoirs of the Right Honourable Lester B. Pearson. Volume II. 1948–1957.* Edited by John A. Munro and Alex I. Inglis. Toronto 1973

Perlin, Albert B. *The Story of Newfoundland.* St John's 1959

Pickersgill, J.W. *My Years With Louis St Laurent. A Political Memoir.* Toronto 1975

– *The Road Back: By a Liberal in Opposition.* Toronto 1986

Pickersgill, J.W., and D.F. Forster, eds. *The Mackenzie King Record*. 4 vols. Toronto 1960–70

Pottle, Herbert L. *Newfoundland: Dawn without Light. Politics, Power and the People in the Smallwood Era*. St John's 1979

Pross, A. Paul, and Susan McCorquodale. *Economic Resurgence and the Constitutional Agenda: The Case of the East Coast Fisheries*. Kingston 1987

Public Papers of the Presidents of the United States: Harry S. Truman. Vol. 4. *1949*. Washington 1964

Reader, W.J. *Bowater. A History*. London 1981

Reid, Escott. *Radical Mandarin: The Memoirs of Escott Reid*. Toronto 1989

Roberts, Leslie. *C.D. The Life and Times of Clarence Decatur Howe*. Toronto 1957

Rowe, Frederick W. *The Development of Education in Newfoundland*. Toronto 1964

– *Education and Culture in Newfoundland*. Toronto 1976

– *A History of Newfoundland and Labrador*. Toronto 1980

– *Into the Breach: Memoirs of a Newfoundland Senator*. Toronto 1988

– *The Smallwood Era*. Toronto 1985

Ryan, Shannon. *Fish out of Water: The Newfoundland Saltfish Trade, 1814–1914*. St John's 1986

Sinclair, Peter R. *From Traps to Draggers: Domestic Commodity Production in Northwest Newfoundland, 1850–1982*. St John's 1985

– *State Intervention and the Newfoundland Fisheries: Essays on Fisheries Policy and Social Structure*. Aldershot 1987

Smallwood, Joseph R. *I Chose Canada. The Memoirs of the Honourable Joseph R. 'Joey' Smallwood*. Toronto 1973

– *No Apology from Me*. St John's 1979

– *The Time Has Come to Tell*. St John's 1979

–, ed. *The Book of Newfoundland*. 4 vols. Vol. 3. St John's 1967

–, ed. *Encyclopedia of Newfoundland and Labrador*. 3 vols. St John's 1984

Smith, Denis. *Diplomacy of Fear: Canada and the Cold War, 1941–1948*. Toronto 1988

Spencer, Robert A. *Canada in World Affairs: From U.N. to NATO*. Toronto 1959

Stacey, C.P. *Arms, Men, and Governments: The War Policies of Canada, 1939–1945*. Ottawa 1974

– *Canada and the Age of Conflict: A History of Canadian External Policies*. Vol. 2, *1921–1948: The Mackenzie King Era*. Toronto 1981

Sterns, Maurice, ed. *Perspectives on Newfoundland Society and Culture*. St John's 1974

Struthers, James. *No Fault of Their Own: Unemployment and the Canadian Welfare State, 1914–1941*. Toronto 1983

Swettenham, John. *McNaughton.* Toronto 1969

Thoms, James R. *Newfoundland and Labrador Who's Who.* Centennial Edition. St John's 1968

Thomson, Dale C. *Louis St Laurent. Canadian.* Toronto 1967

United States Treaties and Other International Agreements. Vol. 3, Pt 4, 1952. Washington 1955

Vadakin, James C. *Family Allowances. An Analysis of Their Development and Implications.* Miami 1958

– *Children, Poverty and Family Allowances.* New York 1968

Walsh, Bren. *More Than a Poor Majority: The Story of Newfoundland's Confederation with Canada.* St John's 1985

Whitaker, Reginald. *The Government Party: Organizing and Financing the Liberal Party of Canada, 1930–58.* Toronto 1977

Young, Walter. *The Anatomy of a Party: The National CCF, 1932–1961.* Toronto 1969

III ARTICLES, UNPUBLISHED PAPERS, AND THESES

Alexander, David. 'The Collapse of the Salt Fish Trade and Newfoundland's Integration into the North American Economy.' *Canadian Historical Association Historical Papers,* 1976

Andersen, Raoul. 'Usufruct and Contradiction: Territorial Custom and Abuse in Newfoundland's Bank Schooner and Dory Fishery.' MAST. *Maritime Anthropological Studies* 2, no. 1 (1988):81–102

Baker, Melvin. 'Rural Electrification in Newfoundland in the 1950s and the Origins of the Newfoundland Power Commission.' Paper in possession of the author. 1990

Bassler, Gerhard P. 'Develop or Perish: Joseph R. Smallwood and Newfoundland's Quest for German Industry.' *Acadiensis* 15, no. 2 (Spring 1986): 93–119

Bercuson, David J. 'SAC vs Sovereignty: The Origins of the Goose Bay Lease, 1946–52.' *Canadian Historical Review* 70, no. 2 (June 1989):206–22

Bilous, Marlene Sonia. 'Federal Attempts at Relieving Regional Economic Disparity: Newfoundland's Experience with DREE.' MA thesis, Memorial University, 1973

Blake, Raymond B, 'The Making of a Province: The Integration of Newfoundland into Confederation, 1948–57.' PHD diss., York University 1991

– 'William Lyon Mackenzie King's Attitude towards Newfoundland's Entry into Confederation.' *Newfoundland Quarterly* 82, no.4 (Spring 1987):26–39

Bothwell, Robert, and John Kirton. '"A Sweet Little Country": American

Attitudes Towards Canada, 1952–1963.' *Queen's Quarterly* 90, no. 4 (Winter 1983):1078–1102

Bradley, F. Gordon. 'Why I Joined the Liberal Party.' *Canadian Liberal* 2, nos 3, 4 (Fall 1949):69–72

Bridle, Paul. 'Canada, the U.S. and Newfoundland, 1946–48.' *International Perspectives* (Nov.–Dec. 1983):20–2

Buckner, Philip, P.B. Waite, and William M. Baker. 'CHR Dialogue: The Maritimes and Confederation: A Reassessment.' *Canadian Historical Review* 71, no. 1 (Mar. 1990): 1–45

Campbell, Terry, and George A. Rawlyk. 'The Historical Framework of Newfoundland and Confederation.' In George A. Rawlyk, ed., *The Atlantic Provinces and the Problems of Confederation*. St John's 1979

Cashin, Peter, Harold Horwood, and Leslie Harris. 'Newfoundland and Confederation, 1948–49.' In Mason Wade, ed., *Regionalism in the Canadian Community*. Toronto 1969. 227–63

Cohen, Anthony P. 'The Definition of Public Identity: Managing Marginality in Outport Newfoundland Following Confederation.' *Sociology Review* 23, no. 1 (1975):93–119

– 'The Management of Myths: The Legitimation of Political Change in Newfoundland.' CPSA Annual Meeting 1971

Conliffe, Christopher. 'The Permanent Joint Board of Defense, 1940–1988,' in David G. Haglund and Joel J. Sokolsky, eds. *The U.S.–Canada Security Relationship*. London, 1989. 145–66

Copes, Parzival. 'The Fishermen's Vote in Newfoundland.' *Canadian Journal of Political Science* 3, no. 4 (Dec. 1970):579–604

Cuff, Robert. 'The Conservative Party Machine and the Election of 1911 in Ontario.' *Ontario History* 58, no. 3 (Sept. 1965):149–56

Dunn, P.D.H. 'Fisheries Re-organization in Newfoundland.' Radio address, St John's, 21 Jan. 1944

Dupré, Joseph S. 'Fiscal Policy in Newfoundland.' PHD diss., Harvard University 1958

Fairley, B. 'Development of the Fishing Industry in Newfoundland.' MA thesis, Queen's University 1980

Forbes, Ernest R. 'Consolidating Disparity: The Maritimes and the Industrialization of Canada During the Second World War.' *Acadiensis* 15, no. 2 (Spring 1986):3–27

Gilmore, William C. 'Law, Constitutional Convention and the Union of Newfoundland and Canada.' *Acadiensis* 18, no. 2 (Spring 1989):111–26

Graham, T. 'The International Behaviour of the Canadian Provinces: The Case of Newfoundland.' MA thesis, Memorial University 1977

Greening, W.E. 'Some Recent Changes in the Economy of Newfoundland.'
Canadian Geographical Journal 55, no. 4 (Oct. 1957):128–49

Gushue, Raymond. 'Newfoundland Fisheries in 1951.' *Newfoundland Journal
of Commerce* 19, no. 1 (Jan. 1952)

Hackett, W.D.B. 'Newfoundland's Union With Canada Favoured.' *Saturday
Night* 61 (April 1946)

Harrington, Michael. 'How Newfoundland Joined Up.' *Atlantic Advocate* 64
(April 1974):39–42

– 'The Canadian Connection. The Newfoundland Referendums: How It All
Happened.' *Atlantic Advocate* 69 (Sept. 1978):46–53

Hayman, Kathryn E. 'The Origins and Function of Canada's High Commission in Newfoundland, 1941–49.' MA thesis, University of Western Ontario
1978

Hiller, James. 'The Career of F. Gordon Bradley.' *Newfoundland Studies* 4, no.
2 (Fall 1988):163–80

– 'Confederation Defeated: The Newfoundland Election of 1869,' in James
Hiller and Peter Neary, eds. *Newfoundland in the Nineteenth and Twentieth
Centuries. Essays in Interpretation*. Toronto 1980. 67–94

– 'Twentieth Century Newfoundland Politics: Some Recent Literature.'
Acadiensis 19, no. 1 (Autumn 1989):180–91

Hiller, J.K., and Michael Harrington, eds. 'Report of the Fisheries Committee of the National Convention. Proceedings and Reports of the National
Convention 1990

Kia, Amir. 'Evaluating Regional Policies in Canada: The Case of Newfoundland.' PHD thesis, Carleton University 1985

McAllister, I. 'Newfoundland: From Dependency to Self-Reliance.' *Canadian
Public Policy* 8, no. 1 (Winter 1982):122–8

McCann, Phillip. 'Confederation Revisited: New Light on British Policy.
Lecture presented to the Newfoundland Historical Society 1983

McCay, Bonnie Jean. 'Appropriate Technology and Coastal Fishermen of
Newfoundland.' PHD thesis, Columbia University 1976

McCorquodale, Susan. 'Newfoundland. The Only Living Father's Realm.'
In Martin Robin, ed., *Canadian Provincial Politics: The Party System of the
Ten Provinces*. Scarborough 1972. 138–70

MacKenzie, David, 'Canada and the Entrance of Newfoundland into Confederation, 1939–49.' PHD diss., University of Toronto 1983

MacNamara, Raymond E. 'The Economy of Newfoundland, Canada's
Newest Province.' MA thesis, Columbia University 1951

Matthews, Ralph. 'Perspectives on Recent Newfoundland Politics.' *Journal
of Canadian Studies* 9, no. 2 (1974):20–35

- 'The Pursuit of Progress. Newfoundland's Social and Economic Development in the Smallwood Era.' In Neil B. Ridler, ed., *Issues in Regional/Urban Development in Atlantic Canada*. Saint John 1978
- 'The Smallwood Legacy: The Development of Underdevelopment in Newfoundland, 1949–72.' *Journal of Canadian Studies* 13, no. 4 (Winter 1978–9):89–108
Mayo, H.B. 'The Economic Problems of the Newfoundland Fisheries.' *Canadian Journal of Economics and Political Science* 17, no. 4 (Nov. 1951):482–93
- 'Newfoundland and Canada: The Case for Union Examined.' DPHIL thesis, University of Oxford 1948
- 'Newfoundland's Entry into the Dominion.' *Journal of Economics and Political Science* 15, no. 25 (Dec. 1949):505–22
Morgan, M.O. 'Newfoundland, Our Tenth Province.' *Queen's Quarterly* 56, no. 2 (1949):258–76
Neary, Peter. 'Canada and the Newfoundland Labour Market, 1939–49.' *Canadian Historical Review* 62, no. 4 (Dec. 1981):470–95
- 'Canadian Immigration Policy and the Newfoundlanders, 1912–39.' *Acadiensis* 11, no. 2 (Spring 1982):71–83
- 'Newfoundland's Union With Canada, 1949: Conspiracy or Choice?' *Acadiensis* 12, no. 2 (Spring 1983):110–19
- 'Party Politics in Newfoundland, 1949–71: A Survey and Analysis,' in J.K. Hiller and Peter Neary, eds., *Newfoundland in the Nineteenth and Twentieth Centuries: Essays in Interpretation*. Toronto 1980. 205–45
- 'The Supreme Court of Canada and "the Bowater's law" 1950.' *Dalhousie Law Journal* 8, no. 1 (Jan. 1984):201–15
-, ed. '"Of More Than Usual Interest ...": Sir P.A. Clutterbuck's Newfoundland Impressions, 1950.' *Newfoundland Studies* 3, no. 2 (Fall 1987):251–64
Neary, Peter, and S.J.R. Noel. 'Continuity and Change in Newfoundland Politics,' in Peter Neary, ed., *The Political Economy of Newfoundland, 1929–72*. Toronto, 1973. 217–21
Newell, I. 'Newfoundland, Canada.' *Queen's Quarterly* 56, no. 2 (1949): 258–76
Overton, James. 'Uneven Regional Development in Canada: The Case of Newfoundland.' *Review of Radical Political Economy* 10, no. 3 (1978): 106–16
Paine, Robert. 'The Persuasiveness of Smallwood: Rhetoric of Cuffer and Scoff, of Metonym and Metaphor.' *Newfoundland Studies* 1, no. 1 (Spring 1985):57–76
Pearson, Lester B. 'Canadian Foreign Policy in a Two-Power World.' In *The Empire Club of Canada Addresses, 1950–51*. Toronto 1951. 46–58

Perlin, George. 'The Constitutional Referendum of 1948 and the Revival of Sectarianism in Newfoundland Politics.' *Queen's Quarterly* 75, no. 1 (1968): 155–60
– 'Patronage and Paternalism: Politics in Newfoundland,' in Maurice Sterns, ed., *Perspectives on Newfoundland Society and Culture*. St John's, 1974. 117–24
– 'Political Support in a Transitional Society: Newfoundland in the Smallwood Era.' Paper presented to a colloquium on Community Aspects of Political Development with Special Reference to Newfoundland, St John's, 4–6 Mar. 1971
Rothney, Gordon O. 'The Denominational Basis of Representation in the Newfoundland Assembly, 1919–63.' *Canadian Journal of Economics and Political Science* 28 (1962):557–70
Russell, Ted. 'My Political Memoirs.' *Evening Telegram*, 28 Oct. 1966
Sinclair, Peter R. 'Fishermen of Northwest Newfoundland: Domestic Commodity Production in Advanced Capitalism.' *Journal of Canadian Studies* 19, no. 1 (Spring 1984):34–47
Smallwood, Joseph R. 'Newfoundland: An Address to the Empire Club.' *The Empire Club of Canada Addresses, 1959–60*. Toronto 1960
Stevens, P.D. 'Laurier, Aylesworth, and the Decline of the Liberal Party in Ontario.' *Historical Papers*, 1968
Tuck, Marilyn. 'The Newfoundland Ranger Force, 1935–50.' MA thesis, Memorial University 1983
'Union of Newfoundland With Canada.' *External Affairs* 1, no. 4 (April 1949):25–31
Webb, Jeff A. 'Newfoundland's National Convention, 1946–48.' MA thesis, Memorial University 1987
– 'The Responsible Government League and the Confederation Campaigns of 1948.' *Newfoundland Studies* 5, no. 2 (Fall 1989):203–20
Wolinetz, Steven B. 'Party Organization in Newfoundland. The Liberal Party Under Smallwood.' Paper presented to Annual Meeting of the Canadian Political Science Association, 1975
Yannopoulos, G.N. 'The Development of the Newfoundland Economy since Confederation.' PHD thesis, University of London 1965
Young, R.A. 'Teaching and Research in Maritime Politics: Old Stereotypes and New Directions.' In P.A. Buckner, ed., *Teaching Maritime Studies*. Fredericton 1986. 153–73

Index

Abbott, D.C. 35, 67, 118–19

Acheson, Dean 133–4; and Leased Bases Agreement 135, 139; and Canadian sovereignty 139; and Pearson's frustration with 140

Addison, Lord 14; meets with Newfoundland delegation to London 16

Airbases Agreement 11

Alderdice, Frederick C. 14

Amulree, Lord 148

Angel, John B. 95, 100, 102, 107, 111; special concessions for 109–110

Anglo-Newfoundland Development Company 25

Argentia 122–3, 129, 134

Associated Newfoundland Industries Limited (ANI) 95, 97, 100, 102, 108; submission to delegation 95–6; and Smallwood 112, 113

Atlantic Canada 48. See also Maritime provinces

Attlee, Clement 14–15

Ayre, Lewis M. 23, 102

Ballam, Charles 47

bank fishery, decline of 158

Bates, Stewart 28, 169; on development of Newfoundland fishery 165

bedding factory 105

Bell, Richard A. 48, 58; organizes PC party in Newfoundland 49–50

Bisson, J.G. 83

Bland, C.H. 40

boats, fishing. See trawlers

boot-and-shoe industry 96

Bowater, Sir Eric 116, 117, 118, 120–1

Bowater pulp-and-paper mill 94; early history 115; tax concessions 115, 116, 117–18

Bowring Brothers 164–5

Bradbury, L.S., joins federal Department of Fisheries 152

Bradley, F. Gordon 18, 41, 42, 46, 49, 57, 65, 100, 142; secretary of state 8; at ceremony to mark union 8, 177; calls for petition to put union with Canada in referendum 18; and delegation to Ottawa 25; and appointment of lieutenant-governor 41–3; and Liberal party 52, 62, 183; at Liberal convention 52, 56; and other

Liberal MPs 69; on the importance of Confederation to fishery 154–5; and the fishery 159, 166ff; on Smallwood 166–8

Bridle, Paul 7, 22, 29, 76, 115; remarks on Canada's role in union 9

Britton, J.C. 96

Brooks, Alfred J. 61

Browne, W.J. 67

Bryce, R.B. 167

Bull, W.F. 96, 98, 106, 108; makes survey of secondary industries 96–7, 99, 101

Burchell, Charles J. 7, 42; as high commissioner 11, 28; on terms of union 38

Butt, A.B. 68

'Buy Newfoundland Products Campaign' 113–14

Cabinet Committee on Newfoundland 28, 29, 31, 75, 87, 99, 115; conciliatory with Newfoundland delegation 29. See also Newfoundland delegation

Cabinet Defence Committee 125

Cahill, Michael 135–6

Cameron, G.D.W. 74

Canada 177; assumes responsibility for Newfoundland 36–7, 146, 177–9; and U.S. military in Newfoundland 122ff, 141–3 (See also military bases); relationship with United States 124ff, 130, 133, 134, 135, 139, 141, 143–4, 182–3; and post-war hopes 177–8

Canadian Commercial Corporation 98–9

Canadian Fisheries Act, proclaimed in Newfoundland 152

Canadian National Railway 103, 167

Carnell, Andrew 55

Carter, Chesley 69

Cashin, Peter 21; and PC party 60

centralization of outports. See fishermen, centralization of

ceremonies, to mark union 8

civil aviation 10, 12, 127, 134, 178

civil servants 39–40, 64, 80, 90; role in extending federal services 71ff

Civil Service Commission 39–40; effects of recruitment in Newfoundland 90

Cheeseman, John T. 22, 49, 68, 174

Clark, W.C. 30

Claxton, Brooke 29, 33, 34, 128; visits Newfoundland 68, 79, 135–7; and U.S. military bases 125–6, 127, 134, 141; and Dean Acheson 139–40; offers lease to Goose Bay to United States 142–3

clothing industry 96, 103

Clutterbuck, P.A. 13, 30; visit to Ottawa 13; on terms of union 37; and Bowater 117–18

Coldwell, M.J.: invites Smallwood and Bradley to join CCF 45–6; visits Newfoundland 47

Collins, W.L. 22, 49; approaches PC party 48

Colonial Cordage Company 112–13

Commission of Government 3, 4, 16, 21, 41, 47, 65, 76, 82, 93, 117; reconstruction plan 13, 27; appointed 14; support for in referendum 22; and old-age pensions 87–8; and Bowater pulp-and-paper company 116; and fishery policy 148–9, 153–4; creates Newfoundland Fisheries Board 148–9, 169

Commonwealth Relations Office
117, 118
Confederate, The 20
Confederate Association 19, 42, 183;
ties to Liberal party 52, 54, 56, 61, 63
Confederation 177, 182; early history
of in Newfoundland 9; reasons
for 9, 84, 177–8, 182–3; benefits
of 65, 78, 84–6, 88, 93, 178–9, 180,
183–4; and economic dislocation
79, 95–114; and fisheries 146, 150–2,
153, 162, 164
Cook, Eric 56, 68
Co-operative Commonwealth Federation (CCF) 12, 45–8, 57, 68, 69, 88
cordage industry 96, 112,
cost of living, royal commission on
104–5, 110–11
Courage, John R. 61, 63,
Coy, R.J. 82
Coyne, James 32
Cranborne, Lord 13
criminal law 36
Crosbie, Chesley 20, 22, 50, 53; appointed to Newfoundland delegation 23, 25; refuses to sign
terms of union 37, 99–100; and
Liberal party 63
Currie, J.S. 49, 59
Curry, L.J. (Leo) 80; coordinates
unemployment insurance 81–3
Curry, R.B. 80; and family allowances 72–3, 75–6, 77, 78; in Newfoundland 76
Curtis, Leslie R. 119, 144
customs duties 94, 105, 108, 123;
removal of 103, 179

Davidson, George 72, 74, 75, 77; and
old-age pensions 86–9, 92–3

defence 10, 126; Canada's defence
of Newfoundland 11, 12, 178;
arrangements between United
States and Canada 123, 124, 130,
135, 143–4
denominational schools 29
Department of Education 90
Department of External Affairs 11,
30–1, 75, 134, 137, 141; and St
Laurent's visit to Washington
132; and Blair Fraser 139
Department of Finance (Canada)
30–1, 33, 102, 120, 151; and unemployment assistance 83
Department of Finance (Newfoundland) 90
Department of Fisheries (Canada)
155, 168, 175; administration of
Newfoundland fisheries 152; and
Newfoundland Fisheries Board
152; announces development plan
152–3; marketing difficulties 154–5,
168–9; plans reform of industry
155, 172
Department of Justice (Canada) 132
Department of Labour (Canada) 79,
80–1
Department of National Health and
Welfare 72, 76, 78
Department of Public Welfare 91–2
Department of Trade and Commerce
96, 98; and secondary industries
96–7, 99, 106–7, 109; absorbs
NAFEL 169–70
Diefenbaker, John 5, 37
Dominion Bureau of Statistics 77,
167
Dominion Steel and Coal Corpora-
tion 109–10
Double Taxation Convention 142

Drew, George 38, 49, 58; campaigns in Newfoundland 59–61
Dunn, P.D.H., emphasizes need for fresh and frozen fishery 148
Duplessis, Maurice 17, 38

economic survey 37
education 29–30, 73, 178
elections 78, 84; provincial (1949) 44, 56ff, 90, 153; federal (1949) 47, 48, 57, 67–8, 152–3; federal (1953) 160–1; federal (1954) 48
electoral districts 36
Emerson, Sir Edward 43
Erskine, D.M. 104
European Recovery Plan 133
Evans, Michael 135–6
extension of federal services 39–41, 64, 71ff, 81, 102

Fahey, Ronald 47
family allowances 5, 19, 37, 58, 64, 70, 71, 80, 111, 179; registration for 72–5; administration established 73–4; and Newfoundland immigrants 74; impact of 77–9, 93, 179
Family Allowances Act 73
Farquhar, H.S. 89
Fenwick, Peter 48
ferry service 36, 108
finances. See transitional payments
fish prices 151; effect of Second World War on 149; preoccupation with 155; investigation into 167
fishermen 151, 155; incomes 146, 153, 157, 161, 172–3, 174–6, 180; centralization of 147, 153, 160, 162, 163, 172, 174, 180–1; and standard of living 147, 149, 152, 156–8, 160, 162, 170, 180; productivity of 148, 149, 153, 155, 160, 161, 173, 180; reduction in numbers 153, 160, 163, 170–1, 174–5, 180; reluctance to continue traditional fishery 159–60
fishery 5, 37, 100, 122, 153, 156, 164; inshore 146; curing 147, 158, 159, 162, 163, 166, 173; marketing 147, 150, 152, 153–5; economic importance 149–50; negotiations in Ottawa (1948) 151–2; comes under federal jurisdiction 151–2; role of women in 157–8
fishery, fresh and frozen 147, 148, 158, 174–6, 178; emphasis on 153, 160, 180; and Smallwood 153, 165–6; and federal government 155
fishery, salt-cod 147, 148, 156, 158, 162–5, 168, 172–3, 176; marketing of 148, 149, 150, 153, 164–5, 169, 170; and transition to fresh and frozen production 148, 153, 155, 159, 172, 180–1; exchange difficulties 150, 153–5; and NAFEL 150–1; federal aid for 154–5, 163
fishery policy and development 172; and Government of Canada 147, 152–3, 155, 156–7, 160–2, 163–4, 165, 168–9, 171–6, 180–1; and Government of Newfoundland 147, 155, 156, 162–5, 181; Lord Amulree on 148; P.D.H. Dunn on 148; Raymond Gushue on 148, 165–6; National Convention on 148; Commission of Government on 148–9; and R.W. Mayhew 152–3, 162, 163–4, 165; and financial aid for 162–3

Fleming, Donald 69
flour 29
Fogo, Gordon 56
Fogwill, Irving 47
Forrestal, James 129
Fort Pepperrell 129, 137
Fortune-Hermitage 61, 63
Frampton, Bill 47
France 122
Fraser, A.M. 22
Fraser, Blair, on U.S. rights in New-
  foundland 139
Frecker, G.A. 90
freight rates 5, 95, 103, 107, 112
Furlong, R.S. 57

Gander 10, 36, 127, 129, 134, 138
Garland, C.F. 54, 69
Garson, Stuart 144
Gill, Burnham 40
Gillis, Bill 48
Goldenberg, H. Carl 97, 99
Goose Bay 125, 126, 127; establish-
  ing U.S. military base at 125ff,
  137, 138, 182; strategic impor-
  tance of 137–8, 145; United States
  offered lease to 142–3, 144
Gordon, Walter 172
Granatstein, J.L. 11
Gregg, Milton 28, 86
Grey Book. See 'Proposed Arrange-
  ments for the Entry of Newfound-
  land into Confederation' (1947)
Grisdale, Frank S. 110–11
Grosart, Allister 60
Gruchy, Philip 25
Gushue, Raymond 50; and future
  of Newfoundland fishery 148;
  appears before Newfoundland
  delegation 150–1; joins federal

Department of Fisheries 152; on
  economic development in Newfoundland 165–6

Harrington, Julian 125, 126; and
  U.S. military bases in Newfound-
  land 138
Harrington, Michael 21
Harris, Walter 42, 66
Hartley R.P. 82, 84
Haynes, C.V. 126
health grants 37
Heeney, Arnold 124, 135, 137; on
  negotiations with United States
  over military bases 138, 139, 140
Hefferton, Sam 47
Henry, Guy V.: and U.S. bases in
  Newfoundland 135; obtains
  lease for U.S. military to Goose
  Bay 143
Hickerson, J.D. 127; on U.S. military
  bases in Newfoundland 130, 132,
  134, 138
Hickman, Edgar 50
Higgins, Gordon F. 22, 49, 68; and
  Brooke Claxton 143
Higgins, John 64
Hodgson, Jack C. 126
Hoganson, E.F. 77
Hollett, Malcolm 22
Honderich, Beland 171
Horwood, Charles 47
Horwood, Harold 47, 71
Howe, C.D. 32, 67, 96, 97; views
  of union with Newfoundland 17;
  and secondary industries 97–8,
  99, 101, 102, 105, 108–9, 179; ad-
  dresses Newfoundland Board of
  Trade 101–2; and John B. Angel
  109–10; and NAFEL 170

income–support programs, and
fishermen 147
Independent, The 20–1
Industrial Development Bank 161
industries. *See* secondary manufac-
turing
Interdepartmental Committee on
Canada-Newfoundland Relations
(ICCNR) 15
Interdepartmental Committee on
Newfoundland (ICN) 28, 30, 39,
53, 71
Interdepartmental Sub-Committee
on Newfoundland Secondary In-
dustries and Purchasing (ISNSIP)
102, 103, 104–5, 107, 111; and fed-
eral premium 103–4, 105, 107, 108,
109
International Woodworkers of
America 69

Jackman, D.I., 'Nish' 47
Jackson, Rupert 62
James, R.L. 116
James Baird Limited 165
Jamieson, Donald 20, 41, 50; on
NAFEL 151
Job, R.B. 16, 22
Job Brothers 159
Johnson, Louis 137
Jones, J. Walter 55

Keenleyside, Hugh 13; appointed
acting high commissioner 12
Keough, W.J. 162; on changes in
fishery 159
Kidd, H.E. 68–9
Kidd, W.H. 68
King, William Lyon Mackenzie 10,
27, 124; and defence of Newfoundland 10, 123, 137; and union with
Newfoundland 12–14, 15, 16, 17,
22; as a Father of Confederation
16, 24; accepts results of referendum 24; with Bradley and Smallwood at federal Liberal convention 53

Laberge, E.P. 80, 82
labour movement 46–7, 136
Labrador 10, 17, 36, 103, 177
Labrador fishery, decline of 158–9
LaCroix, Wilfred 38
Laurier, Wilfrid 5, 8
Laws, F.A.J., manager of NAFEL
150
Leased Bases Agreement 5, 10, 28;
history of 122–3; Canadian reaction to 123–4, 125, 126; negotiations for modification of 125, 126–7,
128, 129–30, 131, 132–3, 134, 135,
137, 138, 140, 182; revised 134–5,
141–4, 145
Lewin, H.M. Spencer 116
Lewis, David 47
Liberal party 38, 48, 52ff; convention 44–5, 50, 52ff, 62, 89; organization and leadership 52; policy
of 56, 64–5; candidates 56, 63;
and elections (1949) 57–69. *See
also:* Bradley; Confederate Association; Smallwood
lieutenant-governor, appointment
of 41–3
Lord Addison. *See* Addison
Lord Amulree. *See* Amulree
Lord Cranborne. *See* Cranborne
Lovett, Robert A. 128, 129

McCord, C.R. 80

McDonald, D.M. 106, 107
Macdonald, Sir Gordon 23, 88, 116;
and F.A.J. Laws 150
Macdonald, John A. 5, 6
Macdonald, J. Scott 53; on Ameri-
can interest in Goose Bay 138
MacDonald, Malcolm 12, 14
MacDonald, Vincent C., and effects
of union on NAFEL 150
Macdonnell, J.M. 48; organizes PC
party in Newfoundland 49–50
McEvoy, John B. 25, 53
MacFarlane, J.W. 88–91
MacKay, R.A. 12, 28, 31, 53; visits
Newfoundland 22–3; and role in
negotiations with Newfoundland
29, 30, 33–4, 75; coordinates fed-
eral services 39ff, 71, 80, 137; on
Canada's negotiations with United
States over military bases 137–8,
141
MacKenzie, David 10–11
MacKenzie, W.C. 155, 168
McNair, John 17
MacNamara, Arthur 80
McNaughton, A.G.L.: discussion on
U.S. bases in Newfoundland 135,
138; authorized to offer United
States a lease to Goose Bay 142–3
Mallory, G.D. 106–7, 111–12
Maritime provinces 6, 45, 46, 53,
95, 105, 182, 183; and Confedera-
tion with Newfoundland 17, 22,
25, 28, 168, 178; and Newfound-
land fishery 147, 151, 164, 168–9,
171, 174, 175, 181
Marshall, W.M. 26
Martin, Paul 57; and family allow-
ances 72–3, 75–6; and old-age
pensions 86–9

Mayhew, R.W.: as federal minister
of fisheries 152; announces development plan 152–3, 155; and
marketing difficulties 154–5; and
Newfoundland Fisheries Development Committee 155
Mayo, H.B. 149
Mews, Harry 50; leader of PC party
50–1; in 1949 elections 57–69; defeated 66
military bases (U.S.) 83, 114; effect
of Confederation on 122; history
of 122–3, 126, 129, 135–6. See also
Leased Bases Agreement
Mitchell, Humphrey 79, 85
Morgan, M.O. 21
Morley, Godfrey 116
Morris, Edward 45
Mundell, D.W. 119

National Convention 4, 20, 24, 25,
46–7, 50, 56, 111; created 14; support for Confederation in 15, 47;
appoints delegation to Ottawa
(1946) 15–16; debates Canadian
proposals for union 18; and Fisheries Committee of 148
National Liberal Federation 52, 54,
56; and Smallwood 68–9
National Military Establishment 130,
131
national policy 5, 94
natural resources 36
negotiations with Ottawa (1948) 31;
and subsidies 25–6. See also: Newfoundland delegation; Terms of
Union
Newell, Isaac 21
Newfoundland 36; strategic value
of 3; and economic development

27, 165–7, 181; financial surplus
of 33–4; reaction to U.S. military
bases in 136–7, 182; living standards (*See:* fishermen; standard
of living); social change in 157–8
Newfoundland Associated Fish Exports Limited: created 149; and
Confederation 150–2; Canadian
reaction to 151, 169; disliked by
Maritime politicians 151; becomes
a federal agency 151, 169–70
Newfoundland Bill 38, 88, 118,
139
Newfoundland Board of Trade 25,
38, 95, 96, 101–2, 113, 151
Newfoundland Boot and Shoe Factory 101, 105
Newfoundland delegation to London
(1947) 16
Newfoundland delegation to Ottawa
(1947) 16ff, 79
Newfoundland delegation to Ottawa
(1948) 4, 23, 29, 33, 38, 182; appointed 25, 116; plans for Ottawa
negotiations 25–7, 96, 101, 150;
memorandum presented to Canadian government 27, 96, 149–50;
and negotiations in Ottawa 27–36,
37, 74, 75, 79, 87, 96, 97–8, 99,
115–16, 150–2, 181–2; and financial
matters 30–6, 37; on post-union
government 41; and secondary
manufacturing 96–100; and fisheries 149–52, 169; reaction of
Maritime politicians to 151, 181
Newfoundland Employment Service
80
Newfoundland Federation of Labour
47, 64, 65
Newfoundland Fisheries Board 148;

created Newfoundland Association
of Fish Exporters Limited 149; and
Confederation 150–2; associated
with prosperity 151; absorbed by
federal Department of Fisheries
152
Newfoundland Fisheries Branch.
See Department of Fisheries
(Canada)
Newfoundland Fisheries Develop-
ment Authority 164, 173
Newfoundland Fisheries Develop-
ment Committee (Walsh Commit-
tee) 159, 162, 164, 166–7; appointed
155; *Report* and recommendations
157–8, 160, 161, 162–3, 165, 166,
168, 173, 174; results of 172–6
Newfoundland Hotel 167
Newfoundland Railway 36
Newfoundland Rangers 135–6
Newfoundland School Attendance
Act 73
Nicholson, A.M. 46
Noel-Baker, Philip 18, 116, 117
North Atlantic Treaty 127, 128, 132,
178
Noseworthy, J.W. 12
Nowlan, George 48–9

O'Keefe, G.P. 40
old-age pensions 37, 57, 58–9, 64,
70, 71; introduction of 86–9; in
Newfoundland before union 87,
89; registration for 88–91; problems with 91–3, 166–7
Old Age Pensions Agreement 89
Old Age Pensions Board 88, 89–91
O'Leary, F.M. 22
oleomargarine 29, 97, 182
Outerbridge, Sir Leonard 41

Park, Eamon 47–8
Parker, John J. 100, 112
Parker and Monroe Shoe Factory
    100–1
Parsons, J.G. 78
Party for Economic Union with the
    United States (PEU) 20, 47
Pearson, Lester B. 11, 28, 134; on
    negotiations with Newfoundland
    28–9, 32; on Newfoundland
    treaty obligations 122; and nego-
    tiations over U.S. military bases
    124, 125, 126, 129–30, 131–3, 134,
    138, 139–40, 141–4; on Canadian
    sovereignty 124, 127, 131, 141, 143,
    144; and quid pro quo 125, 127,
    130, 131, 133, 142–3; statement on
    foreign policy 139; concern over
    U.S. military in Newfoundland
    144
Perlin, A.J. 61, 76
Permanent Joint Board on Defence
    (PJBD) 124, 133; and Leased Bases
    Agreement 135, 138, 139, 140,
    141–3; and Goose Bay 137
Pett, L.B. 74–5
Petten, Ray 54, 69
Philips, T.F. 77
Pickersgill, J.W. 17, 54, 69, 71, 118;
    as MP 161
Pinsent, Douglas 61
Planta, Clive 166; on federal role in
    fisheries 168–9, 171
Pond, James 47
Pottle, Herbert 86, 88, 89, 91–2
Power, Gregory 47, 54, 67–8, 69;
    and demand for change in New-
    foundland 158
price control 65
Price Support Board 168, 169, 171;

and low income for fishermen
    153
Progressive Conservatives 38, 44–5,
    47, 48ff, 88, 183; and organization
    45, 49–50, 66; leadership of 50, 61,
    66; and elections (1949) 57–69;
    and policy 64
'Proposed Arrangements for the
    Entry of Newfoundland into
    Confederation' (1947), (Grey
    Book) 17, 24, 25, 29
provisional government 41
Pushthrough 61

Quinton, Herman W. 70, 88, 89

referenda 7, 22, 52, 58, 67, 100; first
    referendum 4, 19; options on
    18–19; second referendum 22, 49,
    53; and public reaction to results
    23–4
Reid, Escott 35, 127, 137
Report of the Newfoundland Fisheries
    Development Committee. See New-
    foundland Fisheries Development
    Committee
resettlement 172. See fishermen,
    centralization of
responsible government 7; return
    to in Newfoundland 18, 21, 29;
    support for 20ff, 38, 48, 49, 51,
    58, 66–7, 182, 183; and surrender
    of 148
Responsible Government League
    (RGL) 19, 22, 29, 48, 49, 51
Rice, G.J. 77
Rinfret, Thibaudeau 120
Robertson, Norman 11, 12, 106; vis-
    its Newfoundland 155
Roche, Archbishop Edward 42

Rowsell, George 61
Royal Commission on Canada's
Economic Prospects 172
Rusk, Dean, admits United States
has been remiss 140–1
Russell, Edward 47
Russell, Hazen A. 159, 166

St John's District Labour Party 46
St Laurent, Louis 6, 17, 28, 67, 71,
106, 108–9, 167, 178; at ceremonies
to mark union 8, 183–4; in negotiations with Newfoundland 29,
31, 32, 33–4, 88, 97, 98, 156–7; and
parliamentary debate on Newfoundland 38–9, 139; and provisional
government 41–3, 53–4, 62, 65;
on appointment of lieutenant-
governor 41–3; and Bowater pulp-
and-paper company 115–21; and
visit to Washington 131–4; and
fisheries 160, 163
Salt Codfish Association 151
school attendance 73, 79
Second World War 3, 6, 10
secondary industries 5, 37, 94–6,
98, 102; impact of union on 96,
97, 99, 105, 107, 114, 179–80; federal survey of 96–7, 99, 106–7,
111; special assistance for 97–8,
115, 179; and Smallwood 100,
108–9, 110, 111–12; adjusts to
union 103, 106, 108, 113–14; and
federal premium 103–4, 105, 107,
108, 109, 179; and Canadian attitude towards 104–5, 107–8
Senate 36, 65
Senate Foreign Relations Committee
128
Sharp, Mitchell 28, 30, 41; role in

negotiations with Newfoundland
30, 31, 32, 151; on the provisional
government 41; and NAFEL 151;
on Newfoundland's economic
development 167
Sims, R.H. 82
Sinclair, James 174; views on Newfoundland fishery 160, 168–9
Skelton, Alex 32–3
Skelton, O.D. 11
Smallwood, Joseph R. 5, 8, 20, 41,
48, 49, 67, 71, 136; early career of
15, 46, 52; in National Convention
15–16, 18, 47, 56; calls for petition
to put union with Canada in referendum 18; and delegation to
Ottawa 25ff (See also Newfoundland delegation); understanding
of Canadians 25–6; and negotiations in Ottawa 30, 37, 100; and
provisional government 41–3, 65;
appointed premier 42, 64; and
Liberal convention 44–5, 52ff;
and CCF 45–6; and socialism 47,
52; and leadership 52, 183; in
1949 election 57–69: appoints
cabinet 61–2, 166; and Ottawa
68–9, 84, 153, 160–1, 162–5, 166–9,
170, 171–2, 184; and MPs 69 (See
also Bradley); and unemployment
71, 83–6, 136, 180–1; and social
programs 78, 84–5, 88–9, 93, 180;
and Newfoundland entrepreneurs
100, 108–9, 110–12, 162, 164–5;
and economic development 147,
172; and fisheries 147, 153, 155,
156–7, 162, 163–4, 166, 168–9,
171–6; in 1953 election 160–1
Smith, R. Campbell 100, 105
social programs 61, 70, 71, 86, 178–81;

implementation of 5; impact of 93, 180; and fisheries 174, 181. *See also:* family allowances; old-age pensions; unemployment insurance

Sparkes, Grace 21

Squires, Lady Helena 55

Squires, Sir Richard 45, 52

Standard Bedding Company Limited 105

standard of living 147, 148, 149, 156–7, 179, 180–1, 182, 184. *See also* fishermen

State Department (U.S.) 125–6, 128–9, 130, 131, 132, 134, 137, 139, 140; and debate in Parliament on bases 132; wants military concessions from Canada 138–9

Steel Company of Canada 109–10

Stehelin, Paul 72–3, 75; establishes family allowances offices 76–7

Steinhardt, Laurence A., on Canadian concessions to United States 134

Stephenville 123, 129, 134

Sterling, Geoffrey 50

Supreme Court Act 119

Supreme Court of Canada 94, 178; and Bowater pulp-and-paper company 119–21, 180

Swettenham, E.R. 88–92

tariffs. *See* customs duties

Taschereau, Robert 120

taxation 35; and special concessions 94

Taylor, Billy Bond 47

Terms of Union 5, 29, 36, 37, 58, 70, 76, 82, 87, 98, 99, 101, 115, 116, 156, 167, 183; response to in Newfoundland 37–8; Term 17 29; Term 18 119–20, 132; Term 24 33; Term 27 35–6; Term 29 5, 34–5, 37; Term 38 29; Term 39 40; Term 46 29

Torbay 127, 134

transitional subsidy 26, 30–6, 37, 58, 97, 182; increased 34–6, 181

trawlers 147; Commission of Government support for 149

Truman, Harry 124; and U.S. military bases in Newfoundland 133–4, 137–8

unemployment 83–5, 96, 97; and Ottawa 85, 106

unemployment assistance 79, 81, 97, 179, 181; registration for 82–4; impact of 83–4, 85, 93, 179

unemployment insurance 37, 64, 70, 71, 79, 81, 107, 136, 167, 179, 180; introduction of 82–3; consequences of 86, 93, 179, 180; and fishermen 174, 181

Unemployment Insurance Act 79

Unemployment Insurance Commission 80–1, 83

United Kingdom 16, 122, 136; role in Confederation 9, 12–13, 14, 18, 117; and Newfoundland's sterling debt 33; and Bowater pulp-and-paper company 117–18

United Nail and Foundry 109–10

United States 3, 5, 16, 122, 125, 146, 178, 182; and Confederation 20, 125, 126; and rights in Newfoundland 123, 126, 135–7, 138, 143–4; and relationship with Canada 130, 132, 138, 144–5, 182–3; and role of Permanent Joint Board on Defence in modifying Leased Bases Agreement 139, 141–3;

offered lease to Goose Bay 142–3;
and market for fish 148ff, 168
United States Air Force 127, 129,
134, 136

Valdmanis, Alfred 112, 166
Valleyfield–Badgers Quay 163
Varcoe, F.P. 119
veterans' benefits 37
Visiting Forces Act 124, 135, 142, 144

Walsh, Albert 7, 65, 160; becomes
lieutenant-governor 8, 42–3; and
delegation to Ottawa 25ff, 79, 95;
and terms of union 26–7, 29, 30,

34; and Bowater pulp-and-paper
company 115; and Newfoundland
Fisheries Development Committee
155–68, 173, 175
Webb, Jeff A. 19
Wershof, M.H. 143
White, Eric 107, 112, 113
Wilgress, Dana 143
Winter, Gordon A. 25
Winters Robert 57
workmen's compensation 136
Wrong, Hume 12, 124, 137; on U.S.
military bases 127, 128, 131, 134,
140; presents Canada's demands
128–30, 139–40